First Catch
Your Gingerbread

Indian Gingerbread Biscuits.

First Catch Your Gingerbread

Sam Bilton

PROSPECT BOOKS
2020

This edition published in 2020 in Great Britain and the USA by Prospect Books at 26 Parke Road, London, SW13 9NG.

British Library Cataloguing in Publication Data:
A catalogue entry for this book is available from the British Library.

ISBN 978-1-909248-69-4

Set in Adobe Garamond Pro and Cochin by Catheryn Kilgarriff and Brendan King.

Printed by the Gutenberg Press Ltd., Malta.

CONTENTS

Contents

PART II: THE RECIPES

Author's Note

> 'It was inevitable: the scent of bitter almonds always reminded him of the fate of unrequited love.'
>
> Gabriel García Márquez, *Love in the Time of Cholera*

The fragrance of gingerbread will forever to remind me of the coronavirus pandemic that swept the world in 2020. When I began this project I had so many plans. The preliminary research had me blissfully bound to a desk at the British Library (one of my happy places). I had dreams of visiting the gingerbread museum in Toruń, of retracing Wordsworth's steps in the Lake District to sample the famous Grasmere gingerbread, and being enveloped in the aromas of a *pain d'épice* from Dijon, like M.F.K. Fisher, author of *The Gastronomical Me*. None of these trips were able to happen as we were urged to stay at home in order to stay safe. On the upside, there is nothing quite like a lockdown to focus the mind of a writer. At times, the recipe testing was a challenge but I have been grateful to my neighbours for rescuing more than one batch of gingerbread with the donation of a tin of treacle or half a bag of flour (all conveyed to me in a socially responsible manner). It is hard to say whether this is the book I set out to write. Had I been able to visit those gingerbread havens, would the book have been any different? Possibly, but I am content with the end result and hope you will be too. The gingerbread museums, shops and markets will still be there once life gets back to normal (whatever that normal may be), so I will look forward to exploring them when that day arrives.

Sam Bilton, June 2020

DEDICATION

*To my gingerbread boys Billy, Charlie and Alex for
wading through rivers of treacle, cascades of honey
and scaling mountains of gingerbread.*

Part I

The Story of Gingerbread

Pain d'épice with Game Terrine.

Introduction

What is it About Gingerbread?

'An I had but one penny in the world, thou shouldst have it to buy gingerbread.'

William Shakespeare[1]

By all accounts Fanny and Johnnie Cradock were gingerbread addicts, which I guess makes us kindred spirits.[2] Not that I ate mountains of gingerbread as a child but the scent of spicy treats being baked has always beguiled me. I was more likely to choose a slice of sticky ginger cake over a Victoria sandwich (a good ginger cake has a reassuring matronly squidginess about it). I would always fish out a ginger nut from amongst the custard creams and chocolate digestives (a crisp ginger cookie invigorates the palate like no other biscuit can). There is just something so satisfying and comforting in a gingerbread that no other cake or biscuit can equal.

Gingerbread has been defined as 'a product which is always spiced, and normally with ginger, but which varies considerably in shape and texture. Some modern British gingerbreads are so crisp that they might qualify to be called ginger biscuits. Others are definitely cake-like.'[3]

'Normally' suggests there are exceptions to the rule. French gingerbread, *pain d'épice*, rarely contains ginger and is texturally nothing like British gingerbreads. Scandinavian gingerbreads are often heavily laced with cardamom or pepper, from which they get names like *pepparkakor*.[4]

First Catch Your Gingerbread

Even in the British Isles we have gingerbreads that do not contain ginger, such as the Welsh *Teisen sinsir heb sinsir* (literally 'ginger cake without ginger').[5]

Irrespective of what spices the cake or biscuit contains, gingerbread has existed in various guises across Britain and Europe for centuries. It is among the oldest of our sweet treats that has endured and evolved with time. It may not be everyone's favourite patisserie but the fact that we still find recipes in modern cookbooks and buy commercially produced gingerbread products surely demonstrates there is an affection for it?

The history of gingerbread is a complex one. Its roots are obscure, with hints that it may have descended from a medicine in the ancient world or perhaps from an oriental delicacy. Spices like pepper, cinnamon and ginger insinuated their way into Britain's cuisine, arriving with the Romans and remaining long after these invaders had dispersed. Perhaps these opulent spices – and their equally lavish cousins, nutmeg, clove and anise – were always destined to make a love match with honey, and what better way to seal their union than in the form of a cake?

By the medieval era the West's passion for spices had been invigorated, bringing gingerbread, by this time a mixture of honey, breadcrumbs and spices, to the fore. Whoever decided this concoction would make a luxuriant after-dinner treat was probably both inspired and brave (imagine if you had wasted most of your master's expensive store of spices making experimental gingerbreads and he hated it). These gilded morsels, eaten in moderation as a digestive by the elite of the medieval and Tudor eras, were most definitely not for the riff-raff.

Then a slick dark player comes on the scene by the name of treacle, changing gingerbread's fortunes forever. No longer the preserve of the rich it was now in the reach of most people's pockets. A glittering souvenir from the fair – perhaps a gingerbread man or woman, or heart for the one you admire, or an edible pet like a pig, or a reward for learning your letters. When the fair was out of town you could take your chances in a gingerbread 'lottery' run by silver-tongued vendors who roamed the city streets touting their wares.

History does not stand still and as our social, political and culinary pathways have moved with the times, gingerbread has followed suit. The wonderfully ornate kings and queens moulded in gingerbread have been ousted by amorphous figures, but gingerbread houses (even entire cities), caked in sugar snow and adorned with jewelled jellies, still capture our imagination. Commercially produced ginger cakes and biscuits grace our supermarket shelves, and some artisan bakers are lovingly recreating age-old recipes to preserve the taste of the past, ensuring traditional gingerbread is never far from our plates.

What follows is a taste of gingerbread's past. It does not encompass everything in the world of gingerbread, but focusses primarily on the confection's journey in Britain, with occasional forays overseas. To some there may appear to be glaring omissions in terms of regional recipes, but alas there was not enough space to include them all. The book is designed to whet the appetite and to show you how diverse gingerbread can be. I hope you will go forth and explore the recipes so that your home can be filled with the comforting waft of sugar and spice.

A NOTE ON THE RECIPES

All of the dishes in the recipe chapters are based on or inspired by historical sources, but they have been adapted to suit the modern kitchen. The recipes have been written to capture the flavours enjoyed by our ancestors, though they may have been tweaked or presented in an alternate fashion to make them more palatable (there have been several near misses with broken teeth in the Bilton household while testing some of the gingerbreads). Where applicable, the source of each recipe is listed in the notes and there is an extensive bibliography should you wish to look up the original for yourself.

Naturally, I have tested all of the recipes in this book, so I am certain they work in my oven. Many Russians still believe in the *domovoi*, a house spirit, who lives under the cooker. The *domovoi* is a mischievous sprite responsible for all manner of culinary mishaps, from sunken soufflés to burnt toast (and any number of household electrical faults). He is not all bad though, often helping to heal the sick and quell domestic quarrels.[6] Whether you believe in household spirits or not you will appreciate the vagaries of your own oven. Cooking times are given as a guide and in most instances will be accurate. However, only you know if your oven is particularly fierce (in which case you should perhaps reduce the temperature a little), or of a lackadaisical persuasion causing the recipe to take slightly longer to cook than expected.

Chapter One

Ancient Origins of Gingerbread

Would you let yourself and your children fall into the hands of a vengeful enemy and risk suffering a torturous and barbaric death? Or would you opt for a swift and relatively painless demise by poison delivered by your own hands? It is a decision no parent would want to make, but it was the one faced by Mithridates VI, King of Pontus in 63 BCE, as the Roman legions besieged his kingdom.

You could say poison was written into Mithridates' destiny. When it comes to politics, poisoning has been seen throughout history as the most efficient way to rid yourself of your opponents. Mithridates' father was killed by poison, and his own mother had tried to dispose of her son in the same fashion. A feared and powerful leader he may have been, but the threat of assassination always loomed over Mithridates' head like the Sword of Damocles. Mithridates made it his life's ambition to find a way to make himself immune to poison by creating the ultimate antidote. He is remembered in history as the 'Poison King' and his name will forever be linked to the antidote mithridatium.[1]

Mithridatium has taken on a mythical status over the centuries. The 'Poison King' left no written prescription for how to make this cure-all elixir (or at least if he did, no written record of it has survived). What little we do know is based on studies made of Mithridates' personal documents after the king had died. Pliny (AD 23/24–79) studied Mithridates' notes and praised him for being 'a more accomplished researcher into biology than any man before him'. Mithridates conducted numerous experiments, involving poison on prisoners, courtiers and even himself, to deduce the effects these toxins would have and how they could be combated. The king soon realised that in minute quantities poisons could have a remedial effect.[2] Mithridates' antidote probably included spices such as cinnamon, ginger, cardamom, saffron and anise, along with substances like charcoal, curdled milk and garlic, all believed to counteract poisons.[3] These would be combined with small amounts of toxins in an electuary (a paste made from honey) that Mithridates would take daily in the form of an almond-sized pill. Far from having any detrimental effect on his health, this quotidian elixir appeared to make Mithridates exceedingly virile, and was credited for his excellent health and sexual vigour throughout his long life.[4]

Jars for Mithridatium, a popular antidote for poison. © *Wellcome Collection.*

Dabbling in pharmacology would ultimately backfire on Mithridates. Trapped in Pantikapaion, with no hope of escape and Pompey's soldiers about to descend, Mithridates decided to commit suicide. Fortunately, Mithridates always carried a vial of an extremely effective poison which even his antidote could not remedy. He administered some of the poison to two of his young daughters. The effect was swift and both girls died quickly. However, when Mithridates took the remainder of the vial, the poison did not have the desired effect. He had achieved his life's ambition – immunity to poisoning. In the end, Mithridates instructed his bodyguard to administer a fatal blow with his sword, thereby ending the king's life.[5]

It would be a stretch (and a very long one at that) to suggest that mithridatium was an early form of gingerbread. Clearly mithridatium and gingerbread share some of the same ingredients in the spices and the honey used to bind them. What this tale really reveals is the reverence given by ancient civilisations to the medicinal properties of spices, which would trickle down the centuries and see them grow in importance in the culinary world. And as we will see, the mystical powers of spices would become omnipresent as more diverse uses were found for them.

Spices have long been revered for their aromatic properties. They were used by many ancient civilisations as part of the embalming process following death (peppercorns were found in the nose of the Egyptian Pharaoh Ramses II who lived between 1279 and 1213 BCE).[6] The ancient Greeks imported spices primarily to make perfumes and perfumed oils, medicines, and to give aroma to their drinks. Cinnamon in particular was used for divine sacrifices, funerals and in perfumed oils for the hair and body. Spices in general were not utilised to a great extent to flavour the food of the ancient Greeks, although wine could be infused with them. In his work *On Odours*, Theophrastus (c.371–c.287 BCE) declared: 'One might wonder why exotic and other fragrances improve the taste of wines when, so far from having that effect on foods – whether cooked or uncooked – they invariably ruin them.'[7] It took some time before the spicing of food became commonplace in Greece, but by the Byzantine era it was the accepted norm.[8]

The cookery manuscripts named after Roman gourmet Marcus Gavius Apicius, who lived sometime during the first century AD, indicate that spices, such as pepper, were used extensively in the cooking of that era.[9] Pepper was also used as a currency.[10] The Romans used two routes to import spices, both starting in the Red Sea ports of Egypt. The first travelled down the African coast stopping at various towns until the traders reached Mozambique. However, the favoured route by which most of the spices reached Europe was across the ocean towards India.[11] 'They arrive with gold and depart with pepper', wrote Tamil poet Tāyan-Kannanār speaking of Roman traders seen at the port of Muziris in southern India, which even sported a temple dedicated to the Emperor Augustus.[12] Initially, long pepper (*Piper longum*) was favoured by the Romans, although in time they would begin to import the cheaper round black pepper (*Piper nigrum*).[13] After the kingdom of Egypt was annexed by the Romans in 30 BCE – and Rome had acquired control of the Red Sea ports and worked out how to optimise the monsoon winds – the trade route to India became much easier.[14]

Ginger did not garner as much culinary favour with the Romans as pepper. Ginger (*Zingiber officinale*) was domesticated in India, South East Asia and South China. In its dried form, ginger had reached Western Europe by the first century, although it was also preserved and converted into an oil.[15] The Greek for ginger, *zingiberi,* is thought to be derived from *singivera,* a word in the Pali language used in Sri Lanka during Roman times.[16] Ginger was not widely used in Roman cookery at this period. Only 3 % of the dishes in *Apicius* contain ginger compared to 81 % containing pepper.[17] Even so, Greek pharmacist Dioscorides declared in his *De materia medica* that ginger 'is very nice to eat; it is eaten pickle and all',[18] so perhaps it was enjoyed more as a condiment than as a culinary ingredient.

Ginger was prized in both the eastern and western worlds for its medicinal qualities, which possibly explains why it was one of the ingredients in Mithridates' antidote. In China, it has enjoyed a reputation for maintaining health and well-being since ancient times (it is said that Confucius always had ginger when he ate). Ginger had many therapeutic uses. Its 'hot' properties meant that it could be used to remedy the symptoms of colds, flu and headache. It was also used to treat flatulence, indigestion and roundworm, and was even believed to enhance sexual prowess and fertility.[19]

In terms of gingerbreads, the spicing element is critical to separate them from other cakes and biscuits. When looking for the origins of this confection we need to disregard spices for the moment and look towards the early forms of cake.

If ancient civilisations were slow to embrace certain spices such as ginger and cinnamon in their diet, they were not so reticent when it came to sweeteners such as honey.[20] Like spices, honey was prized for its medicinal properties but it was also used in cooking as 'the universal sweetener of the ancient world'.[21] The Greeks and Romans particularly valued honey from the thyme-covered slopes of mount Hymettus outside Athens, as it was considered the best in the known world (thyme was believed to give the best aroma to honey). Both of these civilisations subscribed to the theory of the four humours – blood, yellow bile, black bile, and phlegm – and their influence on the body and its emotions. The food and drink you consumed could have a considerable impact on your humoral balance. Honey (and latterly sugar), alcohol (such as wine), and spices were all considered to be 'hot' ingredients. For this reason, spiced honey wines, like the Roman *mulsum*, were served before a meal, as their potential ill effects could be balanced out with 'cold' foods, such as fish, that were served afterwards.[22]

There is limited information about, and few recipes for, cakes from the ancient world. Despite covering a wide range of recipes for vegetables, meat and fish, *Apicius* does not include a book on cakes or sweets, although there are a few recipes for homemade sweets in Book Seven for 'The Gourmet':

Dulcia piperata: <teres piper.> mittis mel meruim passam rutam, *eo mittis nucleos nuces alicam elixatum. Concisas nucas auellanas tostas adicies et inferes.*

Peppered sweets: pound pepper; add honey, wine, *passum*, and rue. Add to the mixture pine nuts, nuts and boiled *alica*. Add chopped roasted nuts and serve.[23]

Rather than being an oversight on the part of the original author it has been suggested the book on cakes from the *Apicius* collection has been lost.[24] The knowledge we have of the sweet things eaten by the ancient Greeks and Romans is based on texts from that period such as Cato's *On Agriculture,* as well as comedies and poems.[25] From these descriptions we know that cakes, sweets and nuts were served at the end of the meal with wine. These were known as the *tragémata*, 'what one chews alongside wine'.[26] Paintings on vases found in archeological digs also show pyramid-shaped cakes being served at feasts:[27]

In his book, *On Cakes*, Iatrokles makes mention of *khoirinai* and what are called *pyramous*, which he says are no different from what people call *pyramis*. For these are made from toasted wheat soaked in honey. They are served to those who have stayed up all night for religious festivals.[28]

(From *The Deipnosophists* by Athenaeus)

Where cakes are mentioned they usually include honey. Athens was particularly renowned for its oven-baked cakes and bread which were often soaked in honey.[29] Perhaps the most notable cake from this period is the Greek *plakous* (known as *placenta* to the Romans[30]), which was a type of dessert made with thin pastry sheets and filled with sheep's cheese and honey.[31]

There has been some debate whether cakes were used purely for ceremonial purposes at temples, or were specifically designed for feasts.[32] In *The Deipnosophists,* Athenaeus describes a cheesecake called *amphiphon* offered to the Roman goddess of hunting, Diana (Artemis in Greek mythology), which was served with 'figures of lighted torches round it'.[33] One type of honey-drenched cheesecake from Argos was presented to the bridegroom by his bride for his friends to eat.

Another cheesecake from Sparta was shaped like a breast and carried by the female friends of the bride as they sang a song praising her virtues.[34] Even the Celts, who were viewed by the Romans as barbarians – in part due to their penchant for dairy products – ate honey cakes.[35] In Irish mythology the 'Champion's Portion', awarded to the best warrior at Bricriu's Feast, concludes with 'five-score wheaten cakes made with honey'.[36]

Cakes from these periods were most likely flat and dense rather than the fluffy sponge creations we favour today. While no mention is made by Athenaeus or similar authors of spices in these cakes, their compact form survived into the medieval period in the form of gingerbread made from compressed breadcrumbs and honey.[37] It is difficult to pinpoint exactly when spices were added to the honey cake mixture to create something we would recognise as gingerbread.

The *Dictionnaire de Trévoux* (originally published in 1704) identifies gingerbread as *panis mellitos*: 'The ancients called it *panis mellitos*; they also called it *panis nauticus* or *Alexandrinus*, the sea biscuit.'[38] Although *panis mellitos* was certainly used to describe a 'honey bread' in the medieval period, earlier references to this phrase have been impossible to trace.[39] Chauney has concluded that the modern-day gingerbread of France, *pain d'épice*, is descended from the tenth century honey bread from China, called *Mi-Kong*.[40]

Honey (*mi* or *fêng-mi*) is not mentioned in Chinese literature until the third century BCE. It is believed the honey used in China at that time came from the west via Samarkand.[41] It was exchanged for silk and precious stones, which gives some indication of its value.[42] Like Mithridates, the Chinese used honey as a medicine rather than as a cooking ingredient. The Chinese believed honey could promote longevity and included it in their tonics. Like the Romans, the Chinese aslo used honey in savoury and sweet dishes, and it was a highly regarded ingredient for Han feasts.[43]

Foreign food – particularly steamed or fried cakes, described as 'the gold of the T'ang dinner table'[44] – became popular at aristocratic banquets from the eighth century onwards. The most popular cakes were made from wheat or rice. *Shih-mi* were small cakes which included honey and milk, and were produced along the Yangtze basin from Szechwan to Hangchow Bay.[45] Foreign cakes (*hu*) from the west, quite often in the form of steamed or fried breads containing sesame seeds, were particularly popular.[46] As Edward Shafer has observed: 'Some of these fancy pastries that enriched the T'ang cuisine, many of them newly introduced from abroad, were distinguished by their incorporation of foreign ingredients, especially spices and other aromatic substances, while others were based on foreign recipes, although the ingredients might be readily available in China.'

Based on this evidence, perhaps the origins of gingerbread lie a little closer to western Europe. There is some indication that wheat-based 'foreign' cakes topped with sesame seeds were sold on the streets of Chang'an (modern Xi'an) by Iranians.[47] As the major trade routes for silk and spices crossed Persia it is easy to see how spice would eventually find its way into a sweetened bread or cake.

Islamic ambassadors from Rum (formerly known as Rumieh under the Romans) were recorded as presenting the T'ang emperor with a gift of mithridatium in AD 667.[48] Meanwhile, rulers across Europe from Charlemagne to Elizabeth I consumed mithridatium every day in the hopes of achieving the same immunity afforded to the Poison King.[49] But as we shall see, the medicinal value of spices extended beyond general well-being.

CHAPTER TWO

MEDIEVAL GINGERBREAD

Within the stomach, loins, and in the lung
Praise of hot ginger rightly may be sung.
It quenches thirst, revives, excites the brain
And in old age awakes young love again.
(From the *Regimen sanitatis Salernitanum*[1])

Spices were a vital part of the medieval apothecary's armoury in an era where you figuratively were what you ate. Just about any ailment could be cured (in theory, at least) by consuming a combination of spices and herbs, often mixed with honey or any number of less palatable ingredients (and not only poisons). The hot and dry nature of spices particularly endeared themselves to remedies for sexual issues. The leading sex manual of the Middle Ages, *De coitu* (*On Sexual Intercourse*), was written by an eleventh-century African physician who later converted to Christianity called Constantine the African, who played an important role in establishing the medical school at Salerno. Constantine helpfully provided several prescriptions in his treatise for sexual difficulties, such as a cure for impotence which included ginger, pepper, galangal, cinnamon and various herbs 'to be taken sparingly after lunch and dinner'. Another Constantine special was designed to boost libido, combining spices with rocket and carrot, which the monk modestly claimed to be 'the best there is'.[2]

An early form of gingerbread may have evolved from a thirteenth-century electuary called *diazinziberos* (listed as *gingibrati* in the accounts of Robert Montpellier, apothecary to Henri III): 'take very well cooked parsnips, mince them and cook them with clarified honey until all the honey is absorbed, stirring well so that the mixture does not stick to the vessel; then put in aromatic powders, gimigibre, pepper, nutmeg, and galingale; and cook together to a candy'.[3] The parsnips would eventually give way to breadcrumbs to produce a more familiar style of confection.[4] It is unclear what purpose Montpellier's electuary served, but given the examples suggested by Constantine we can hazard a guess.

At one time it was believed the spices that play such an important role in gingerbread arrived in Europe when soldiers returned from the Crusades.[5] One theory is that Genghis Khan's horsemen carried a supply of honey bread with them when they went into battle, possibly based on an ancient Chinese recipe for *Mi-Kong* which combined wheat and honey. The Arabs and Turks inherited a taste for these sweet, energy giving breads from the Mongols, who in turn passed it on to the Crusaders.[6] This seems unlikely as the Mongolian diet centres around meat and dairy products. The Mongols are better known for carrying dried dairy products such as yoghurt and milk, which could be reconstituted with water. These provided protein and other nutrients in a portable form. Even today there are very few wheat-based dishes in traditional Mongolian cooking.[7]

The truth is spices never left Europe. Even after the fall of Rome, spices continued to be imported into Britain throughout the Middle Ages (possibly from China or Persia) although they were much scarcer than they had been in Roman times.[8] Although peasants did not use spices on a regular basis, the presence of 'Spicers' or 'Pepperers' (merchants selling spices) in small towns suggests people may have been able to enjoy them for special occasions.[9] Pepper was the most important and widely-used spice in culinary terms (other spices were available but they appear to have been limited to medicinal uses).[10] Monks even had a sign for pepper when they were forbidden to speak.[11] When he died in 735, the Venerable Bede bequeathed a number of spices to his brethren including cinnamon, cloves, cubebs, grains of paradise, ginger, liquorice and sugar.[12] Where the Crusades did influence the spice trade was by enabling European merchants to establish a foothold in the Levant, thereby creating a substantial presence in the region not witnessed since the fall of the

Roman Empire.[13] Greater quantities of the luxury ingredient sugar were also imported from the Mediterranean after the First Crusade (1096–9).[14]

Chronicles of the Crusades, such as those by the thirteenth-century abbot Arnold of Lübeck, give us a glimpse of the elusive *panis mellitos* mentioned in the *Dictionnaire de Trévoux*:

> They now entered Rum, a deserted, unwelcoming and waterless land, and bread was lacking in their packs since they did not have supplies. There were, however, those among them who had prepared themselves honeyed bread [*panis mellitos*], since this was plentiful, and they were sustained as best they could. Those who had not made similar preparations ate either horseflesh and water or roots. Those who no longer had the strength to walk fell on their faces on the ground, so that they might receive martyrdom for the Lord's name. Rushing down upon them, the enemy slew them without mercy in the sight of all the others.[15]

There is evidence to suggest the Anglo-Saxons ate fine breads made from enriched doughs on special occasions, a legacy from the preceding Roman era.[16] Feasts were generally held for special occasions such as the arrival of an important guest, celebrating or commemorating a rite of passage, related to a season (for example, harvest time) or religious event, and to celebrate a victory or coronation. These finer 'feasting' breads could be spiced (*gesyfled*) or sprinkled with seeds (*wel besewen*) like dill, caraway or poppy. They may have been enriched further with eggs, butter or cream and sweetened with honey or dried fruits, and could have been a forerunner of our modern festival breads, like hot cross buns.[17]

Once spices became more abundant in the West, Europeans would soon begin to include them in sweet confections made with honey and a variety of flours. In pre-Christian Russia, the original *pryaniki* (a Russian-style gingerbread still made today) was made from rye flour, honey and berry juice, with the addition of spices after the Middle Ages.[18] Gingerbread has been made in Toruń, Poland since the thirteenth century.[19] In the Netherlands *Deventer koek* (a compact loaf flavoured with honey and bitter orange which dates back to 1417), is one of the oldest spice cake recipes still being made. The earliest record of gingerbread in Sweden comes from the nuns of Vadstena in 1444. The cakes were sold in the convent pharmacy primarily as a medicine, as they were considered to have a calming effect and alleviate digestive problems. Vast quantities of gingerbread were sent to Johan II, King of Denmark, Sweden and Norway,[20] from a pharmacy in Copenhagen in the late fifteenth century. The confection had be prescribed by the royal physician to cure the king's wretched mood.[21] Philippe le Bon, the Duke of Burgundy, is believed to have been so impressed with a gingerbread he sampled in Flanders that he brought the baker back with him to France in 1452 so that he could have a constant supply of it.[22] The beautiful mistress of King Charles VII, Agnès Sorel, shared the Duke's love of gingerbread (or *pain d'épice* as it is known in France). Charles' son, the future King Louis XI, has been accused of orchestrating her early demise. He was said to be so jealous of the influence Agnès had over his father he sent her some poisoned gingerbread.[23] In the sixteenth century, during the reign of Henri II, this confection would again be tainted with poison when rumours spread that Italians were doctoring their beloved *pain d'épice* with toxic substances (one imagines sales of mithridatium went through the roof at this time). It would not regain favour at the French court until the reign of Louis XIV.[24]

One of the earliest known recipes for gingerbread in Britain is found in *Two Fifteenth-Century Cookery-Books*:

> Gyngerbrede. Take a quart of hony, & sethe it, & skeme it clene; take Safroun, pouder Pepir, & þrow ther-on; take gratyd Brede, & make it so chargeaunt þat it wol be y-leched; þen take pouder Canelle, & straw þer-on y-now; þen make yt square, lyke as þou wolt leche it; take when þou lechyst hyt, an caste Box leaves a-bouyn, y-stkyd þer-on, on clowys. And if þou wolt haue it Red, coloure it with Saunderys y-now.[25]

This stiff paste of breadcrumbs and honey, flavoured with pepper, saffron and cinnamon, omits ginger altogether, although it is called 'gyngerbrede' rather than 'pepper bread'. The paste was shaped into a square before being sliced and decorated with box leaves impaled by a clove. It could also be coloured red with sanders or sandalwood.[26] C. Anne Wilson believes the omission of ginger to be an oversight on the part of the original author or transcriber. However, there are many recipes on the continent for gingerbreads and pepper breads which include neither ginger nor pepper, so it is conceivable that this recipe is as its original author intended it to be.

In Chaucer's *Canterbury Tales* the gingerbread enjoyed by Sir Thopas, a Flemish knight, has been interpreted as being preserved ginger. Indeed, ginger preserved in syrup was eaten during the medieval period. It was one of the few occasions where a fork would be used at the dining table in order to lift the sticky sweetmeat to the mouth.[27]

> And roial spicerye
> Of gyngebreed that was ful fyn,
> And lycorys, and eek comyn,
> With sugre that is trye.[28]

However, Constance Hieatt explains there is evidence in contemporary manuscripts to suggest that some gingerbreads from the medieval period were 'a chewy but fairly hard candy, a confection resembling toffee, made of nothing more than honey and spices'.[29] She is rather amused by the childish treats enjoyed by Sir Thopas, which comprised 'two kinds of sweet drinks and three kinds of expensive candy: gingery "toffee", liquorice and candied cumin seeds'.

Medieval gingerbread was served as a sweetmeat at the end of a meal as part of the 'void' or 'voidee'.[30] Initially the 'void' was the term used for the clearing of the table between courses. By the fifteenth century the voidee described the sweet course served at the end of the meal to aid digestion and sweeten the breath.[31] As well as gingerbread, the voidee could include comfits,[32] wafers and hippocras.[33] As food historian Peter Brears observes: 'Considered hot and moist in nature such sugary foods helped to break down the food received into the body's cauldron, the stomach, a practice we still follow with our after-dinner mints and liqueurs.'[34] The spices and honey used in this early recipe were luxury items, so gingerbread was only accessible to the wealthy. Only the greatest of households, with large kitchens that included a 'Confectionary' or a 'Wafery' area, would be making and serving them on a frequent basis.[35]

As a stand-alone ingredient, ginger had long been praised for its abilities to aid digestion. Anthimus, a Byzantine doctor at the court of Merovingian King Theuderic I (AD 511–533) praised the spice for its positive effect on digestion and included it in many of his dishes.[36] In the Elizabethan era, ginger's hot nature was believed to be good for flatulence and cold stomachs, as well as 'provoking' sluggish husbands and sharpening the sight.[37] During the same period, gingerbread itself was described as 'a kinde of cake or paste made to comfort the stomacke'.[38]

Spices, and especially ginger, were thought to be aphrodisiacs. Any food infused with spices would be in danger of inflaming passion (or in cases of impotence, restoring it). Add hot and moist sugar into the equation and you were asking for trouble. The custom of providing spiced wines at medieval weddings could have been intended to serve a different purpose than being a simple means of toasting the happy couple.[39] It is perhaps no wonder then that gingerbread was offered as a gift (along with other spices and precious foods such as sugar and figs) to Margaret, the 'Maid of Norway' who was being courted as a desirable match for Edward I's son.[40]

During the sixteenth century the medieval voidee would be replaced by the 'banquet'.[41] Like the voidee, the banquet was a separate course served after a formal feast in large households, frequently in a separate room, building, or even on the roof (a post dinner 'after-party' if you like). It was an opportunity to flirt outrageously beyond the wagging tongues of the servants. Invitations to the host's banquet were usually only extended to a select few.[42] Gradually, this trend would filter down the social scale and soon banqueting houses gained a somewhat ribald reputation. They were described by Philip Stubbes in his 1583 pamphlet *Anatomie of Abuses*:

> In the suburbes of the citie, they [women] have *gardens* either paled or walled round about very high, with their harbers and bowers fit for the purpose; and lest they might be espied in these open

places they have their *banqueting-houses* with galleries, turrets, and what not, therein sumptuously erected; wherein they may, and doubtless do, many of them, play the filthy persons.[43]

As in the medieval period, the treats served at the banquet were laden with sugar and spices. The purpose was to demonstrate the confectionary skills of the provider, as well as being a display of wealth. These luscious tidbits were designed to tantalise and titivate all of the senses in order 'to promote the hot and moist humours of lust'.[44] Although larger quantities of sugar were being imported into Britain by the seventeenth century it was still considered a luxury item. This resulted in a high level of tooth decay in the upper classes. This in turn sparked a fashion for tooth picks, many of which were made from precious metals like silver. To have bad teeth indicated you had joined the ranks of the elite banqueters.[45]

In *The Good Huswife's Jewell* (1596–97), Thomas Dawson includes a list of 'all things necessary for a banquet':

> Sugar: Cinnamon: Liquorice: Pepper: Nutmegs: Saffron: Sanders: all kinds of Comfits: Aniseed: Coriander: Oranges: Pomegranate Seeds: Damask water: Lemons: Prunes: Rose water: Dates: Currants: Raisins: Cherries, conserved: Barberries, conserved: Rye flour: Ginger: Sweet oranges: Pepper, white and brown: Cloves: Mace: Wafers: For your marchpane, seasoned and unseasoned spinach.[46]

Many of the ingredients listed above were used to make the gingerbreads of the period, of which there were two kinds: red and white. White gingerbread recipes usually centre around marchpane, an almond paste like marzipan, as in this recipe from John Murrell's *A Delightfull Daily Exercise for Ladies and Gentlewomen* (1621):

> To Make White Gingerbread[47]
> Take half a pound of marchpane paste, a quarter of a pound of white Ginger beaten and [sieved], half a pound of the powder of refined sugar, beat this to a very fine paste with dragagant[48] steeped in rose-water, then role it in round cakes and print it with

your moulds: dry them in an oven when the bread is drawn forth upon white papers, and when they be very dry box them and keep them all the year.

Murrell's marchpane was moulded into a large disk up to 45 cm in diameter with crimped edges. The centre was decorated with a tower or castle, lions or birds (both the structure and the animals were also formed from the marchpane in the centre of the disk) and decorated with comfits, before being dried in the oven. The finished article was then iced with sugar mixed with egg whites and rose water, oven dried again, and finally gilded before being served. Murrell's contemporary, Sir Hugh Plat, provides a slightly different take on the concept of the almond-based gingerbread in his cookery book, *Delightes for Ladies*, published in 1600. His recipe calls for grated cake as well as sugar, almonds, egg yolks, lemon juice and grains of musk. When you scroll though his book to find a corresponding cake recipe it is quite a surprise to discover that Plat's 'Sweet Cakes without Either Spice or Sugar' are made from dried parsnips combined with fine wheat flour and absolutely no sugar.[49]

The other recipe Plat provides for gingerbread is much closer to its original medieval incarnation (the wine included in this recipe lends it a scarlet hue rather than sanders):

To Make Gingerbread[50]
Take three stale Manchets[51] and grate them, dry them, and sift them through a fine sieve, then add unto them one ounce of Ginger being beaten, and as much cinnamon, one ounce of Liquorice and Aniseeds being beaten together and [sieved], half a pound of sugar, then boil it all there together in a posnet,[52] with a quart of claret wine till they come to a stiff paste with often stirring of it; and when it is stiff, mould it on a table and so drive it thin, and put it in your moulds: dust your mould with cinnamon, ginger and liquorice, being mixed together in a fine powder. This is your Gingerbread used at the Court, and in all Gentlemen's houses at festival times. It is otherwise called dry Leach.[53]

Dawson, Murrell and Plat's books belong to a genre of manuals emerging at the end of the sixteenth century to provide advice on how to manage households.[54] As well as recipes for sweetmeats like gingerbread, these books would include remedies for common ailments of the period. Some gentlewomen even created their own collections of recipes and remedies which make fascinating reading.[55]

Although sweetmeats such as gingerbread and marmalades[56] were made at home, it was also possible to buy them from professional confectioners who set up business in Britain from the mid-sixteenth century.[57] In a contrast to other European nations there are no records from this time to indicate whether there was a dedicated gingerbread guild in Britain. In countries such as France and Germany, making gingerbread was a highly skilled profession and guilds were established for these craftsmen to regulate how their local gingerbreads should be made.[58] The French King Henri IV declared in 1596 that nobody could become a master gingerbread maker until he was at least twenty years old and had spent four years or more as an apprentice. Furthermore, the said apprentice had to bake three loaves of *pain d'épice,* flavoured with cinnamon, nutmeg and cloves, weighing twenty pounds each for his master to prove he had reached the desired level of expertise.[59] In the Netherlands, a Deventer council decree in 1417 stated exactly what ingredients the town's *Deventer koek* (a spiced honey cake) should contain, and bakers could be fined 666 guilders if they failed to comply.[60]

English cookery has long doffed its cap to the French kitchen, but there is a 'valid contrast' between the two countries' recipes from this time, none more so than when you look at gingerbread.[61] Continental gingerbreads, such as *pain d'épice*, seem to be more akin to cake (if a little on the dense side)[62] compared to our own largely honey-based and breadcrumb-based confections of this period. This could be a question of available ingredients. Several European gingerbreads use rye flour (like the *pain d'épice* of Reims) or a combination of rye and wheat. Rye was being grown in Britain during the medieval period although rye bread was seen as poor man's fodder.[63] Presumably, rye flour or bread would have been deemed unsuitable for such luxurious confection. Where you do see regional variations in British gingerbread is in the use of oats. Samuel Johnson somewhat derisively describes oats as 'a grain, which in England is generally given to horses, but in Scotland supports the people.'[64] It is true that oats do feature in Scottish recipes such as broonie (an oatmeal gingerbread from the Orkneys. See page 136 for a recipe) or Yorkshire parkin. However, oat-based recipes (albeit not necessarily gingerbread) are found in cookbooks of the period such as *The Art of Cookery Made Plain and Easy* by Hannah Glasse.[65] Honey, which still features significantly in many European gingerbreads even today, had also been dropped in favour of the more exclusive sugar.[66] The manuscript copy of Mary Doggett's 'Booke of receits' (1682) contains a gingerbread recipe which includes sugar and honey, but this is unusual for the period.[67] The spicing element of gingerbread appears to vary according to the personal taste of the baker, although from here on most British gingerbreads do contain ginger.

Gingerbread would remain a treat for festivals and special occasions for many years to come. But it was about to undergo a further evolution by embracing a substance that would help make it more accessible to the masses.

CHAPTER THREE

EVERYMAN'S GINGERBREAD

As disasters go, the Great Molasses Flood of 1919 in Boston, Massachusetts, should rank as one of biblical proportions, although you will clearly find no trace of it mentioned in either Testament. The catastrophe occurred in January of that year when a giant tank of molasses burst. Imagine the horror as two million gallons of black syrup careered though the streets of the city's North End district at an estimated thirty-five miles per hour, leaving in its wake a trail of destruction. Many people were trapped by the debris and some were asphyxiated by the gooey sludge. In total, twenty-one people lost their lives and over one hundred and fifty suffered injuries as a result of the deluge. Rescue workers were still looking for bodies five days after the tragedy, and it is said the smell of molasses lingered for decades.[1]

Experts have attributed the Great Molasses Flood to engineering flaws in the structure of the tank, which had been built quickly in 1915 to meet the rising demand for the industrial alcohol that could be brewed from molasses. This was used to make dynamite and other explosives which had been in high demand during the Great War.[2] However, long before the inundation, molasses were highly prized, both in America and Britain, as an ingredient in the kitchen and the distillery.

Molasses, or treacle as we prefer to call it in Britain, is a by-product of sugar production. After the sweet juice has been extracted from the canes by pounding or soaking, it is heated to create crystals which eventually become 'refined' sugar. The dark, viscous, sweet substance resulting from this process is treacle.

Europeans were no strangers to the idea of treacle, although it would take a while for it to be adopted as a sweetening agent in recipes. The word 'treacle' comes from the Greek *theriaca antidotos* (literally an antidote for the bite of a wild beast). The Roman Emperor Nero's physician, Andromachus, applied the term to a mixture of honey, spices and drugs as a cure-all for venomous bites and poisons (not unlike Mithridatium). This concoction was still

Eighteenth-century pharmacy storage jar used for Theriac, Bordeaux, France. © Science Museum, London.

available in the Middle Ages as *theriaca* or *triacle* from apothecaries and treacle mongers. Venetian treacle, an electuary reputedly made to Andromachus' very recipe, was the most costly. Venetian treacle would eventually be usurped by a new electuary called London treacle, which used cheap molasses rather than honey as its base.[3] This association of treacle as a medicine could explain why it was slow to be adopted as a culinary ingredient.[4]

Sugar and its derivatives had been slowly winding their way westwards long before the Crusades in the eleventh century, courtesy of the Arabs who had been growing sugar cane in Sicily, Cyprus and even Spain.[5] Not surprisingly, given their influence over the spice trade in the Middle Ages, the Venetians were quick to capitalise on this fledgling industry, setting up new enterprises in the Mediterranean, with other merchant states like Genoa following suit.[6]

In England, treacle's transformation from medicine to food came about largely as a result of the country's colonial expansion during the seventeenth century. Early English settlers in the Caribbean tried growing crops such as cotton and tobacco with some success, but it was sugar that helped make them rich.[7] Colonialists from all over Europe soon realised that the climate in the Caribbean and Americas was much better suited to growing sugar than the Mediterranean. Sugar exports from Barbados alone in the late 1640s were worth over three million pounds, making it England's wealthiest colony.[8] Sugar production is particularly labour intensive. Twenty thousand new African slaves were required each year to maintain the labour force in the 'sugar islands', fuelling England's slave trade.[9] The country became embedded in a trade triangle. English products were exchanged for African slaves, who in turn were shipped to the colonies to provide the labour required on the sugar plantations. The sugar then returned to the motherland for consumption by the English and her neighbours.[10]

Until the middle of the sixteenth century, New World sugar was refined in the Low Countries, but from 1544 England began refining its own sugar.[11] By the end of the seventeenth century there were nineteen sugar refineries in the City of London and a further nineteen in Southwark.[12] This meant that treacle could be produced on home soil. As England's colonial interests expanded, so the price of sugar and treacle would come down.[13] As well as a medicine, treacle was used to distil rum (particularly in New England, which we will return to),[14] but as the production of treacle outstripped the demands of apothecaries and distillers it was sold as a cheap unmedicated sweetener known as 'common treacle', later simplified to 'treacle'.[15]

It was not long before honey was usurped by sugar or treacle in gingerbread recipes. Robert May's gingerbread recipe from *The Accomplisht Cook* (1685) clings to the habit of using breadcrumbs and ground almonds, but these are combined with sugar and spices rather than honey.[16] In the 1705 edition of *The Family Dictionary* William Salmon records that a gingerbread was made for King Charles II (1660–85) containing three pounds of treacle, half a pound each of candied orange, lemon and citron peel, plus two ounces of coriander seeds and enough flour to make a paste.[17] John Nott's gingerbread in *The Cook's and Confectioner's Dictionary* (1723) is similar:

17. To make Ginger-Bread[18]
Take four Pounds of Treacle, of Citron, Lemon and Orange Peel, and candy'd Ginger, of each half a pound; slice all these thin, add also beaten Ginger, Coriander-seeds, and Caraway-seeds, of each two Ounces; mix all these with as much Flour, as will make it a soft Paste; then lay it in Cakes on Tin-plates, and bake it in a quick Oven.

Interestingly, gingerbread is conspicuously absent from some of the more courtly cookbooks of the early eighteenth century, such as Charles Carter's *Complete Practical Cook* (1730).[19] So had gingerbread fallen out of favour with the elite by the eighteenth century? If you look at Carter's recipes, spices are used far more sparingly than perhaps they would have been in Elizabeth I's reign, although they are still present, particularly in his sweet dishes.[20] These and other contemporary recipes, such as those by John Nott, indicate that there was still a taste for spiced sweet treats.

The absence of gingerbread recipes from some books of the period may have been a question of the availability of the materials required to make them. The price of sugar had plummeted during the course of the seventeenth century, from over one shilling per pound at the beginning to around six pence or less per pound by 1700.[21] While sugar was by no means an everyday item for the majority of the population, many more people could afford to buy it for use in puddings and tarts.[22] Diarist Samuel Pepys, the tailor's son who rose to become Chief Secretary to the Admiralty, mentions eating gingerbread in his diary entry for 28th February 1668: '...she gave me some ginger-bread made in cakes, like chocolate, very good, made by a friend'.[23] As Sidney Mintz has observed, 'the regular consumption of sugar, particularly cheap brown sugar or treacle, even in modest quantities, gradually reduced sugar's status as a glamorous luxury and a precious good'.[24]

By the end of the seventeenth century, London would boast forty confectioners.[25] Perhaps having access to these merchants removed the need to make sweet treats like gingerbread at home, enabling your cook (if you were lucky enough to have one, luckier still if he had worked in France or happened to be French) to concentrate on producing French-inspired dishes like *Beef à la Mode*. Further innovations in the way that sugar was processed during the eighteenth century – not to mention 'the systematic exploitation of slave labour'[26] – reduced the cost of this commodity to the consumer even more. The Lathams, a smallholding family from Lancashire, consumed an average of 50 lbs of sugar and 20 lbs of treacle per year during the 1740s, and they were by no means considered to be wealthy.[27] Although the high-end cookbooks of the era may have omitted gingerbread recipes, they were included in the more homely books of Hannah Glasse (1747) and Maria Rundell (1806):

Gingerbread – Another Sort[28]
To three quarters of a pound of treacle beat one egg strained;

mix four ounces of brown sugar, half an ounce of ginger sifted; of cloves, mace, allspice and nutmeg, a quarter of an ounce, beaten as fine as possible: coriander and caraway seeds, each a quarter of an ounce; melt one pound of butter, and mix with the above; and add as much flour as will knead into a pretty stiff paste; then roll it out, and cut into cakes.

Bake on tin plates in a quick oven. A little time will bake them. Of some, drops[29] may be made.

There were notable differences between the diets of the labouring classes in the south of England and those in the north of the country. Due to the climatic conditions in the north of England oats were the staple cereal in this part of the country whereas wheat was favoured in the south.[30] Oats could withstand the harsh wet climate found 600–800 ft above sea level. They were a key ingredient for the popular 'Hasty Pudding' (a kind of porridge which could be eaten with treacle or milk[31]). Oatcakes were a principal element in the diet for the majority of Yorkshire's working population. They were cooked on a 'bakstone' or bakestone, a smooth, flat heated slab often built into the fireplace. Oatcakes were either made from a stiff dough rolled into a thin bread known as clapbread, haverbread or havercake (from the old Norse *hafri* meaning oats) or from a batter poured directly onto the bakestone.[32]

Oatmeal would be combined with treacle (also popular in the north due to its affordability, where wages and the cost of living were significantly lower[33]) to make parkin, another type of gingerbread. The recipe below is from Mrs Hailstone's 'Receipt Book', a household notebook kept by a Bradford solicitor's wife at the beginning of the nineteenth century:[34]

To Make Parkin
3 lbs Oatmeal, 6 Ounces of Butter rubbed in, 1 oz of Ginger, 1 oz of Coriander Seeds, a Glass of Brandy, 3 lbs of Treacle make hot to mix it up with, a good spoonful dropped upon your Tins, and baked in a tolerably hot Oven.

Romantic poet William Wordsworth (1770–1850), who lived in the Lake District, was evidently fond of gingerbread. His sister, Dorothy, wrote about his longing for it in the last entry of her Grasmere journal in January 1803:

> Wm. had a fancy for some ginger bread. I put on Molly's cloak and my Spenser, and we walked towards Matthew Newton's. I went into the house. The blind man and his wife and sister were sitting by the fire, all dressed and very clean in their Sunday clothes, the sister reading. They took their little stock out of the cupboard, and I bought 6 pennyworth. They were so grateful when I paid them for it that I could not find it in my heart to tell them we were going to make ginger bread ourselves. I had asked them if they had no thick – 'No,' answered Matthew, 'there was none in Friday, but we'll endeavour to get some.' The next day the women came just when we were baking and we bought 2 pennyworth.[35]

Jane Grigson casts doubts on the links between the gingerbread so sought after by Wordsworth and the renowned Grasmere variety available today. Modern Grasmere gingerbread has a crumbly, almost shortbread-like texture and is based on a closely guarded recipe by Sarah Nelson from 1855.[36] Given the prevalence of oats in the diet of northerners in the eighteenth and early nineteenth centuries, there does appear to be a case for the gingerbread enjoyed by the Wordsworths being more like the parkin made by Mrs Hailstone (which produces a thin, chewy gingerbread, possibly not dissimilar to that sold by Matthew Newton).

As well as its famous literary resident, Grasmere was also known for its rush-bearing ceremony, originally held on 5th August or the Saturday closest to it.[37] For centuries, similar ceremonies took place all over the country but particularly in northern towns and villages. The festivals would differ slightly from village to village but typically rushes and other greenery were borne to the church, usually by young women adorned with the 'fairest flowers of the field',[38] and spread over the floor. The rushes were strewn over the earth or flagstones to provide the congregation with comfort and warmth when kneeling for prayer.[39] Rushes were chosen with care for their durability (much as you would a carpet) or for their fragrance.[40] Once the formal ceremony was complete, the singing, dancing and – for children the most important bit – the eating could begin.

> One highly important ceremony, to the minds of the children, was yet to come – the presentation of the gingerbread. As they filed out of the church, twopenny slabs of a peculiarly black and solid substance were given into their eager little hands. The rain had ceased, and we grown-ups all waited in the churchyard, looking down on the issuing file of red tam-o'-shanters, ribboned straw hats, worn grey caps, and, wavering along very low in the line, soft, fair-tinted baby hoods, often cuddled up against some guardian knee. Under the varied headgear ecstatic feasting had begun even in the church porch, though some of the children were too entranced with excitement to find their mouths. One chubby urchin waved his piece of gingerbread in the air, and another laid his on a gravestone and inadvertently sat down on it. A bewildered wee damsel in robin's-egg blue had lost hers in the basket of wild flowers that was slung about her neck. One spud of a boy, roaring as he came, was wiping his eyes with his. In general, however, the rush-bearers were munching with such relish that they did not trouble themselves to remove the tissue paper adhering to the bottom of each cake, but swallowed that as contentedly as the rest. Meanwhile their respective adults were swooping down upon them, dabbing the smear of gingerbread off cheeks and chins, buttoning up little sacques and jackets, and whisking off the most obtrusive patches of half-dried mud. Among these parental regulators was a beaming old woman with a big market-basket on her arm, who brushed and tidied as impartially as if she were grandmother to the whole parish.[41]

While American travel writer Katharine Lee Bates (1859–1929) may not have been overly enamoured with Ambleside's 'peculiarly black and solid' gingerbread, her compatriots clearly had different views on the confection. When the English pilgrims, who included women, arrived in seventeenth-century America, they brought with them their culinary knowledge. It is also feasible that they carried cookbooks from England or at least recipes copied from culinary manuscripts such as Gervase Markham's *The English Huswife* (1615).[42] Karen Hess believes the recipes in Martha Washington's *Booke of Cookery* are far earlier than the date of her marriage to her first husband Daniel Custis in 1749.[43] The first gingerbread recipe in Martha's *Booke of Sweetmeats* contains honey and breadcrumbs, harking back to the gingerbreads of medieval times.[44] Although early American cookery reflected its English roots, the settlers adapted the recipes to suit the ingredients available. In the cookbook written by New Englander Amelia Simmons, Hasty Pudding is transformed into 'A Nice Indian Pudding' by substituting cornmeal for the traditional oats.[45]

West Indian molasses were particularly important to the settlers in North America. One of the primary uses for this product was to distill rum. Although rum could be imported from the Caribbean, New Englanders brewed more than half a million gallons of it themselves a year.[46] Molasses from the French sugar islands was far cheaper than that from the British colonies like Barbados (France did not have its own rum industry so the French were happy to sell their molasses off cheap). The 1733 Molasses Act imposed a 6d tax on molasses imported into America sourced from outside of the British empire, causing outcry across the thirteen mainland colonies and leaving a bitter taste the Americans would remember in decades to come. The foodstuff most commonly associated with the American Revolution is tea, but John Adams would later reflect that 'molasses was an essential ingredient in American Independence'.[47]

It would also become an essential ingredient in American gingerbread. There are six gingerbread recipes in Simmons' *American Cookery* (1796), largely recognised as the first homegrown American cookbook,[48] although not all of them include molasses:

Molasses Gingerbread
One table spoon of cinnamon, one spoonful ginger, some coriander or allspice, put to four tea spoons pearlash, dissolved in half pint of water, four pounds flour, one quart molasses, six ounces butter (if in summer rub in butter, if in the winter warm the butter and molasses, and pour to the spiced flour) knead well till stiff, the more the butter, the lighter and whiter it will be; bake brisk fifteen minutes, wash it with whites and sugar beat together.[49]

One hundred years later several of the gingerbread recipes in the *Boston Cooking School Cook Book* (1896) by Fannie Merritt Farmer would contain molasses. Much as it had been in England, gingerbread was something that was acceptable for the lady of the house to make. Evidently it was the only thing Jo March in *Little Women* could make that was 'fit to eat'.[50] Although molasses is not a commonly used ingredient in French cookery, it features in many of the French-sounding cake recipes (such as 'Gateau au Gingembre') in *The Picayune's Creole Cook Book* (1901).[51] Even the *pain d'épice* recipe uses molasses in place of the traditional honey. The recipe for 'Stage Planks or Gingerbread without Butter or Eggs' was apparently a hard confection (as suggested by the name) that would keep for weeks. The nickname for this cake was 'Estomac Mulâtre' or 'The Mulatto's Stomach', as it was 'only fit for the stomach of a mulatto to digest'.[52]

From the seventeenth century another spice was also to enter the gingerbread sphere. Allspice had been discovered by Columbus and other early European explorers at the end of the fifteenth century. The small, brown, pea-like seeds with a rough surface were mistaken for pepper, hence the Spanish name *pimienta* or *pimiento* in English. Following the conquest of Jamaica in 1655, England received regular imports of allspice.[53] 'Jamaica pepper', as it came to be known, took a while to become fully entrenched in English cuisine but its clove-cinnamon-nutmeg-like qualities soon endeared it to cooks.[54] Maria Rundell provides a recipe for Kitchen Pepper including ground ginger, cinnamon, nutmeg, cloves, black pepper, allspice and salt to keep on hand in the kitchen for use in pickles and sauces (barring the salt it would probably have made an admirable seasoning for gingerbread).[55] Her contemporary Dr Kitchiner uses equal quantities of ginger and allspice in his orange gingerbread.

Generally speaking, the Victorians were a little more circumspect when it came to spicing gingerbreads. The key spice used is almost always ginger, sometimes partnered by allspice or cloves. Eliza Acton provides very detailed, if labour intensive, instructions (very rare for the time) on how to prepare her 'Acton Gingerbread':

Whisk four strained or well-cleared eggs to the lightest possible froth (French eggs, if really sweet, will answer for this purpose), and pour to them by degrees, a pound and a quarter of treacle, still beating them lightly. Add, in the same manner, six ounces of pale brown sugar free from lumps, one pound of sifted flour, and six ounces of good butter, just sufficiently warmed to be liquid, and no more, for if hot, it would render the cake heavy; and it should be poured in small portions to the mixture, which should be well beaten up with the back of a wooden spoon as each portion is thrown in: the success of the cake depends entirely on this part of the process. When properly mingled with the mass, the butter will not be perceptible on the surface; and if the cake be kept light by constant whisking, large bubbles will appear at last. When it is ready, add to it one ounce of Jamaica ginger and a large teaspoon of cloves in fine powder, with the lightly grated rind of two full sized lemons. Butter thickly, in every part, a shallow square tin pan, and bake the gingerbread slowly for nearly or quite and hour in a gentle oven. Let it cool a little before it is turned out, and set it on its edge until cold, supporting it, if needful, against a large jar or bowl. We have usually had it baked in an American oven, in a tin less than two inches deep; and it has been excellent. We retain the name given to it originally in our own circle.[56]

From the eighteenth century onwards gingerbread was enjoyed by all levels of society. The future Queen Victoria gave her beloved King Charles Spaniel, Dash, 'two bits of gingerbread surrounded with branches of holly and candles' for Christmas in 1833.[57] Prince Albert, the queen's consort would introduce some traditions from his homeland into the royal household:

> Albert arranged a surprise for the Children. In Germany, the old saying that St Nicholas appears with a rod for naughty children, & gingerbread for good ones, is constantly represented, & Arthur hearing of this begged for one. Accordingly Albert got up a St Nicholas, most formidable he looking, in black, covered with snow, a long white beard, & red nose, – of a gigantic stature! He came in asking the Children, who were somewhat awed & alarmed, – 'are you a good child,' & giving them gingerbread & apples.[58]

Agnes B. Marshall bucks the trend of the time for treacle-laden gingerbreads by including a sugar-based recipe for 'Nuremberg Gingerbread' in her cookbook, which may have been a nod to the late Prince Albert's German heritage.[59] However, Charles Francatelli, who worked for the royal household for a short time, gives a honey-based recipe for 'Swiss Lecrelets' which are probably closer to the style of gingerbread enjoyed on the continent than Marshall's sugar-based one.[60] According to Swiss chef Joseph Favre,[61] *lecrelets* is the French spelling of the Swiss *leckerlis* (derived from the German *lecker* meaning delicious). These spiced lozenge-shaped biscuits containing almonds and mixed citrus peel were highly regarded both at home and by travellers passing through Basel. Francatelli describes them as being 'well adapted for dessert, luncheon, or as a pleasant adjunct for the supper tray'. Quite unusually for 'domestic' English gingerbread recipes of the period, Francatelli recommends leaving the dough in a cool place for three days prior to use.[62]

Gingerbread was not only eaten during the festive period in Britain. It was available from bakers and confectioners in towns and from vendors at fairs and markets across the country all year round. While staying on the Isle of Wight the Royal Family visited a fête on Prince Alfred's sixth birthday (6th August 1850) where they witnessed 'jingling, blindman's buff, wheelbarrow races, coits, hurdle & running races, jumping in sacks, bobbing for gingerbread, &c'.[63] In Charles Dickens' heyday, gingerbread was still a popular treat:

> Mr. Dick was very partial to gingerbread. To render his visits the more agreeable, my aunt had instructed me to open a credit for him at a cake shop, which was hampered with the stipulation that he should not be served with more than one shilling's-worth in the course of any one day.[64]

Frederick Vine devotes a number of pages to different types of gingerbread in his *Saleable Shop Goods for Counter Tray and Window* (1898), ranging from the traditional 'block' style gingerbreads pressed into special moulds to lacy brandy snaps.[65] Although the ingredients in his 'Thick Gingerbread' may be simple, it is clear that Vine believes a decent gingerbread requires considerable care to achieve good results:

> The longer this dough stands, the better will be the resultant gingerbread. In the old days it was always the rule to put away the gingerbread sponges early in the spring, and then it would be in prime condition for use about September; but at the present time it would, most probably be deemed ripe in from one to three months.[66]

By the end of the nineteenth century the consumer's attitude towards the traditional block gingerbread was changing. Vine would lament:

> This is the ordinary plain lump gingerbread that was so much in vogue a few years ago, but of late years it has gone considerably out of sight. Why it should have done so is perhaps to be explained by the very much greater variety of confectionary before the public. But I do not think that is the reason – which

I believe is, because the same attention is not bestowed upon its manufacture now as formerly, and the sponges are not given sufficient time to ripen.[67]

As the twentieth century dawned, was gingerbread about to fizzle away into obscurity?

CHAPTER FOUR

GINGERBREAD CREATIONS

Eminent food historian Ivan Day has rightly lamented the evolution of the elegant gingerbread creations of yesteryear to 'the currant-eyed homunculus of the modern bakery aisle'.[1] At one time there was a real art to making gingerbread both in terms of the dough itself and the moulds used to produce gingerbread royalty.

We are fortunate that a fair number of these moulds have survived, thanks to collectors like Edward Pinto, who wrote extensively on the subject of treen: simple household items, including gingerbread moulds, made from wood. The subject matter of these moulds varies immensely from era and country but provides a fascinating insight into European social history. From 'everyday' objects like hats, pistols, and swords (well, at least they would have been everyday objects in seventeenth-century Paris) to saints and royalty, just about anything or anyone could be reproduced in gingerbread with the appropriate mould.[2]

Like any recipe, the standard of the finished item was dependent on the quality of the ingredients used. When it came to gingerbread moulds it was important to use an odourless wood to ensure no unpleasant flavours would taint the finished product. The best wood by far was box wood. Box (*Buxus sempervirens*) is slow growing and though it is hard to carve it is incredibly durable, so perfect for moulds where many distinct impressions are required. Some fruit woods like pear, cherry, apple or plum could also be used, as well as chestnut and ash. Beech and elm were occasionally used but produced less defined gingerbreads.[3]

The thickness of these moulds varied from one to three centimetres but most were carved on both sides and were sometimes referred to as cards.[4] This meant you could have completely different subjects on one card – the crucifixion on one side, say, and puss in boots on the other. On a more practical note, as Frederick Vine explains in his book *Saleable Shop Goods*, you could have a halfpenny gingerbread mould on one side and a penny mould on the other.[5] The original moulds were produced freehand with the designs carved in reverse, known as intaglio carving. Mirrors were only used for letters or crests. As this was such skilled work it is understandable that the craftsman would want to leave some kind of identifying mark or name on the mould.[6] In Russia, craftsmen would receive prizes for their wooden artistry, and intricate gingerbread boards have been found in excavations at Novgorod. Large ceremonial gingerbreads in Russia could weigh several poods – a pood was the equivalent of 36 lbs – and include up to eighty individual squares which were particularly handy for feasts. At the end of the meal, farewell 'cookies' could be broken off these enormous slabs and given to guests as a signal that it was time to leave.[7] By the time Vine published his book in 1898, bakers could buy bespoke gingerbread moulds with their name on, made by confectioner machinists, perhaps marking the beginning of the end of this particular art form.[8]

As the desire to eat elaborately stamped gingerbreads decreased, so the demand for collecting moulds grew. On the one hand this has helped preserve our heritage although perhaps the respect due these objects has been somewhat abused. Andrew Tuer describes how some 'unregenerate person' had sawn several of the moulds he had acquired in two thereby halving the thickness.[9] Many of the moulds that once served bakers so faithfully are cherished as ornaments or heritage pieces in museums rather than being used in the kitchen.[10] Antique gingerbread moulds have become so sought after it has prompted a spate of forgeries, which include crudely carved moulds usually in the form of dogs, cats and other 'undatable items' from Holland and

Belgium. Sometimes the wood has even been charred to persuade people that the mould was used in an oven (gingerbread was never baked in the actual mould).[11]

The popularity of gingerbread through the ages cannot be attributed to its appearance alone. Ultimately, it had to taste good too. The key is letting the flavours of the gingerbread develop by leaving the dough to rest for a period of time, as described by Vine. This fermentation process was the preserve of the professional baker in Britain. Although some continental gingerbread recipes written for the home cook require the dough to be left for a period of time it is rare to find similar instructions in British household manuals. Vine was clearly writing for the bakery trade and provides detailed descriptions with images of how to 'block out' the gingerbread dough. The quantities given in his basic recipes are immense. Recipe number 209 for 'Thick Gingerbread' contains 56 lbs treacle; 1 lb ash; ¾ lb hard and 1 quart of water combined with enough household flour 'to form rather a stiff dough'. 'Ash' is the old-fashioned word for sodium carbonate (which was originally extracted from the ashes of plants growing in sodium-rich soils) and 'hard' refers to alum (aluminium sulphate) both of which are found in modern baking powder. Portions of the fermented dough could be cut off as required. Sometimes caraway seeds or comfits – sugar-coated nuts, spices or seeds – were added.[12] The dough was then pressed into moulds or rolled out and cut into shapes such as fluted squares for Parliament cakes (a recipe for which you can find on page 104) providing the baker plenty of opportunities to air his creativity.[13]

OF DOUGH AND MEN

I've run away from a little old woman,
A little old man,
And I can run away from you, I can.[14]

If I were a gingerbread boy I would run too. Not from any sense of bravado but purely as an act of self-preservation. The cocky little biscuit sprints away from his elderly creators like an errant toddler, avoids the clutches of a number of farmworkers and animals before eventually getting his comeuppance in the jaws of a fox.[15] There seemed to be no escape for gingerbread figures in the nineteenth century. In Hoffmann's *Nutcracker* (originally published in 1816 and immortalised as a ballet by Tchaikovsky in 1892) the titular hero's gingerbread reinforcements are soon defeated by the mouse king's soldiers:

> And there did, in fact, advance a small contingent of brown gingerbread men and women, with gilt faces, hats and helmets… And the enemy's chasseurs soon bit their legs off, so that they tumbled topsy-turvey, and killed several of Nutcracker's companions-in-arms into the bargain.[16]

Bakers of yesteryear have kindly left us numerous wooden artefacts detailing the figures and shapes that were popular for gingerbread. The significance of some of these moulds is more obvious than others. For example, many pictured famous or patriotic figures, like the Duke of Wellington sitting on his horse.[17] Royalty was clearly a popular subject, although sometimes the same design could be utilised for different monarchs, making it quite tricky to date some moulds.[18] In the early nineteenth century a gilded King George on horseback was popular and 'was eaten with great relish by his juvenile subjects'.[19] While the distinctive moulds may have fallen out of use, the generic gingerbread figure is as much a part of our social fabric as it would have been several hundred years ago. How we love to dismember these biscuit people by plucking off an arm or leg, or perhaps going for outright decapitation before plunging the body into a vat of hot tea. Could there be a link between how we devour our gingerbread men now and their original purpose? The authors of a late nineteenth-century article entitled 'Mythological forms of bakers' cakes' certainly appear to think so:

> The gingerbread man can be traced back to the sacrifice of prisoners, knights and footsoldiers. Human sacrifices, however, even in the most ancient times, were sacred to the gods alone, and were not eaten by the worshippers themselves, but only their baked

and painted effigies. These figures were originally painted with the blood of the victims. It is for this reason that these gingerbread figures are still ornamented with red. The blood was considered the seat of the soul, therefore very precious and by devouring it they added to their own strength and lessened the power of the enemy as an evil spirit.[20]

In his study of mythology and religion, *The Golden Bough*, Sir James George Frazer describes how the Aztecs in Mexico would make 'the likeness of a man fashioned out of seeds of various sorts, which were kneaded into a dough with the blood of children' (it is not clear whether the children were sacrificed or merely 'donated' their blood for the purpose).[21] This dough effigy represented the Aztec god Huitzilopochtli and after great ceremony it was sacrificed then divided into small pieces and given to the male inhabitants. However, there appears to be little evidence to support the theory that painting dough effigies with the blood of sacrificial victims or kneading their blood into dough was a common practice in the past. Frazer dismisses the notion that all dough effigies in Europe were a type of sacramental bread eaten by worshippers to replace an earlier practice of human sacrifice.[22] Humanoid artefacts fashioned in dough, dating from as early as 1400 BCE, have been found in Deir-el-Medinah in Egypt, including a feast cake made with honey that appears to resemble a child's face and body. Eva Crane has suggested this could be a prototype gingerbread man, though she does not make any connection between the effigy and human sacrifice.[23]

Effigies, edible or otherwise, have long been used to denigrate particular groups of people or individuals. In the past, the English had a penchant for having a jibe at Welsh nationalism.[24] In England on St David's Day (1st March) it used to be the custom to hang or burn effigies of Welshmen (the same way the British still do with 'Guys' on 5th November). This was witnessed by the seventeenth-century diarist Samuel Pepys:

> In Mark Lane, I do observe, it being St David's Day, the picture of a man dressed like a Welchman, hanging by the neck upon one of the poles that stand out at the top of one of the merchants'

houses, in full proportion, and very handsomely done; which is one of the oddest sights I have seen a good while, for it was so like a man that one would have thought it was indeed a man.[25]

A century later, references were still being made to this practice as indicated in a stanza from a poem printed in *Poor Robin's Almanac* of 1757:

> *But it would make a stranger laugh*
> *To see th'English hang poor Taff:*
> *A pair of breeches and a coat,*
> *Hat, shoes, and stockings, and what not,*
> *All stuffed with hay to represent*
> *The Cambrian hero thereby meant:*
> *With sword sometimes three inches broad,*
> *And other armour made of wood,*
> *They drag hur to some publick tree,*
> *And hang hur up in effigy.*[26]

While Horatio Smith (1779–1849) scorned this English insult to the Welsh inhabitants of London, though he conceded that they did on occasion retaliate.[27] At some point the effigy switched from being made of straw to the more innocuous gingerbread:

> On this day, also, 'taffies' – small figures of white 'parlement', like gingergread, moulded into the semblance of 'a Welchman riding on a goat, affixed to a skewer of wood' – were wont to be exhibited in the shop windows of the gingerbread bakers, small pastry cooks, and chandlers in the metropolis and large towns in the country.[28]

Generally speaking, gingerbread depictions of famous people were made because the person in question was renowned for a particular act or they were popular in their own right.[29] But occasionally, they had far more seditious connotations. In 1827 a confectioner, Billy-Baidar, from Metz was hauled in front of a tribunal for producing a gingerbread figure of the deeply unpopular King Charles X. The local prefect declared the image disrespectful as the king was depicted wearing a *calotte*, a type of skullcap worn by priests. The implication was that the king was in cahoots with the Jesuits. Fortunately for Billy-Baider some local mould makers testified that the offending cap was in fact hair, pointing out that it was impossible to achieve fine detail such as individual strands in *pain d'épice*. The gingerbread maker was acquitted but the court ruled that the mould should be destroyed. As to whether or not the 'Jesuit-King' mould was in fact destroyed remains something of a mystery. Although there is no trace of the mould itself there is a gingerbread fashioned from it tucked away in the National Archives in Paris. Even after all these years when you see a photograph of the gingerbread figure, the 'hair' in question clearly resembles a cap so Billy-Baider was very lucky indeed to escape prosecution.[30]

Occasionally, edible figures reflected a more localised rather than national fame, and served as objects of public commemoration.[31] The Museum of English Rural Life has a gingerbread mould in its collection which features two ladies side by side, so close in fact that they appear to be joined together.[32] It bears a striking resemblance to the design of the Biddenden Cakes handed out on Easter Monday. The custom is believed to date back to at least the early seventeenth century. A charitable dole of bread, cheese and beer is given to the widows and pensioners of Biddenden while onlookers receive cakes with the figures of two ladies stamped on them known as the Biddenden Maids.[33] W.T. Marchant refers to these maids as having 'the peculiar form of twin figure gingerbread cakes'.[34] However, the cakes are in fact hard, plain biscuits simply made from flour and water.

Aside from the famous personages moulded in gingerbread there were the generic human shapes sold at fairs, known as 'gingerbread husbands'. Gingerbread husbands seem to have been particularly popular in the southern counties of England.[35] The *Chelmsford Chronicle,* for instance, on Friday 14 May 1847 reports of the Spring Fair that, 'there were upon the stalls rows of gingerbread husbands for little ladies, and on the pavement rows of young gentlemen for larger ones, looking almost as gay if not quite so soft and tender'.[36] Founder of the English Folk Cookery Association in 1928 Florence White comments 'just imagine a child's joy in the gingerbread husband, and her grief when the gilt wore off!'[37] Gingerbread wives were also available and are mentioned by John Keats in reference to Dawlish fair,[38] as well as John Newbery in his 1764 children's story, *The Fairing*:

> Please buy a Gingerbread wife, Sir? Here is a very delicate one. Indeed, there is too much Gold upon her Nose; but that is no Objection to those who drive Smithfield bargains, and marry their wives by weight.[39]

The trend for moulded figures would gradually dwindle as lamented by an article in the *Daily Telegraph* in 1929:

> Before and on Feb 14th gingerbread valentines, or gingerbread husbands were on sale; they were famous fairings, for one of the principal fairs of the country was held not that day in Bath over one hundred years ago. Gingerbread husbands were little figures of men made in gingerbread biscuit: sometimes the gentlemen would be carrying a stick, sometimes an umbrella. He was decorated with touches of gold. It was much a custom to buy a gingerbread husband on Valentine's Day as it was in Durham and the North to make or buy a Yule dough baby at Christmas, or a three cornered god-cake at Coventry for the New Year; a seed-cake at the close of wheat sowing in October, or soul cakes in November and parkin on November 5th at Leeds…But up to fifteen years ago gingerbread husbands could still be bought at an old established shop at Bath. Alas! The Great War ended this also, and gingerbread husbands are no longer obtainable.[40]

I Left My Heart In…

For Richard the Lionheart (King of England 1189–1199) Normandy was his happy place. The monarch was so fond of this area of France that he ordered his heart to be buried at Rouen cathedral while the rest of his body was interred at the feet of his father in Anjou. This was far from an unusual request in twelfth-century Europe. Medieval nobility believed the heart was the seat of love, so it was natural to have it buried in a place which they associated with personal happiness, while their bodies were laid to rest elsewhere. From this period onwards the heart shape would come to symbolise love, both spiritual and profane.[41]

The Christian church would embrace the symbol through its devotion of the Sacred Heart to illustrate the love and suffering of Jesus Christ.[42] In the religious context the shape is usually embellished further. A flaming heart became the symbol of the love of man (or God), particularly during the second half of the seventeenth century. This image is frequently associated with Saint Augustine although sometimes the heart is pierced with an arrow.[43] Nuns would be presented with a gingerbread 'heart of vows' on their spiritual marriage to Christ. These ornate gingerbreads included the monogram of Christ, IHS (a transliteration of the name 'Jesus' in Greek), and sometimes depictions of the crown of thorns or the nails of the cross. The carved relief could be embellished further by 'painting' or gilding the gingerbreads. Gilding was particularly popular in Europe on gingerbread hearts featuring patron saints, which were often given as gifts by parents or godparents to children.

In the end, romantic love would win the day and, from the eighteenth century onwards, the heart became the symbol of affection, a fact exploited by confectioners in Britain who sold heart-shaped cakes called sweethearts or Royal Hearts.[44] The probate inventory of John Reynolds, a chapman (street hawker) from Boston, Lincolnshire, listed quantities of 'Ginger Bread in Rowls & sweethearts' valued at 12 shillings.[45]

Given the association with love it is understandable that heart-shaped gingerbread and cakes should be given as engagement or wedding presents.[46] This has particularly been the case in eastern Europe as discussed by Edith Hörandner. A heart featuring a padlock or bar could (rather depressingly) represent 'the finality of marriage', while a pair of doves represented faithfulness and affection. By the end of the eighteenth century it was common for the bride and groom's names to appear on the gingerbread.[47] At the gingerbread museum in Radovljica, they have a heart-shaped mould dating from the sixteenth century which belonged to a nobleman.[48]

In the Netherlands, gingerbreads were used as edible love letters or even a covert marriage proposal. Known as *hylikmaker* they were sold at fairs and could be heart-shaped although sometimes they were plain rectangles. At the horse and cattle market in Goes, many young girls dreamed of being presented with a cow-shaped cake decorated with her name or verse. Depending on where you lived in the Netherlands there appears to have been various interpretations on how to react when you received the *hylikmaker*. If a girl received a *hylikmaker* then she had an admirer. In certain areas, the way to signal she shared the boy's affections would be to share the cake with him. In the Achterhoek, if the admirer came to coffee fourteen days later and was offered the first slice of the love cake, the engagement became a fact. A trial by love cake took place in Deventer. The cake was put into the mouths of the happy couple and if they were able to consume it without using their hands, the engagement would be confirmed. However, if they failed, the young man was sent packing. And woe betide if your amour should return the whole or even a portion of the *hylikmaker* – that was an outright rejection.[49]

The honey-based *lect* of Slovenia (known as *licitar* in Croatia) have been popular love tokens in all levels of society since the nineteenth century. The shiny red icing which coats the exterior of the honey bread (which symbolises passion and love) and the elaborate floral decoration makes the *lect* appear more like an ornament rather than something you would eat. Often these biscuits include a small mirror for the recipient (usually a young woman) to admire themselves.[50] Despite appearances the *lect* are entirely edible. However, in the past, some of the ingredients used to achieve the bright colours on gingerbread hearts were not safe to eat.[51]

Sometimes there are no strings attached to the giving of love tokens. Gingerbread hearts are presented to everyone as a gift of friendship in the Austrian town of Gmunden on the fourth Sunday of Lent. This custom of 'presenting love' was revived after the Second World War but has roots in a centuries-old practice when the well-to-do citizens of the town would give the poor gifts.

ANIMAL MAGIC

As diplomatic envoys go, few have attracted as much fervour and attention as the glamorous Zarafa. Her journey from Africa to France had been long and slow, covering almost five thousand kilometres over many months. Wherever she went she was greeted by crowds – thirty thousand welcomed her in Lyon alone. Well, it's not every day you get to see a giraffe in the flesh, especially in the nineteenth century.[52]

Eager to curry favour with European leaders (and to gloss over his suppression of the Greek uprising against Ottoman rule) Muhammad Ali, the viceroy of Egypt, had sent a giraffe to King Charles X of France as a gift which was presented to him in 1827. To say she took Paris by storm would be an understatement. Sixty thousand people visited her at the Jardin des Plantes in Paris over a three-week period in the July she arrived.[53] The journal *Le Pandore* would declare 'from the modest gingerbread to the sumptuous bronze, everything in fashion offers a giraffe'.[54] Women began styling their hair *à la girafe* and wearing giraffe coloured dresses.[55] Like so many famous personages before her, Zarafa – as the giraffe came to be popularly known – would be immortalised in gingerbread by Dijon bakers such as Barnabé Boittier.[56] The year after Zarafa arrived in France, Muhammad Ali also sent Emperor Franz I of Austria a giraffe.[57] The Austrians were equally as enamoured as the French with their exotic acquisition. The Museum Brot und Kunst in Germany has an Austrian gingerbread mould featuring a giraffe dating from 1828. Up until the outbreak of the First World War you could still buy 'Giraffeln' pastries in some Viennese bakeries.[58]

Throughout history, depictions of animals and birds in gingerbread have been popular. Some, like the giraffes described above, are directly linked to specific events. Other figures could have more symbolic meaning. Some were just downright bizarre.

An early reference to using animal-shaped moulds to shape biscuits is found in *The Baghdad Cookbook* (c.1226). A recipe for a boiled honey and almond sweetmeat spiced with musk, called *Samak wa-Aqrās* (fishes and cakes) instructs the cook to:

> …make it into fish and loaves in the carved wooden moulds which are made for that purpose…You might make it into chickens and lambs and other shapes, all with the mould according to what is desired.[59]

The oldest form of gingerbreads in Russia were moulded into shapes (rather than stamped in moulds). Known as *lepnye pryaniki* one of the most popular forms was a 'sun deer' – a reindeer with antlers that resemble the sun's rays. They were baked at the winter solstice and exchanged to bring good fortune for the year ahead. The cookies were given to mummers, who dressed in scary animal costumes, as a reward for singing carols, and to wish them well for the year ahead.[60]

Roosters and peacocks were also popular gingerbread subjects in Russia, and in Britain too it would seem.[61] One of the most popular, if a tad unusual, gingerbread moulds features a cockerel wearing trousers. Henry Mayhew describes this type of gingerbread as an 'edible toy'[62] which was in decline by the mid-nineteenth century. Horsham Museum in Sussex has a good example of a cockerel in breeches on display.[63] Andrew Tuer explains that gingerbreads like this would be given to good customers as makeweights. There could be humour behind these gifts too. According to Tuer, the theme of the cockerel in breeches is 'since the world was young who is to wear the breeches and rule the roost?'[64] Mayhew declares that the gingerbread cockerel was a 'formidable-looking bird, with his nether garments of gold'.[65] There are other theories as to what the cockerel in breeches symbolises. One suggestion is that the symbol is taken from the coat of arms for the Dutch town of Hensbroek (which literally translates as 'hens pants'), a famous example of 'canting'. Derived from the Anglo-Norman *cant*, meaning song or singing, the image represents a play on the bearer's name in the form of a visual pun.[66]

Other gilded animal subjects were sheep and dogs, 'looking as if they had been formed in close and faithful imitation of children's first attempts at cattle drawing',[67] which were moulded in white and brown gingerbread.

While cockerels were busy strutting their stuff at British fairs it was gingerbread pigs that ruled the roost at the Foire du Trône in Paris. Richly decorated with pink sugar and filigree icing they were a nod to the animals that used to roam the city's streets during the medieval period.[68] An accident involving a horse, a pig and a king would see swine banished from the city of Paris in the twelfth century. Phillippe, who co-ruled France with his father Louis VI from 1129–31, was riding through the city when his horse was startled by a stray pig and he was catapulted from the saddle. Phillippe never recovered from his injuries and his grief-stricken father banned pigs from roaming the streets of Paris. The Cistercian Abbey of Saint-Antoine, which was established some years after Phillippe's death in what is now the 12th *arrondissement*, had to abide by this rule. However, in the fifteenth century Louis XI granted a dispensation for the abbey's pigs. These monastic swine could wander the streets providing they wore a bell marked with a cross around their necks. In centuries to come, the pigs would be immortalised in gingerbread sold at the Foire de Trône. Gingerbread pigs were sometimes featured as part of the mid-Lent festivities in Paris. In amongst the showers of confetti, coins and cigarettes 'Gingerbread pigs would be dangled on the end of a piece of string just above the heads of the crowd, and finally given to some enterprising person who jumped a little higher than the others.'[69]

HOME SWEET HOME

Nibbling, nibbling like a mouse,
Who's nibbling at my house?[70]

If you were to come across a life-sized house made of gingerbread and confectionary, could you resist snapping off a roof tile or smashing a window for a morsel of sugared glass? It is no wonder Hansel and Gretel were seduced by the sticky charms of the witch's abode. The question is, which came first – the gingerbread house or the fairy tale?

While there is plenty of evidence, both physical and documentary, to illustrate the zoomorphic and anthropomorphic shapes created in gingerbread, the same cannot be said of gingerbread houses. One popular belief is that these edible structures originated in sixteenth-century Germany.[71] Others have suggested that the origins are closer to the eighteenth century. In his history of spices, Jack Turner writes 'around the year 1400 Parisian merchant Jacques Duché had a walk-in gingerbread house constructed, its walls inlaid with precious stones and spices'. Perhaps the account of the size and magnificence of this structure was exaggerated. Medieval authors (who were often monks probably looking for a diversion from the endless routine of prayers and chores) were prone to fanciful descriptions, as illustrated in this excerpt from a poem about the mythical 'Land of Cockaygne':

An abbey's there, a handsome sight,
Of monks with habits grey and white.
The house has many rooms and halls;
Pies and pasties form the walls,
Made with rich fillings, fish and meat,
The tastiest a man could eat.

Flour-cakes are the shingles all
Of cloister, chamber, church, and hall.
The nails are puddings, rich and fat
Kings and princes might dine on that.
There you can come and eat your fill,
And not be blamed for your self-will.
All is common to young and old,
To strong and stern, to meek and bold.[75]

With so many conflicting views it is hard to pinpoint an exact period for the creation of the first gingerbread houses, particularly as the structures in question would have been gnawed away leaving no evidence of their existence.

There is of course one glaring problem with the theory that the story of Hansel and Gretel resulted in the building of gingerbread houses. In the original version from 1812 the witches house is not made from gingerbread:

> When they got quite near, they saw that the house was made of bread, and it was roofed with cake; the windows were transparent sugar.
> 'This will be something for us,' said Hansel. 'We will have a good meal. I will have a piece of the roof, Gretel, and you can have a bit of the window, it will be nice and sweet.'[76]

In fact, if you look at the illustration Arthur Rackham produced for the 1920s edition, the house looks remarkably like an entirely inedible stone cottage and the children appear heartbreakingly young to be left to fend for themselves. It is a far cry from the gaudy, sweet-encrusted gingerbread houses produced in the twenty-first century. What people tend to forget with this story is the underlying issues of hunger and abandonment. The entire family is on the brink of starvation so the mother (in later editions the stepmother) decides the children should be left in the forest to ultimately perish, in order that she and her husband may live. Placed in the context of Germany's social history it is easy to see why the tale of Hansel and Gretel would strike a chord with its readers. The country had suffered several periods of famine as a result of wars and conflict in the seventeenth and eighteenth centuries, and endured further hardship during the Napoleonic wars which were being fought while the Brothers Grimm were researching and collating their collection of folk tales.[77] As Joan Alcock explains: 'For peasants, especially, the imaginative and magic elements of tales about houses of food and hidden treasure had specific attraction.'[78] The witch's house did not need to be made of gingerbread to tantalise the Grimms' readers. The promise of abundant bread alone (considered a staple food in so many European cultures) would have been sufficient to seduce them.

In December 1853 Engelbert Humperdinck's opera *Hansel and Gretel* opened in Wiemar, triggering a 'gingerbread renaissance'.[79] His telling of the Hansel and Gretel saga even includes some additional gingerbread children (who return to their human form at the end of the opera).[80] Gingerbread houses came into their own. Apprentice bakers and confectioners would often produce a gingerbread house as their 'masterpiece' at the culmination of their internship. Hansel, Gretel and the witch became popular subjects which were painted onto gingerbread 'plates' in white and coloured icing.[81]

One hundred years after Humperdinck's opera, Germany would be rocked by the revelation published in a book by Hans Traxler called *Die Wahrheit über Hänsel und Gretel* ('The Truth About Hansel and Gretel') which claimed the Grimm's fairytale was based in part on a true story. Rather than abandoned children the siblings were grown up bakers who, in the seventeenth century, murdered Katharina Schraderin, a 'baker witch', for her gingerbread recipe. Katharina had rejected a marriage proposal from Hans Metzler, a fellow baker who was desperate to get his hands on the recipe. Hans sought revenge by accusing Katharina of witchcraft but she was acquitted and left the town of Wernigerode to live in the woods. Hans and his sister Grete found Katharina and killed her but failed to find the recipe. In 1963, Traxler published an account of amateur archeologist, Georg Ossegg's, search for the witch's house. Ossegg's dogged exploration of the Spessart woods resulted in him locating not only the charred foundations of the house but also a small tin box containing the famous recipe. Germany was once again spellbound by this folk tale and the morbid turn it had taken. But none of it was true. Traxler, a children's author, had concocted the elaborate hoax to coincide with the centenary of the death of Jacob Grimm. Ossegg was a character from Traxler's own imagination, and he even falsified a seventeenth-century manuscript providing details of Katharina's trial. The recipe, however, was real. Traxler had copied it from a Dr Oetker cookbook.[82]

The trend for gingerbread houses must have spread to Britain at some point during the nineteenth century. In Thomas Hardy's *Jude the Obscure* (1896), Jude Fawley, who had grown up in his aunt's baking business, takes to building gingerbread houses, called Christminster cakes, when illness prevents him from working as a stonemason. His ex-wife Arabella sees Jude's partner Sue selling the gingerbread houses at the Kennetbridge spring fair and exclaims:

> 'I never saw any like 'em. Why, they are windows and towers, and pinnacles. And upon my word they are very nice.' She had helped herself, and was unceremoniously munching one of the cakes.
> 'Yes. They are reminiscences of the Christminster Colleges. Traceried windows, and cloisters, you see. It was a whim of his to do them in pastry.'[83]

It is probably no coincidence that one of the names for a gingerbread house in German is *knusperhäusen*. *Knuspern* means to nibble or munch in German. After all, the ultimate fate of all gingerbread structures and figures is to be consumed.[84]

EAT YOUR WORDS

I mention'd different ways of breeding;
Begin we in our children's reading,
To master John the English maid
A horn-brook gives of gingerbread,

And, that the child may learn the better,
As he can name, he eats the letter.
Proceeding thus with vast delight,
He spells, and gnaws from left to right.
But show a Hebrew's hopeful son
Where we suppose the book begun,
The child would thank you for your kindness,
And read quite backward from our finis.

Matthew Prior, *Alma: Or, The Progress of the Mind* (1718)[85]

When it comes to children and undertaking an onerous task, such as doing homework, the promise of a sweet treat is often a very effective form of bribery (unless of course you happen to be Mr Brocklehurst's little boy in *Jane Eyre,* who would rather learn a psalm than have a ginger nut).[86]

Teaching aids, such as 'hornbooks' – an early form of children's primer – were employed to help engage young students in learning how to read. Hornbooks have been in use from at least the mid-fifteenth century if not earlier. The original hornbooks had the alphabet written on animal skins which were stretched over boards. The board was then covered with a thin transparent layer of horn to protect it from dirty hands. Eventually this skin was replaced by carved or printed boards containing the alphabet, nine digits and sometimes the Lord's Prayer. The boards would have a handle so that they could be easily held and in time the protective layer of horn would disappear although the name 'hornbook' would stick.[87]

Somewhere along the way a clever soul hit upon the idea of using gingerbread as a suitable material for making hornbooks. Gingerbread hornbooks had the benefit of being both educational and providing a delicious incentive for the pupil to learn his or her letters – every letter correctly memorised could be nibbled away. In a children's book called *Fortune's Football* (1806) the author Isaac Jennings speaks of learning his alphabet by 'feasting on my gingerbread book with associates only on condition of performing well my task'.[88] Of course the major drawback of an edible hornbook is that once it has been eaten you no longer have anything to refer to should you need to refresh your memory, as William Hone, author of the *Every Day and Every Year Book,* illustrates:

> Among my recollections of childish pleasures I have a vivid remembrance of an alphabet called the Horn-Book, price one farthing, published by the Gingerbread Bakers and sold by all dealers in gingerbread in town and country. There was a superior edition with a wider margin, handsomely gilt, price a half penny. I formerly purchased for my own use several copies of different editions of this work, but have not preserved one. It was larger than the common horn-book, and made of dark brown gingerbread.[89]

Occasionally the alphabet gingerbreads were called 'book gingerbread'. The letters were carved into the mould in reverse (usually done freehand[90]) so they would appear correct on the gingerbread when it was turned out. Hornbook gingerbread, such as that described by Hone, generally sold for a halfpenny a slice, particularly at fairs. However, a finer white gingerbread was available for children who had been especially good, although it came at a premium price of one penny per slab.[91]

Part of the allure of hornbook and other shaped gingerbreads was the gilding. In the Middle Ages it was popular to decorate gingerbread with gilded cloves and box leaves in the form of a fleur-de-lis.[92] Describing his visit to Bartholomew Fair in 1825, William Hone noted 'the gingerbread stalls varied in size, and were conspicuously fine, due to the Dutch gold on their different shaped wares.[93] Dutch gold is actually an alloy of copper and zinc that convincingly mimics the tone of real gold (and is consequently a lot cheaper to use).[94] According to tradition 'a lick of the tongue preceded the application of the foil'.[95] During his lifetime Andrew Tuer had amassed a sizeable collection of gingerbread moulds, many of which came from a Mr Edward Jeboult of Taunton. Mr Jeboult, whose grandfather had carved moulds in the eighteenth century, claimed the phrase 'taking the gilt off the gingerbread' comes from the custom of selling damaged or broken bits at half the ordinary price.

Gingerbread alphabets were not exclusive to Britain. This style of gingerbread was popular in the Netherlands and can occasionally be found in the still life paintings of seventeenth-century artist Pieter Claesz. Edible letters (*Bankelette*), nowadays made from pastry or chocolate rather than gingerbread, are popular gifts in the Netherlands on 6th December, the start of *Sinterklaas* season.[96]

CHAPTER FIVE

ALL THE FUN OF THE FAIR

Now the Fair's a filling!
O, for a tune to startle
The birds o' the booths here billing,
Yearly with old saint Bartle!
The drunkards they are wading,
The punks and chapmen trading;
Who'd see the Fair without his lading?

Nightingale, A Ballad Singer
in *Bartholomew Fair,* Ben Jonson (1614)[1]

The first thing that reaches you is the low thrumming of the bassline in the music. As you get closer to its source the beats invade your body, a cacophony of tunes competing to draw you to their attractions. Then the scents of the fair envelop you. The savoury tang of fried onions and grilled meats mingle with the sickly notes of syrupy treats and the engine oil that lubricates the wheels of the rides. And what rides! – centrifuges of fun that leave multicoloured streaks in the air as they sprint past and a few passengers are parted from their lunch. You may find the occasional sedate ferris wheel or a vintage carousel with its grinning steeds as a nod to a bygone age, but what passes as a fair today would be largely unrecognisable to a fair-goer of two hundred years ago.

The ancestry of the fair can be traced back to the medieval era when the right of the monarch to hold a fair in a particular town was granted by royal charter. The aim of these charters was to provide revenue for the crown by way of an annual fee payable by the city or town. Between 1199 and 1350 over fifteen hundred charters were issued across England.[2] The priory of Burscough in Ormskirk, a town in Lancashire renowned for its gingerbread, was granted a charter by Edward I and Edmund, earl of Lancaster, to hold a weekly market on a Thursday at their manor, and a five-day annual fair from 29 August.[3]

The main focal point of most fairs was commerce in terms of buying or selling livestock, or hiring labourers. But whatever the purpose of the fair, those in attendance would still require refreshment. In Ben Jonson's seventeenth-century play *Bartholomew Fair* there is a hog roast available, a man selling trinkets, puppeteers and a lady selling gingerbread. By the nineteenth century the stalls selling comestibles would be joined by an assortment of 'peep shows, toy-stands, waxworks, inspired monsters, disinterested medical men who travelled for the public good, thimble riggers, nick-nack vendors, and readers of Fate'. The consumables and entertainment would lend the proceedings a festive feel and become the main draw for the local population. Once the business of the day was concluded the fun could begin. In Thomas Hardy's *The Mayor of Casterbridge,* Michael Henchard gets into the spirit of the fair at Weydon-Priors by consuming several bowls of furmity – a boiled grain dish like porridge – liberally laced with rum. In his drunken stupor he sells his wife and child to a passing sailor for five guineas.[4]

Gingerbread has been synonymous with fairs for hundreds of years. It was considered good luck to eat a piece of gingerbread bought at a fair.[5] Known as 'fairings' they could be moulded into different shapes and were often gilded. In Cornwall 'a proper and complete' fairing was a spicy ginger biscuit adorned with lambs tails (caraway comfits[6]), candied angelica, almond comfits and macaroons.[7]

One of the most famous fairs was Bartholomew Fair at Smithfield in London. It was started by the prior of the Hospital of St Bartholomew in the twelfth century and lasted for three days over the feast of St Bartholomew on 24th August. Like many fairs, the original purpose was to sell cattle and merchandise, particularly cloth. By the time Ben Jonson wrote his play of the same name the emphasis had shifted from business to pleasure.[8] After the restoration of the monarchy in 1660 the fair would become a fourteen-day event that was opened by the Lord Mayor of London.[9] Bartholomew Fair (and almost every other fair) gained a reputation for being exceptionally rowdy with freak shows, like the pig-faced lady, and performing animals joining the fray. West Smithfield was nicknamed Ruffian's Hall because it was renowned for fights. The fair became so disreputable during the seventeenth century that Queen Anne ordered it to return to a three-day event.[10]

The Greenwich Fair held over Easter was equally notorious. Charles Dickens described it as 'a sort of spring-rash, a three-day's fever, which cools the blood for six months afterwards'.[11] Streams of fair-goers would pour through the streets of Greenwich before descending into the park, passing through the fair's entrance 'occupied on either side by the vendors of gingerbread and toys', and taking in games like find the pea under the thimble, melodramas ('with three murders and a ghost'), 'natural curiosities' such as 'a dwarf, a giantess, a living skeleton, a wild Indian', and gingerbread nuts, 'of which the majority of the regular fair-goers carry a pound or two as a present supply, tied up in a cotton pocket-handkerchief'.[12] In a *Punch* article of 1845, Mrs Caudle berates her husband for having too much fun at Greenwich Fair (a thoroughly disreputable thing for a married man and father to do) and for not bringing his children home a single gingerbread nut.[13] Edward Walford recalls: 'The crowd was so dense and disorderly as to threaten each minute the erection of barricades of brandy-snaps, and the overthrow and deposition of the gilt gingerbread kings ranged on each side.'[14]

The British did not have the monopoly of fairs or indeed fairings. The Parisians had their own gingerbread fair. It was first held over Easter week in 1719 inside the Abbey of Saint-Antoine and involved around twenty gingerbread merchants. One hundred years later it had spilled out onto the streets and the gingerbread vendors were joined by other traders. By 1883 it had stretched right up to Place de la Nation (formerly the Place du Trône which would eventually lead to the fair being called 'La Foire du Trône') and the surrounding streets.[15] In many ways this Parisian fair resembled the large fairs in London. There were gingerbread figures for sale (the president of France, Adolphe Thiers had been very popular in 1873, as of course were gingerbread pigs), gingerbread lotteries, merry-go-rounds, circus booths, shooting galleries and waxworks. An article in the *North British Daily Mail* describing the Parisian gingerbread fair in 1874 commented: 'The great thing of the show, however, was the huge crowd; its good humour, the utter absence of drunkenness, of horse play, and even of that kind of chaff which a crowd of upwards of 100,000 Englishmen would be sure to indulge in.'[16]

This rather sober description of the Foire du Trône seems somewhat at odds with how the novelist J.-K. Huysmans portrayed this famous Parisian fair in his novel, *The Vatard Sisters* (1879). Huysmans's crowd was quite unruly, 'people stepped on each other's toes, they shoved each other', and 'clutches of children boistered about, blowing on toy trumpets, faces smeared with gingerbread, snotty-nosed and full of life'.[17] Like their British counterparts, this French fair sported refreshment stalls although wine 'so bitter it would curl hair' took the place of ale and waffles provided sustenance rather than the furmity enjoyed by Michael Henchard. The gingerbread stall, 'with its pretty red pompoms of tinsel and its gold spangles', manned by an impudent and solemn old matron', stood out from the rest:

> This woman was flanked on her right by heaps of honeyed gingerbread, by gingerbread cakes, gingerbread hearts and gingerbread rings, all wrapped in glazed paper flecked with gold letters and covered in blue ribbons, and cutting a swathe through the whole display were gigantic puff-pastries, coated in yellow, lilac and green icing which was swirled with silver spirals and emblazoned with genial mottos. To her left lay an army of little gingerbread men, soft and pale, some plain, others skilfully spruced up with festoons of pastry, speckled with aniseed or sprinkled with dots of sugar; all manner of people were represented: cooks,

A child eating a piece of gingerbread with his name on it at the Foire du Trône in Paris,
1939. © Excelsior – L'Equipe/Roger-Viollet.

shopkeepers, infantrymen, generals – there was even a lion with the legs of a bassethound and the snout of a pig.[18]

Despite all the side shows, the main attraction of this Paris fair was the gingerbread. Pierre Larousse described the spectacle in his *Grande dictionnaire universel du XIXe siècle* (1866):

Around six or seven o'clock, we come up against waves of men, women and children laden with gingerbread. They have their pockets stuffed, they hold it in each hand, they hold it under each arm, they carry it hanging from canes and parasols: gingerbread of all tastes, of all shapes, with almonds, lemon, orange, angelica, fruit, this and then that; in pavés, slabs, crowns, squares, rectangles, diamonds, hearts and especially gingerbread men; good Lord! how many men, from the size of a Lilliputian to that of a drum major! Never have we seen so many gingerbread men; there is not a child who does not have his (his papa bought him the largest possible), so that more often than not, it is the baby who looks like the gingerbread man![19]

So far, the fairs discussed have been regular events taking place on a specific date or festival of the year, but there was one type of fair that was entirely dependent on the weather. The river Thames froze solid twenty-five times between 1092 and 1814 thereby becoming the location of an impromptu 'frost fair'. Unlike the fairs of Greenwich and Bartholomew they could last several months (so long as the ice held) and were a source of temporary but highly lucrative business for street vendors, including those who sold gingerbread.[20] Diarist John Evelyn described the frost fair of 1684:

Coaches plied from Westminster to the Temple, and from several other stairs to and fro, as in the streets, sleds, sliding with skates, a bull baiting, horse and coach races, puppet-plays and interludes, cooks, tippling, and other lewd places, so that it seemed to be a bacchanalian triumph, or carnival on the water.[21]

Piping hot gingerbread and other eatables were sold at inflated prices by pedlars who would buy their wares from professional bakers. These bakers had ovens large enough to cook the quantities required to satisfy the demand from the vast number of visitors. If the gingerbread failed to warm your cockles, some hawkers also sold gin to accompany it: a gin tent and gingerbread stall feature in a woodcut print of the 1715–16 frost fair.[22] George Cruickshank's illustration of the 1814 frost fair shows revellers gambolling on the frozen Thames in front of a tent with a placard announcing 'Gin and Gingerbread sold here wholesale'.[23] The gingerbread was often marketed to appeal to children in the form of educational toys like alphabet hornbooks (one can only hope the gin was purely an enticement to get the child's parents to visit the stall rather than being doled out to the children themselves). The Museum of London has a fragment of an alphabet gingerbread from the 1814 frost fair still wrapped in blue sugar paper, bought by a Thomas Moxon for his child.[24]

Old-fashioned fairs, with their vestiges of agricultural trade, began to decline in the mid-nineteenth century. By 1840 Bartholomew Fair was a shadow of its former self. Increasing lawlessness (on one September morning alone in 1815 forty-five felonies were reported at Bartholomew Fair) and consequent public outcry saw the great carnival diminish to a few wild beast shows and a handful of gilt gingerbread booths. After more than seven hundred years the final Bartholomew Fair was held in 1855.[25] The Colchester fair successfully combined amusements and livestock sales (around 2000 bullocks, 800 sheep and 40 horses were sold at the fair in 1822). However, by 1848 it too had dwindled to 'a toy and gingerbread fair of the lowest description' and by 1910 the fair had reverted completely to the sale of cattle and horses.[26]

The Fairs Act of 1871 (further amended in 1873) gave local authorities the right to ban travelling fairs in their districts. The onus was on itinerant fairs to demonstrate the recreational benefits they could provide to the local population. Fairs, once the source of entertainment in so many towns, had competition from theatres, music halls and travelling exhibitions such as lantern shows.[27] The fact that fairs had a less than glowing reputation in terms of moral standards would not have endeared them to the more temperate of Victorian society. Thomas Frost, the radical writer and printer, was certain fairs had had their time, concluding his book *The Old Showmen and the Old London Fairs* (1874) with the words:

> Fairs are becoming extinct because, with the progress of the nation, they have ceased to possess any value in its social economy [...] What need then, of fairs, and shows? The nation has outgrown them, and fairs are as dead as the generations which they have delighted, and the last showman will soon be as great a curiosity as the dodo.[28]

Frost was mistaken. Menageries of exotic beasts and human curiosities would be replaced by gaily decorated wooden horses undulating on merry-go-rounds powered by steam, and these in turn would evolve into the hair-raising rides of today.[29] Sadly the gilt gingerbread kings and queens would be deposed by candyfloss, toffee apples and popcorn. But even gingerbread would survive albeit in a less elaborate form, finding its way to our stomachs through different channels.

Who'll Buy My Hot Smoking Gingerbread?

Celebrities love a gimmick. Whether it is Michael Jackson's white sequinned glove or the Village People's eclectic mix of uniforms, it is usually something the fans can readily identify the personality with (and very often easily imitate). If a visual cue is not forthcoming, then a catchphrase is the next best thing (or possibly even better). Think of Baldrick's 'cunning plan' in the *Blackadder* series or Del Boy's 'lovely jubbly' in *Only Fools and Horses*. In eighteenth-century London a flamboyant gingerbread vendor known as 'Tiddy Doll' had them both:

> In his person he was tall, well made, and his features handsome. He affected to dress like a person of rank; white gold laced suit

Within the image: NEW FRENCH OVEN for Imperial Gingerbread; Little Dough Viceroys, intended for the next new Batch; BAVARIA, WIRTEMB, BADEN; Ash-Hole for broken Gingerbread; Kings & Queens; Crowds & Sceptre; Sun & Moons; True Corsican Kinglings for Home, Consum & Exportation.

DDY-DOLL, the great French-Gingerbread-Baker; drawing out a new Batch of Kings.—his Man, Hopping-Talley, mixing up the Dough.

In this satirical image created by James Gillray in 1806, Napoleon is depicted as the famous London street-seller of gingerbread, Tiddy-doll, whose wares and patter made him a long-remembered character. © *The Trustees of the British Museum.*

of clothes, laced ruffled shirt, laced hat and feather, white silk stockings, with the addition of a fine white apron.[30]

Mr Ford, Tiddy's real name, made bold claims about his gingerbread, claiming it would 'melt in your mouth like a red-hot brick-bat, and rumble in your inside like Punch and his wheelbarrow.' He acquired his nickname for his penchant for singing 'ti-tid-dy, ti-ti, ti-tid-dy, ti-ti, ti-tid-dy, ti-ti, tid-dy, did-dy, dol-lol, ti-tid-dy, ti-tid-dy, ti-ti, tid-dy, tid-dy, dol' to the tune of popular ballads.[31]

Little is known of the true identity or life of Tiddy Doll but whoever he was he certainly made a lasting impression and he continued to capture the imagination of artists and writers well into the nineteenth century. Tiddy Doll was featured in eighteenth-century prints with Hogarth including the gingerbread vendor in the foreground of *The Idle Apprentice Executed at Tyburn* (1747) brandishing his wares, complete with ruffled

75

shirt, white apron and a feathered hat. In 1806 the caricaturist James Gillray would use Tiddy Doll as the model for his satirical depiction of Napoleon (with an emphasis on the feathered tricorn), as the great French gingerbread maker, shovelling gingerbread kings and queens into an oven. William Hone, the writer and satirist, who documented the everyday manners and customs in Britain from ancient to modern times in *The Every-day Book* (1826), felt compelled to describe Tiddy Doll in his account of the May Fair in London dubbing him the 'king of itinerant tradesmen'.[32] Although Hone does not provide a date for the gingerbread vendor's death he refers to Tiddy Doll in the past tense so it seems unlikely that his account of this character are based on first-hand knowledge. Writing some fifty years after Hone, radical writer and journalist Thomas Frost would state that Tiddy Dolly was so well known that 'on his once being missed for a week from his usual stand in the Haymarket, on the unusual occasion of an excursion to a country fair, a "catch-penny" account of his alleged murder was sold in the streets by thousands'.[33] A 'catch-penny' was a cheap newspaper or pamphlet printed to capitalise on a current event or popular issue.[34] An account of Tiddy Doll's death appeared on Wednesday 17 June 1752, in *The True Briton*, which announced:

> A famous gingerbread seller known by the Name of Tididol, was found murdered in Chelsea Field. It is said, that he was robbed of 20 l. and that they who committed the Murder must have been acquainted with his being possessed of that sum.[35]

Twenty pounds was a significant sum in the mid-eighteenth century.[36] If this report of Tiddy Doll's death were true then Mr Ford had done exceedingly well for himself, which may explain how he was able to afford such fine clothes. When you consider that the Sussex shopkeeper, Thomas Turner, who was relatively well-to-do himself, on one occasion ordered '14 lb. of thick [gingerbread], 2s. 3d., 1 gross of sweethearts 1s., thin bread 5s. 6d', then Tiddy Doll must have sold an awful lot of gingerbread to have amassed such a fortune.[37]

By the mid-nineteenth century, street hawkers of edible goods were not as numerous as they had once been. Henry Mayhew attributed this decline in part to the reduced purchasing power of the labouring classes and the rise of shopkeepers selling 'cheap luxuries' like penny pies. It was, however, possible to eke out a living from selling food on the street. Mayhew believed the dealers in eatables and drinkables were more intelligent than the average kerb-side vendor, particularly when it came to 'dainties' like pastries and cakes. The consumer could be highly critical of these sweet treats so they not only had to be cheap but taste good too. Street traders were identified by the goods they sold rather than their names. So their customers would refer to them as 'a pickled whelk' or 'a sweet stuff'. Cries like 'Hot spiced gingerbread nuts, nuts, nuts! If one'll warm you, wha-at'll a pound do? — Wha-a-a-at'll a pound do?' would ring out in towns and cities across the country as purveyors announced their wares.[38]

For many the ability to sell food on the streets was a godsend. An Irish sailor called Daniel Clarey began selling gingerbread nuts after the loss of his leg during 'an engagement on the "Salt Seas".' Dan's gimmick was to sell the gingerbread nuts by way of a lottery.[39] Endowed with the gift of the gab, Clarey assured his customers that his lottery was no 'South Sea Bubble'.[40] As there were no blanks in Clarey's game every player would win and receive a prize. Clarey boasted that 'some of his gingerbread shot are so highly seasoned that they are as hot as the noble Nelson's balls when he last peppered the jackets of England's foes'.[41]

The lottery took the form of a box with strings attached to the bottom. For a halfpenny you pulled a string and a doll's head would appear in one of the variously numbered twenty-seven holes. If you had chosen the same number that the doll appeared in you would win one hundred gingerbread nuts. If not, you were still rewarded with at least seven gingerbread nuts. Ever the self-assured salesman, Clarey had no qualms in stating that his nuts were far superior to those of the famous Tiddy Doll. In fact his wares were so fine 'should any one of his noble friends prove so fortunate as to draw a prize of one hundred of them, he would be entitled to those of half the usual size, so delicately small that they would be no bigger than the quack doctor's pills'.[42] Sounds like a bit of a swizz to me.

Selling gingerbread nuts by way of a lottery must have been fairly commonplace as it was mentioned in pantomimes, the popular musical comedies of the day. This song, 'Hot Spice Gingerbread!', composed around 1796, is from *Harlequin and Oberon*:

> Come boys and girls, men and maids, widows and wives,
> The best penny lay out you e'er spent in your lives;
> Here's my whirligig lottery, a penny a spell,
> No blanks but all prizes; and that's pretty well.
> Don't send humming and ha'ing, with ifs and with buts,
> Try your luck for my round sound Gingerbread Nuts;
>
> And then here's my glorious spice gingerbread too,
> Hot enough e'en to melt the cold heart of a Jew.
> Hot spice gingerbread hot! Come buy my spice gingerbread, smoaking hot!
>
> Your fine beaux and belles, an your rattle-pate rakes,
> One half are game Nuts, the rest gingerbread Cakes;
> Then in gingerbread Coaches we've gingerbread Lords,
> And gingerbread Soldiers with gingerbread Swords!
> And what are your Patriots? 'Tis easy to tell,
> By their constantly crying, they've something to sell.
>
> [*Spoken*] But it's a query, whether it's as good for the English constitution as my
>
> Hot spice gingerbread, hot!
>
> My gingerbread lottery is just like the world,
> For its index of chances for ever is twirl'd;
> But some diff'rence between 'em exists without doubt,
> The world's lottery has blanks, while mine's wholly without;
> There no matter how often you shuffle and cut,
> It i'n't once in ten games you can get a game nut;
> So I laugh at the world like an impudent elf,

And, just like my betters, take care of myself.

[*Spoken*] There's nobody likes himself better than I do;
Then all the pretty girls are so fond of me, since the death of my
poor wife!

Aye, and for the loss of her I can't help crying –

Hot spice gingerbread, hot![43]

While gingerbread vendors like Tiddy Doll and Dan Clarey were characters in their own right there was still something disreputable about touting wares on the street or at a fair. In Thomas Hardy's *Jude the Obscure*, lovers Sue Bridehead and Jude Fawley have been socially disgraced by leaving their respective spouses to set up home together. They contemplate becoming gingerbread stallholders at markets and fairs, 'where people are gloriously indifferent to everything except the quality of the goods'.[44] Tiddy Doll and Dan Clarey may have espoused the virtues of their goods but often the quality of the gingerbread was in question. An article in *Punch* on the revival of the Brook Green Fair sums up how the attractions of the seller could potentially distract from the quality of the goods being sold:

'Poor maiden,' thought the youth, 'if thou wert sent
With thy long curls and low-neck'd blandishment,
To wake attention to thy canvas mart
Of gingerbread – thou little know'st the art;
For though thy lips should sweetly counsel "Buy,"
Those nuts look far too dusty, stale, and dry.'[45]

A stallholder in Ben Jonson's play *Bartholomew Fair*, Lanthorn Leatherhead, accuses fellow vendor Joan Trash (the name says it all) of selling 'gingerbread progeny' made with 'stale bread, rotten eggs, musty ginger, and dead honey', despite Trash's protestations that her gingerbread is made with 'nothing but what's wholesome'.[46] Leatherhead is not the only person to criticise Trash. Puritan pastor, Zeal-of-the-land Busy, accuses her of peddling a 'basket of popery, thy nest of images, and whole legend of ginger-work.'[47] Convinced that the fair and its attractions create sinful intentions, fuelled among other things by Trash's spicy gingerbread, Busy overturns her basket. The stallholders have the last laugh though when Busy is put in the stocks for preaching at the fair.

Weary travellers between Liverpool and Preston making a 'pit stop' at the Talbot Inn at Ormskirk in the late eighteenth century were impressed by the gingerbread proffered, but less so by the witch-like appearance of the ladies selling it. One passenger concluded that 'the Lancastrians may contend with the Yorkists for crowns and be victors, but must submit to be rivalled by them in the question of the Roses'.[48] In this case, the quality of the gingerbread more than compensated for the lacklustre appearance of its vendors.

If John Thomas Smith, author of *The Cries of London* (1839), is to be believed, selling gingerbread reaped little financial reward as the profits made were 'generally spent in gin and hot suppers'.[49] A stinging indictment for those who were just trying to get by through introducing a bit of spice into the lives of their neighbours.

Chapter Six

Decline and Rise of Gingerbread

Dentists love to lecture us on the importance of avoiding sugary treats in order to maintain the health of our teeth. So it may come as something of a surprise to learn that a dentist was responsible for mechanising the process of spun sugar to produce the ethereal delight that is candyfloss (or cotton candy as it's known on the other side of the pond).[1]

The process of spinning sugar had been around for a good while before dentist William Morrison and partner in crime John C. Wharton, a confectioner, came up with their invention. Over a hundred years before, Elizabeth Raffald (1733–81), a confectioner herself, provided recipes for making a silver and gold web for covering sweetmeats by using melted or lightly caramelised sugar, instructing her readers to:

> …take up as much of the syrup as the point of the knife will hold, and a fine thread will come from the point, which you must draw as quick as possible backwards and forwards, and also around the mould, as long as it will spin from the knife.[2]

In 1897 Morrison and Wharton invented a machine to spin sugar which they revealed to the world at the 1904 World's Fair in St Louis. Initially they called their confection 'fairy floss' and it was an instant success with the duo selling 68,655 boxes at the fair. In 1921 another dentist, Joseph Lascaux, created a similar machine, but called his sugary cloud 'cotton candy' which would become the most common name for this sweet treat in the USA.[3]

Candyfloss was just one of the novel confections available at fairs that replaced gingerbread in our affections. Of course there were other sweets available, such as doughnuts and toffee apples, although Dorothy Hartley believes the latter had been available at outlets like Bartholomew Fair for centuries.[4] Towards the end of Sheila Kaye-Smith's novel *Sussex Gorse* (1924), the principal character, eighty-two year old Reuben Backfield, concludes the fair in 1902 'had gone terribly to pieces since his young days':

> The Fair had moved still further with the times. The merry-go-round organ played Bluebell, Dolly Grey, and The Absent-Minded Beggar, the chief target in the shooting-gallery was Kruger, with Cronje and De Wet as subordinates, and the Panorama showed Queen Victoria's funeral. The fighting booth was hidden away still further, and dancing now only started at nightfall. There were some new shows, too. The old-fashioned thimble-rigging had given place to a modern swindle with tickets and a dial; instead of the bearded woman or the pig-faced boy, one put a penny in the slot and saw a lady undress – to a certain point. [...T]he stalls themselves were of a more utilitarian nature, selling whips and trousers and balls of string, instead of the ribbon and gingerbread fairings bought by lovers in days of old.[5]

Brian Vesey-Fitzgerald surmises that the reason why some fairs were discontinued relates to the importance of certain towns and villages to the local economies. The original purpose of many fairs had been commerce, whether the trade had been livestock or labour. As the social and economic landscape of Britain altered towards the end of the nineteenth century, the purpose of the fair would shift from business to pleasure. From the medieval era through to the early nineteenth century it was the market element of the fair that was important rather than entertainment, so fairs would have been held in reasonably well-populated areas.[6] As the rural population drifted away from the countryside towards cities and towns to find more lucrative work, the requirement for traditional fairs (and their audience) dwindled.[7]

The Sussex market town of Horsham was a case in point.[8] Like may towns and cities across the country Horsham was granted charters during the medieval era to hold markets and fairs. By the fifteenth century Horsham had a market on Monday, Wednesday and Saturday, and three three-day fairs in late spring, mid-summer and early winter.[9] These fairs were largely devoted to the sale of livestock (sheep, cattle and horses). The sheep fair on 18 July was followed by a pleasure fair and lasted between three and eight days depending on the day of the week it commenced.[10] The July pleasure fair was extremely popular. Henry Burstow, the celebrated bellringer and song singer who was born in the town in 1826, recalled people flocking to Horsham for the fair in their 'hundreds and thousands'. The inhabitants of Horsham were less enamoured with the festivities, and complained about the unsanitary conditions the itinerant stallholders lived in, which was 'a source of much annoyance and sometimes of disease to the permanent residents there.'[11] By 1874 local pressure would eventually see the July fair limited to one day and the pre-Whitsun fair, described as worn out, ceased to exist soon after.

When Horsham fairs were going strong, gingerbread could be found there and 'had a great sale among townspeople and 'furriners' alike'.[12] A letter dated 18th July 1803, from the poet Percy Bysshe Shelley to his Aunt Kate who lived in Horsham, indicates the town's gingerbread was fondly remembered:

> Tell the bearer not to forget to bring me a fairing, which is some gingerbread, sweetmeat, hunting-nuts and a pocket book.[13]

One purveyor of gingerbread in Horsham was Abraham Chatfield (1809–78), who had a small confectionery shop in the western part of the town known as the 'Bishopric'. Charlie Parsons started working for Chatfield as a boy and would deliver the confectioner's wares, including brandy snaps and gingerbread, to local villages in a pony and cart. He was employed by Chatfield for over thirty years,[14] likely at a time when the town's gingerbread production was at its height in the 1860s.[15] From museum records we know that there were ten gingerbread makers in the town (some of the moulds in the Horsham Museum collection have the baker's names on them). The 1851 census describes Chatfield as owning a 'confectionery and sweetstuffs shop' which was 'famous for its home-made gingerbreads, cakes and brandy snaps, muffins, and crumpets'.[16] In 1917, the last Horsham gingerbread maker, George Lovekin, died aged eighty-three. Lovekin's moulds made their way to C. J. Attree, who donated his collection to Brighton Museum in the autumn of 1917, though they are now on permanent display at Horsham Museum. According to Attree, there were three types of gingerbread made in Horsham:

Parliament – a fatless gingerbread made of light treacle, with crinkled edges. These sold for a penny each.

Toy – using a similar recipe to the Parliament gingerbread. No further description is provided by Attree regarding the form of the Toy gingerbread. Based on other accounts it is possible that this was the mixture used in the various moulds on display in the museum.

Hard – made with heavy treacle, lard and a little water.

Flour and ground ginger were included in all of the gingerbreads and some bakers added seeds too. They were sold according to size, with small ones being marketed in bundles of six for a penny.[17] However, with Lovekin's death Horsham's gingerbread industry fizzled out.

All was not lost for Horsham's gingerbread legacy. A local business woman, Lesley Ward, had stumbled across a reference to the town's gingerbread while researching old recipes for the historic cooking sessions she was running at Petworth House. She contacted Horsham Museum's curator, Jeremy Knight, to find out more. In 2009, the museum had acquired a two-hundred-year-old cookery notebook from Penshurst Place written by one of Shelley's aunts which included a gingerbread recipe. The curator had been thinking about trying to recreate Horsham's gingerbread from the Shelley family recipe and discussed it and the link to the poet with Ward.[18]

Calling these cookery notes from Penshurst Place 'recipes' is something of a stretch. Ward was presented with a list of ingredients but no method or cooking times (handwritten culinary notebooks were often produced as aide memoirs rather than detailed instruction manuals). After consulting recipe books from the eighteenth and nineteenth centuries, and a bit of trial and error, Ward finally created a gingerbread which captured the taste Shelley would recognise. The buttery, richly spiced gingerbread is sold in slabs rather than printed in moulds and is now widely available across Sussex.[19]

The art of carving gingerbread moulds also began to decline in the nineteenth century, particularly when it came to basic shapes like hearts, which were easy to reproduce as metal cutters.[20] Ornate wooden moulds would be relegated to museums or be collected by admirers of vintage kitchenalia.[21] Where is the need for carved reliefs when sheets of gaily coloured motifs can be printed on rice paper en masse, then cut out and stuck onto the gingerbread with icing? Even metal cutters have been replaced by machines which can produce popular shapes more efficiently.[22]

The Great War had a profound effect on all aspects of British culture and was probably the final nail in the coffin for classically moulded gingerbreads. Lifestyles and tastes were changing. Women who had been farming the land and working in factories while the men were at war had a new sense of independence and were reluctant at first to go back into domestic service.[23] In reality, the economic hardships of the 1920s saw many women returning to service to free up jobs for men who had returned from the war, and simply because there was no other work to be had.[24] Even the opportunities in service were becoming limited as middle-class households were forced to tighten their belts in the face of economic recession.[25]

These social changes would spawn a new style of cookery book. Gone were the Victorian manuals of the Mrs Beeton ilk crammed with blunt instructions, and in came more conversational works like *Kitchen Essays* by Lady Agnes Jekyll, first published in 1922.[26] Gingerbread, like the proverbial bad penny, could still be found among the pages of volumes penned by society hostesses (who in truth had probably never set foot in the kitchen beyond giving the cook some instruction for the day's meals).[27] May Byron's *Cake Book* (1915) provides twenty recipes for gingerbread cakes, five recipes for parkin and ten for various ginger biscuits (including brandy snaps).[28] Jekyll's cookbook includes just one recipe for a gingery Winter Cake, 'black and sticky with treacle, enlivened by whole white almonds', which appears in the chapter 'A Motor Excursion Luncheon' (camp-stools, a waterproof rug and furs were considered essential for this trip).[29] Recipes in general were taking an exotic turn (zabaglione – an Italian dessert made with egg yolks, sugar, and a sweet wine – appears to be a particular favourite of food writers from the interwar period) and Mrs C.F. Leyel and Miss Olga Hartley even promised 'Dishes from the Arabian Nights' in their book, *The Gentle Art of Cookery* (1921).[30] Gingerbread by now must have seemed positively mundane.

Folklorist Florence White was concerned that the 'charm of England's cookery' was being 'completely crushed out of existence' by the nation's fascination with foreign food.[31] She travelled all over the country collecting everyday recipes and anecdotes about how and when traditional dishes were prepared and eaten. Her book, *Good Food in England,* originally published in 1932, was not about putting on a stylish dinner party but sought to record England's culinary heritage, which may otherwise have been lost. Naturally, the collection includes several gingerbread recipes. What makes White's book particularly charming are the little introductions provided by the contributors, with tips such as 'it is done when the parkin springs back when an impression is made with the finger'.[32] Around the same time, F. Marian McNeill was going through a similar process to preserve the old national dishes of Scotland. Like White, her book *The Scots Kitchen* (1929) is dotted with nuggets of information on the origins of everyday Scottish recipes. Thanks to McNeill we have her recipe for Broonie (an oatmeal gingerbread from the Orkney Islands) based on her childhood memories of the 'midday "piece"' one of her friends used to share with her when she was five or six.[33]

One of the reasons gingerbread has endeared itself to consumers over the centuries is its ability to be stored for a number of days (or in some cases weeks). Recipes will often instruct you to leave the gingerbread for a day or two before cutting, as the cake improves with keeping. This quality must have been a godsend in times of privation such as the Second World War, when treats were thin on the ground due to strict rationing. It could also be made with the bare minimum of ingredients, as this wartime recipe demonstrates:

Gingerbread Cake
½ lb self raising flour
6 oz syrup
1 teaspoon ground ginger
1 teaspoon bicarbonate of soda
¼ tepid water

Place the flour and syrup in a basin. Mix the ginger and soda with the tepid water, add to the flour and syrup, and mix all together. Turn into a greased tin, about 11 inches x 7 inches, and bake in a moderate oven for about 1¼ hours. Do not cut for 2 days.[34]

This is an undeniably austere recipe but at least you could eke out the cake for several days without it going stale. Some wartime gingerbread recipes contain a little fat, but most of those I have come across do not contain eggs (which were also on ration) so it is easy to see why this style of cake would have appealed to the nation's housewives.

Decorated gingerbreads were particularly popular in Germany in the interwar years.[35] This is perhaps best illustrated by the work of Lydia Driesch-Foucar, a member of the Bauhaus art movement. A ceramicist by training, Driesch-Foucar turned her hand to making elaborate *formgebäck* (gingerbread shapes) to earn some desperately needed money after the sudden death of her husband in 1930. Initially, the gingerbreads were given to friends as gifts but she eventually opened a small workshop making *lebkuchen*, a type of gingerbread biscuit. While the decoration on her gingerbreads was modern, the subjects themselves, such as horses, hares and cockerels, remained traditional. During the 1930s she became a member of the Association of German Craftsmen and was subsequently invited to sell her gingerbread at the Museum of Applied Art trade fair, legitimising her food product as a handicraft. Driesch-Foucar's style also dovetailed with the Nazi fascination for folk art, which helped boost her success at the time, but would ultimately have repercussions on her reputation as a designing artist after the war. Magdalena Droste concludes: 'Driesch-Foucar's [gingerbread] cookies shifted from a symbol of friendship to a profit-oriented form of *Frauenschaffen* ('women's work'), to works of folk or decorative art, and ultimately to symbols of the Bauhaus.'[36]

When it comes to modern gingerbread art, it is probably best epitomised through gingerbread houses. While the origins of this art form may be obscure or controversial (depending on your take on the situation) it has grown in popularity over the twentieth century and into the twenty-first. Whether you are baking one from scratch or using one of the many kits available, the gingerbread house seems to have become an accepted element of the Christmas festivities, which in some households is almost as essential as the tree and presents themselves.

In Asheville, North Carolina, the Omni Grove Park Inn has hosted the National Gingerbread House Competition since 1992. It was supposed to be a one-off event – just another way to celebrate the holiday season – but it proved so popular it has been run every year since. Competition is fierce with the calibre of the entries getting higher each year. The contestants are judged by a panel of renowned food, art and media professionals. The designs of the structures are astounding (there were 226 in 2019). Some of the houses are more akin to something you would expect to see in an aspirational lifestyle magazine rather than a cake. Hansel and Gretel could easily walk on by dismissing them as inedible. As well as houses, there are other structures like Romany caravans, ships and grand pianos.[37] Technology has played a role in advancing the gingerbread designs. Some competitors use 3D printers to make moulds and other special gingerbread tools, and certain edible components can be printed, too, providing you have access to the right equipment. This has prompted a new rule stating that entries must have no more than 40 % machine-designed, 3D printer or laser-cut components. Ultimately, the final artwork has to be edible but as one competitor summed up: 'It has to be 100 % edible, but 100 % edible doesn't mean it tastes good.'[38]

In Europe, entire gingerbread cities are constructed each winter. Bergen in Norway boasts the biggest, but other towns like Stavanger and Hammerfest create their own *Pepperkakebyen,* or gingerbread towns.[39] Not to be left out of this festive fun, there has been an annual gingerbread city constructed by architects, designers and engineers in Britain since 2015. The project was started by the Museum of Architecture to connect the public with architecture through an innovative display, designed for the holiday season. In 2019 the display included many of London's landmarks such as Battersea Power Station (or 'Buttersea Power Station' as the makers referred to it) and a Gingernut Cracker Ballet (which was awarded first place in the competition).[40] It was an impressive sight, even if the sugar drenched atmosphere was a little overpowering.

All is not lost for the fair. Trade fairs, for the most part, have disappeared (the exception being county shows like the South of England Show), but travelling fairs with their thrill-fuelled rides still roam the country. In the boom years following the Second World War, Vesey-Fitzgerald noted that fairs were 'more popular in Britain than any time since the reign of Elizabeth the First', with 250 fairs being held across the country over the summer months of 1955.[41] The annual fair in Hull is still going strong after more than seven hundred years and is particularly associated with the brandy snaps made by Wright & Co of Brighouse.[42] By the latter part of the twentieth century the fun fair would be joined by the food festival as a source of pleasure. From spring to early autumn, festivals are held across the land to celebrate the diverse range of local food products, including gingerbread. Ormskirk has a dedicated gingerbread festival, and Market Drayton its Ginger and Spice Festival reminiscent of the Gingerbread Fair in Paris.[43] Then there are the Christmas markets which have become as commonplace in Britain as they are on the continent. Every year, cities like York, Bath and Belfast welcome traders from across Europe to create that festive feel. Blenheim Palace in Oxfordshire also hosts a Christmas market to run alongside its illuminated light trail.[44] Christmas markets both at home and abroad attract millions of visitors each year selling decorations, knick-knacks (many of which I'm sure we buy on a whim and regret as soon as we get home) and all manner of food, including that yuletide essential, gingerbread. Nigel Slater, recalling a visit to the Christmas market in Vienna, captures the allure of these seasonal treats rather well:

The scent of gingerbread halts me. A mountain of iced cookies, butterscotch-coloured biscuits that smell of aniseed and ginger. Crisp, iced stars, plum puddings and snowflakes. Each has a hole for ribbon, the occasional silver ball and the temptation that goes with anything home baked and hand iced. For a second I see them, cute as kittens, on my tree at home. Then I see them as crumbs and shattered dreams in my suitcase.[45]

Efforts to sideline gingerbread have been in vain. People seem to love it or loath it for the same reasons, be that the intense (overpowering) heat of spice, or its satisfying stickiness (or cloyingness). In Helen Oyeyemi's modern fairy tale, *Gingerbread*, it is described as 'eating revenge':

'It's like noshing on the actual and anatomical heart of somebody who scarred your beloved and thought they'd got away with it,' the gingerbread addict said. 'That heart, ground to ash and shot through with darts of heat, salt, spice and sulphurous syrup, as if honey was measured out, set ablaze and trickled through the dough along with the liquefied spoon. You are phenomenal. You've ruined my life forever. Thank you.'[46]

Admittedly, gingerbread is unlikely to provoke such extreme reactions in most people. Whether it is nostalgia for something that is 'gratifyingly old-fashioned',[47] or it harks 'back to innocent indulgences and jolly times at nursery',[48] gingerbread looks like it will linger in our larders for generations to come. It could simply be that gingerbread survived because it tastes good, even if it is only preserved as a token recipe in the baking section of a cookbook (invariably attributed to 'Mum' or 'Grandma'). If gingerbread were to have the last laugh it would be because its reach has extended far beyond the fairground or the afternoon tea menu. It has invaded our coffee cups (gingerbread lattes); liquor cabinets (gingerbread vodka); bath tubs (gingerbread bath bombs) and even candyfloss (yes, you can indeed buy gingerbread flavoured sugar). Gingerbread is definitely here to stay and I for one am jolly glad that it is.

Pumpkin Tortellini.

PART II

THE RECIPES

In 1933 Huntley & Palmers launched a large-scale promotion of Ginger Nut biscuits and this tin was probably part of that campaign. The John Ginger character helped to make Ginger Nuts one of the firm's top sellers. © Reading Borough Council (Reading Museum Service).

Biscuits, Wafers & Griddle Cakes

Britain has long been a nation of tea drinkers. For many people a cup of tea is incomplete without a biscuit sidekick. Many of our much loved biscuit varieties like shortbread and digestives are based on recipes formerly baked in the home. The word 'biscuit' has been adopted from the French for 'twice cooked'.[1] Sixteenth-century physician Andrew Boorde believed they could be very nourishing if made with fine flour.[2] The varieties cooked in this period ranged from mass-produced 'hardtack' or ship's biscuits given to soldiers and sailors, to finer varieties which included eggs, sugar, spices and rosewater.[3] That gingerbread evolved into a more crisp incarnation should therefore come as no surprise.

Today, the most famous ginger biscuit in Britain is the Ginger Nut. Although sales of Ginger Nuts have fallen in recent years they remain one of McVities most popular every day biscuits.[4] The modern recipe is based on a mixture of golden syrup and granulated sugar, combined with flour, butter and ginger. The resulting biscuit is hard and spicy, leading the Ginger Nut to be described as the 'Chicken Vindaloo of the biscuit world'.[5] Its firm nature does make it great for dunking in a cup of tea, which may explain why the Ginger Nut's popularity has endured.

Mass production of biscuits in the nineteenth century came about as a consequence of the industrialisation of food production. Quaker businessman Joseph Huntley was one of the first manufacturers to exploit these technological advances at his bakery on London Street in Reading. By the late 1830s Huntley & Palmers were producing around twenty different kinds of biscuit (this would rise to 400 products by 1900). Huntley & Palmers' aim was to produce biscuits to suit every taste and budget, from fancy Rout Cakes at two shillings per pound to the more moderately priced Ginger Nut at a mere eight pence per pound.[6] A kind warder at Reading Gaol (which was situated close to the Huntley & Palmers factory) smuggled in a few Ginger Nuts on occasion for inmate Oscar Wilde to calm the author's temperamental stomach.[7]

Huntley & Palmers cannot be given credit for inventing the Ginger Nut. Recipes for Gingerbread Nuts can be found in eighteenth-century – and no doubt earlier – cookery books, such as Hannah Glasse's *The Art of Cookery Made Plain and Easy*.[8] They have been described as 'travelling biscuits',[9] possibly due to their durable nature or the fact that ginger was believed to be good for digestion. The 'nut' element describes the shape rather than one of the ingredients:

Gingerbread Nuts

To two pounds of sifted Flour, put two pounds of Treacle, three quarters of a pound of Moist Sugar, half a pound of Candied Orange-peel cut small, one ounce and a half of ground Ginger, one ounce of ground Caraways, and three quarters of a pound of Butter oiled: mix all well together, and set it by some time – then roll it out in pieces about the size of a walnut – lay them in rows on a baking-plate; press them flat with the hand, and bake them in a slow oven about ten minutes.[10]

Ginger Nuts would remain one of Huntley & Palmers most popular biscuits into the twentieth century. In 1933 Huntley & Palmers launched a sales promotion featuring the character John Ginger, clad as a traditional seventeenth-century Quaker complete with conical brimmed hat, designed to appeal to children. The John Ginger advertisements for Ginger Nuts often included the tag line 'There are none so good'. His image was still being used as a promotional tool right into the late twentieth century, appearing on mugs in New Zealand demonstrating the nation's nostalgia for interwar design and products.[11]

Historical gingerbread nut recipes produce a rather unforgivingly tough biscuit which challenges even the strongest of teeth. Some liberties have therefore been taken when reproducing them here to make them more palatable to modern tastes.

A Note On Baking Biscuits

Don't be tempted to cook the biscuits for much longer than the time stated in each recipe. Most biscuits will still be a little soft when they come out of the oven but will harden as they cool on the baking sheet. Always leave them on the baking sheet for a few minutes to do this before transferring the biscuits to a wire rack. The exceptions to this rule are Brandy Snaps and Fairy Gingerbread Wafers, as they need to be shaped while they are warm and pliable. Most of these biscuits will store reasonably well in an airtight container.

Ormskirk Gingerbread[12]

During the eighteenth century the Liverpool to Preston stagecoach would stop at the Talbot Inn in Ormskirk to allow its passengers to stretch their legs. On alighting the coach the travellers would be offered packets of gingerbread to buy. Many said this was the best gingerbread they had ever eaten.

Ingredients (Makes around 12 biscuits)
55 g / 2 oz golden syrup
55 g / 2 oz treacle
110 g / 4 oz soft unsalted butter
110 g / 4 oz soft dark brown sugar
2 tsp ground ginger
½ tsp ground cinnamon
Finely grated zest of 1 large lemon or 2 small lemons
275 g / 10 oz plain flour

Method
1. Preheat the oven to 180 °C. Line a good sized baking sheet with non-stick baking paper or a non-stick silicone liner.
2. Gently warm the syrup and treacle together in a small saucepan or for a short while in a microwave.
3. Cream the butter and sugar together in a large bowl. Add the warm treacle and syrup to the bowl then add the spices, zest and flour.
4. Bring the dough together then roll out on a lightly floured board to a thickness of 5 mm. Using a 7.5 cm / 3 in biscuit cutter stamp out rounds from the dough, re-rolling the scraps.
5. Place on the prepared baking sheet and cook for 12–15 minutes.

From front to back: Chocolate Orange Gingerbread, White Buttons and Ormskirk Gingerbread.

WHITE BUTTONS

[handwritten: Made for the foodbank for coronation week May 2023 - v. now nutmeg]

This is one of the many gingerbreads that used to be sold at county fairs, the most famous of which comes from Grantham in Lincolnshire. The Grantham gingerbread has a dome shape and is almost hollow inside. However, I prefer this crazed version (caused by the dough rising and falling in the oven) from Norfolk.[13] Frederick Vine[14] includes nutmeg in his version which I have also included here although you can omit it if you prefer.

Ingredients (Makes around 24 biscuits)
250 g / 9 oz plain flour
3 tsp ground ginger
¼ tsp ground nutmeg (optional)
½ tsp bicarbonate of soda
250 g / 9 oz caster sugar plus 25 g / 1 oz extra
100 g / 4 oz cold unsalted butter, cubed
1 large egg, beaten
Up to 2 tbsp whole milk

Method
1. Sieve the flour, ginger, nutmeg (if using) and bicarbonate of soda into a bowl then stir in the 250 g / 9 oz caster sugar.
2. Rub the butter into the flour and sugar. Add the beaten egg and enough milk to bring the mixture together as a firm, but slightly sticky dough.
3. Divide the dough into 24 pieces then roll into little balls (they should weigh around 25 g / 1 oz each). Roll each ball in the extra caster sugar. Place on a tray and refrigerate for at least one hour or longer. You can freeze the balls on a clingfilm lined at this point to cook later from frozen.
4. Preheat the oven to 150 °C. You will need to cook these biscuits in batches as they spread considerably while they are baking. Place some of the balls on a baking sheet lined with silicone or greaseproof paper ensuring they are well spaced. Bake for around 12–15 minutes or until the buttons are a pale fawn colour. If cooking from frozen, bake the biscuits for 15–18 minutes. *[handwritten: 6 max per tray]*

[handwritten: advised! - wd say 20 leaves them crunchier at 150C fan]

Mrs Dixon's Hunting Nuts[15]

Mary Anne Dixon was the second wife of the Reverend W. H. Dixon who became the rural dean of York in 1842, a decade or so after his wedding. Mary Anne appears to have inherited a book of brewing notes from her mother which includes worm medicine, gout cordial and various dyes. Her book also includes recipes such as the one below, which is a gingerbread nut in everything but name. The editors of of this collection of household recipes refer to these small biscuits as being particularly suited to travelling because they don't crumble, and add that the hunting nuts are 'liked by horses and hounds'. They're very much liked by people too.

Ingredients (Makes 12–14 small biscuits)
25 g / 1 oz sugar
75 g / 3 oz treacle
65 g / 2 ⅓ oz butter
1½ tsp ground ginger
½ tsp caraway seeds
Pinch ground cloves
½ tsp ground cinnamon
125 g / 4 ½ oz flour
¼ tsp bicarbonate of soda
40 g / 1 ½ oz demerara sugar

Method
1. Put the sugar, treacle and butter in a saucepan along with the spices. Heat the mixture until the butter has melted and the treacle is liquid but do not boil. Allow to cool until it is lukewarm.
2. Mix the flour and bicarbonate of soda thoroughly into the mixture. Cover the bowl and place in the fridge for at least an hour (longer is fine).
3. Preheat the oven to 180 °C. Line a good sized baking sheet with non-stick baking paper or a non-stick silicone liner.
4. Roll the dough into walnut-size balls then roll each ball in the Demerara sugar. This adds a good crunch to the outside of the biscuit but you can skip this phase or do half rolled in sugar and leave half plain.

5. Place on the baking tray and cook for 10 minutes. They will have spread a little but should be little cracked domes.

CHOCOLATE ORANGE GINGERBREAD

The 'germ' of inspiration for this comes from the esteemed Regency cook Dr William Kitchiner's recipe for Orange Gingerbread.[16] Chocolate marries beautifully with both ginger and orange although you will not find it in the original recipe (chocolate was primarily consumed as a drink at this time). This is a thoroughly modern interpretation of Kitchiner's work producing a softer, cookie style gingerbread rather than a crisp biscuit. The word 'cookie' comes from the Dutch '*koekje*' meaning 'little cake'.[17] I use a mini food processor to finely chop the mixed peel but you can use larger chunks if you prefer.

Ingredients (Makes 12–14)
100 g / 4 oz unsalted butter
50 g / 2 oz treacle
100 g / 4 oz granulated sugar
150 g / 5 oz plain flour
½ tsp baking powder
2 tsp ground ginger
¾ tsp ground all spice
1 large egg
A few drops orange essence (optional)
50 g / 2 oz candied peel, finely chopped
50 g / 2 oz dark chocolate, roughly chopped

Method
1. Preheat the oven to 180 °C. Line a good sized baking sheet with non-stick baking paper or a non-stick silicone liner.
2. Gently melt the butter and treacle in a small saucepan. Place the granulated sugar in a bowl then pour the melted butter and treacle over the sugar. Allow to cool slightly.
3. Sieve the flour, baking powder and spices.
4. Beat the egg into the sweet buttery mixture then mix in the spicy

flour. Add a few drops of orange essence (if using) followed by the finely chopped candied peel and roughly chopped chocolate.

5. Drop tablespoons of the cookie dough onto the baking sheet leaving plenty of space between each mound. Bake for 8–10 minutes. They will be very soft when you take them out of the oven so leave them on the sheet to firm up before transferring to a wire rack.

INDIAN GINGERBREAD[18]

One of my favourite recipe books is *The Indian Cookery Book* by a 'Thirty-Five Years' Resident'. Written at the pinnacle of the British Raj it is a fantastic combination of fairly authentic Indian curries (for the time at least)[19] and home comforts, like steamed puddings. There are a number of gingerbread recipes in the book, including one which uses a sugar syrup in place of treacle (golden syrup was not available until the 1880s in Britain) and another which includes cayenne pepper as one of the spices. I have picked elements from several of these variations to create this recipe, which is not dissimilar to a modern ginger nut. My husband says this is the best ginger biscuit he has ever tasted.

Ingredients (Makes 16)
125 g / 4 ½ oz self raising flour
1 tsp bicarbonate of soda
1 tsp ground ginger
½ tsp ground cinnamon
A good pinch of ground cloves and cayenne pepper
50 g / 2 oz granulated sugar
50 g / 2 oz cold unsalted butter, diced
1 piece preserved stem ginger (around 25 g / 1 oz drained weight), finely chopped
15 g / ½ oz pistachio nuts, finely chopped
50 g / 2 oz golden syrup

Method
1. Preheat the oven to 180 °C. Line a good sized baking sheet with non-stick baking paper or a non-stick silicone liner.

2. Sieve the flour, bicarbonate of soda and spices into a bowl.
3. Add the sugar then rub in the butter.
4. Stir in the chopped ginger and nuts.
5. Divide into 16 pieces and roll into balls. Place on the prepared baking sheet, well spaced apart. Bake for 8–10 minutes.

PARLIAMENT GINGERBREAD
(WITH APOLOGIES TO THE ENGLISH SUFFRAGISTS)[20]

This particular recipe comes from the *Original Suffrage Cook Book* published in 1915, although the recipe's origins are much older. Fundraising books like this were published to raise money to support the campaign for the vote for women, especially in America.

Meg Dods attributes a similar recipe for 'Parlies' to Mrs Fletcher in her *Cook and Housewife's Manual* (1827). F. Marian McNeill believes Mrs Fletcher is actually the Mrs Flockhart, a vintner in Edinburgh, who features in Sir Walter Scott's novel *Waverley*. As well as an array of spirits she supplied her customers with gingerbread 'in thin, crisp cakes called Parliaments – in round pieces, denominated snaps'.[21] According to Scottish lexicographer Dr Jamieson, members of the Scottish parliament were particularly partial to them, hence the name.[22] When this type of biscuit was sold at fairs they were often decorated with coloured comfits known as 'Glasgow Jam' (or 'hundreds and thousands' in today's parlance).[23]

Ingredients (Makes approx 24, 8 cm biscuits)
225 g / 8 oz plain flour
25 g / 1 oz butter
2 tsp ground ginger
2 tsp mixed spice
110 g / 4 oz caster sugar
½ tsp bicarbonate of soda dissolved in 1 tbsp hot water
225 g / 8 oz treacle

Method
1. Preheat the oven to 180 °C.

Parliament Gingerbread (left) and Ginger Snaps (right).

2. Put the flour in a bowl and rub in the butter, then add the spices and caster sugar.

3. Add the bicarbonate of soda and water along with the treacle then knead to a smooth paste (or cheat and use a food processor!).

4. On a lightly floured board, roll the dough out to a thickness of around 3 mm then stamp out the biscuits using a square, fluted cookie cutter. Make sure you have enough flour on the board as this is an exceedingly sticky dough.

5. Place on a baking sheet lined with silicone paper (or well greased) then bake for 7–8 minutes. Leave on the sheet for a few minutes to harden before cooling on a wire rack.

GINGER SNAPS[24]

In the early seventeenth century a 'snap' meant a light meal or a snack. From the Victorian era it was used to describe a thin, crisp ginger biscuit.[25] These and the Parliament Gingerbread are also delicious with cheese.

Ingredients (Makes 36, 8 cm biscuits)
225 g / 8 oz flour
¼ tsp bicarbonate of soda
1 tsp ginger
1 tsp white pepper
110 g / 4 oz demerara sugar
55 g / 2 oz butter, cubed
120 g / 4 ½ oz golden syrup
50 g / 2 oz treacle

Method

1. Preheat the oven to 150 °C. Line a good sized baking sheet with non-stick baking paper or a non-stick silicone liner.

2. Sieve the dry ingredients into a bowl. Then add the sugar.

3. Rub the butter into the spiced flour.

4. Add the syrup and treacle then mix to a smooth paste.

5. Roll out on a lightly floured board to a thickness of around 2–3 mm

(you need them to be fairly thin but not transparent). Cut out the desired shape then place on a baking sheet. Brush with water and bake for 10–15 minutes.

Brandy Snaps[26]

Golden syrup is used to make brandy snaps today but the original brandy snaps sold at fairs were made from treacle. You really do need asbestos fingers to create the rolled wafer effect (for which I use the handle of a wooden spoon). Alternatively, you could drape them over a rolling pin like the Fairy Gingerbread Wafers (see page 110) or just leave the lacy discs to harden as they are.

Ingredients (Makes 18–20)
50 g / 2 oz unsalted butter
50 g / 2 oz treacle
50 g / 2 oz demerara sugar
A few drops orange or lemon extract (optional)
1 tsp ground ginger
50 g / 2 oz plain flour

Method
1. Preheat the oven to 180 °C. Have a couple of wooden spoons ready to curl the snaps around when they come out of the oven.
2. Melt the butter, treacle and sugar in a small saucepan. Add a few drops of orange or lemon extract (if using) then stir in the ginger and flour.
3. Drop teaspoons of the mixture on a baking sheet lined with silicone or non-stick paper making sure they are well spaced (once again you will need to bake in batches). Bake for 6–7 minutes. As these wafers contain treacle it is very tricky to see whether they are burning so watch them carefully. If they look black they are probably burnt! Remove from the oven and wait for a minute or two for the biscuits to harden slightly. Quickly remove them from the baking sheet with a palette knife and wrap each one around the handle of a wooden spoon (you should be able to get at least two per spoon). Don't wrap them too tightly otherwise you won't be able to take them off without breaking

them. If they start to get too hard on the baking sheet, return them briefly to the oven to make the mixture pliable again.

4. Within a few minutes the snaps will be hard. Slip the hardened brandy snap off the handle. Store in an airtight container. These actually seem to keep quite well so long as the weather is not too humid.

PARKIN PIGS[27]

Pigs were a particularly popular shape for gingerbread biscuits. One of the best-known makers of parkin pigs in Yorkshire was a spice merchant called Chatterton from Bradford. Chatterton's *pièce de resistance* was a gingerbread representation of Daniel in the lions' den.

> Ingredients (Makes 12–16 8 cm / 3 in pigs or shapes, depending on the size of the cutter)
> 50 g / 2 oz treacle
> 50 g / 2 oz golden syrup
> 25 g / 1 oz light brown sugar
> 25 g / 1 oz unsalted butter
> 100 g / 4 oz plain flour
> 100 g / 4 oz medium oatmeal
> ½ tsp bicarbonate of soda
> 1 tsp ground ginger
> ½ tsp mixed spice

Method

1. Preheat the oven to 180 °C. Line a good sized baking sheet with non-stick baking paper or a non-stick silicone liner.

2. Gently heat the treacle, golden syrup, sugar and butter together.

3. Place the remaining ingredients in a bowl. Add the melted treacle mixture then mix to a firm dough.

4. Roll out on a lightly floured board to a thickness of 5 mm. Stamp out pigs or whatever shape you desire. Place on the baking sheet and cook for 8–10 minutes.

FAIRY GINGERBREAD WAFERS[28]

Wafers are probably the oldest type of biscuit around. Historically they would have been made using special wafer tongs and served with spiced wine as part of the 'voidee'.[29] These are basically a gingery tuile which are great to serve with desserts or ice cream. You can spread the mixture out freehand, but I prefer to fashion a template using an A4 acetate sheet into which I cut six circles measuring 7–8 cm / 3 in diameter.

Ingredients (Makes around 18–20)
85 g / 3 oz plain flour
1 ½ tsp ground ginger
50 g / 2 oz soft unsalted butter
60 g / 2 oz icing sugar, sieved
70 ml / 3 fl oz whole milk

Method

1. Preheat the oven to 180 °C. Have a rolling pin ready to curl the tuiles over when they come out of the oven.

2. Sieve the flour and ginger together. Put aside until required.

3. Cream the butter and icing sugar together then beat in the milk. Stir in the flour and ginger. You should have a loose, spreadable batter but it should not be too liquid.

4. Place your template on a baking sheet lined with silicone or nonstick paper. Thinly spread a little of the wafer batter into each of the holes in your template. Remove the acetate (or whatever you are using) leaving six circles on the baking sheet.

5. Place the baking sheet in the oven and cook for around 5 minutes. The fairy gingerbread should just be starting to turn golden at the edges but still pale in the middle. If it seems too pale return it to the oven for another minute or so (be warned, these gingerbreads go from pale to golden very quickly). Leave the tuiles on the tray to firm up a little before using a palette knife to transfer them to the rolling pin. Drape them over the rolling pin and allow them to cool completely. Repeat this process with the remaining batter.

6. You can store these wafers in an airtight container but they are best eaten within a day or so of baking.

MRS HAILSTONE'S PARKIN[30]

Ann Hailstone was born around 1780. She married Samuel Hailstone, a Bradford solicitor, in 1808. Like many women she kept a record of her favourite recipes from the time she married until her death in 1833. Her son Edward bequeathed her household book to York Minster Library in 1890, along with a large collection of books on Yorkshire.

The editors of this recipe compare the end result to a flapjack. Mrs Hailstone doesn't specify what type of oatmeal is required, so I've taken the liberty of using porridge oats instead. I've also increased the quantity of butter in the original recipe to give the parkin a softer texture. Coriander seeds were frequently used in the seventeenth century to flavour biscuits but seem to have fallen out of favour during the following century. It's nice to see them make a reappearance here, although you may want to reduce the amount used slightly if you're not so keen on this particular spice.

Ingredients (Makes 8 pieces)
2 tsp coriander seeds
100 g / 4 oz treacle
50 g / 2 oz soft light brown sugar
100 g / 4 oz unsalted butter
1 tbsp brandy
225 g / 8 oz porridge oats
3 tsp ground ginger

Method
1. Preheat the oven to 180 °C. Line an 18 cm / 7 in square tin with foil-backed baking parchment or grease and line the tin with baking paper.
2. Pound the coriander seeds with a pestle and mortar (or place them in a bowl and use the end of a rolling pin) to coarsely crush them. Reserve until required.
3. Gently heat the treacle, sugar, butter and brandy until warm and very liquid.
4. Place the oats and spices in a bowl. Pour the warm treacle onto the oats then mix well to combine.

5. Spoon the mixture into the prepared tin. Bake for 15 minutes. When the parkin comes out of the oven, immediately divide it into 8 pieces while it is still in the tin. Leave it to cool fully in the tin.

Perkins with Raspberry & Redcurrant Compote

Perkins are a type of individual parkin from northern England and southern Scotland.[31] They would have originally been cooked on a hot griddle or bakestone, not unlike traditional Yorkshire oatcakes or haver cakes which are made from a leavened batter. The texture varies according to where they are made. Those from England tend to be softer and spongier while the Scottish versions are more akin to crisp biscuits.[32] Most modern recipes are baked in the oven but I prefer to follow Julie Duff's lead and cook mine in the traditional way on a griddle to produce something not dissimilar to an oaty Scotch pancake.

Ingredients for the perkins (Makes 12–14)
100 g / 4 oz medium oatmeal
50 g / 2 oz unsalted butter plus a small knob
50 g / 2 oz dark brown sugar
50 g / 2 oz golden syrup
50 g / 2 oz treacle
125 g / 4 ½ oz plain flour
1 tsp baking powder
½ tsp bicarbonate of soda
1 tsp ground ginger
1 tsp mixed spice
1 large egg
200 ml / 7 fl oz whole milk

Ingredients for the compote
150 g / 5 oz red currants, fresh or frozen
150 g / 5 oz raspberries, fresh or frozen
75–100 g / 3–4 oz granulated sugar
1 tbsp water
1 tsp arrowroot mixed with 1 tbsp water

Method

1. Melt 50 g / 2 oz butter, sugar, golden syrup and treacle over a gentle heat. Allow to cool slightly.

2. Sieve the flour, baking powder, bicarbonate of soda and spices into a bowl. Stir in the oatmeal.

3. Beat the egg into the cooled syrups. Make a well in the centre of the flour then add the sugar mixture. Using a balloon whisk or electric whisk start beating the ingredients together, gradually adding the milk as you go. Leave the batter to rest for one hour (this rest period is essential as it helps thicken the batter and to soften the oatmeal).

4. Preheat a griddle or a large, non-stick frying pan over a medium high heat. When it is hot I like to add a small knob of butter just to make sure the first batch of perkins don't stick. Spoon 2 tablespoons of batter per oatcake onto the hot griddle. Depending on the size of your griddle or frying pan, you should be able to cook two to three at a time. This will spread to give you a cake around 8–10 cm / 4–5 in in diameter. Cook for around 2–3 minutes before flipping over and cooking for a further 1 ½ to 2 minutes. Keep the oatcakes warm in a low oven, covered with foil to prevent them drying out, while you use up the rest of the batter. Serve warm with the berry compote on the side or drizzled with honey.

5. To make the compote, place the red currants and raspberries in a saucepan with 75 g / 3 oz sugar and 1 tablespoon water. Cook over a gentle heat until the berries begin to burst and the mixture becomes really juicy. As the fruit approaches boiling point, stir in the arrowroot mixed with water and stir continuously until the compote has thickened. Add more sugar if you prefer a sweeter compote. The compote can be made in advance and is delicious hot or cold.

SAM'S SIMPLE GINGERBREAD

While I love all of the recipes in this book sometimes you just want a straightforward formula for gingerbread, particularly when baking with children. This dough is ideal for making gingerbread men or animals. Feel free to replace the spices in this recipe with the same measurement of the medieval or *lebkuchen* spice mixes. You can also make a slightly lighter mixture by replacing the treacle with honey and the dark brown sugar with light brown sugar.

Ingredients for a dozen or so gingerbread men (depending on the size of your cutter)
100 g / 4 oz unsalted butter
2 tbsp treacle
350 g / 12 oz plain flour
1 ½ tsp ground ginger
½ tsp ground cinnamon
¼ tsp ground nutmeg
Pinch ground cloves
1 tsp baking powder
100 g / 4 oz dark brown sugar
75 g / 3 oz caster sugar
1 large egg, beaten
A splash of milk (if required)
A few currants for decoration (optional)

Method

1. Preheat the oven to 180 °C. Gently heat the butter and treacle until just melted but not too warm. If it does start bubbling leave it for a little while to cool before proceeding with the rest of the recipe.

2. Sieve the flour, spices and baking powder into a bowl. Stir in the sugars then add the melted butter and treacle followed by the beaten egg. Bring the dough together adding a splash of milk if the mixture seems too dry. You can use the dough right away although I like to leave mine to rest for an hour wrapped in clingfilm or foil.

3. When you are ready to make your gingerbread shapes, lightly dust a work surface with flour. Divide the dough in two, keeping one half covered. Roll the dough to a thickness of 5 mm / ¼ in then stamp out your chosen shapes using cookie cutters. Repeat this process using the remaining dough. You can gather up the trimmings and roll the dough out again to cut out more shapes.

4. Place the gingerbread shapes on a greased or lined baking sheet. You can decorate your gingerbread men with currants for eyes and buttons

Små Pepparkakor.

if you like by pressing them gently into the dough figures at this point. Bake for 10–15 minutes until slightly risen and golden. Leave them on the tray for a couple of minutes before transferring to a cooling rack. Once the figures are completely cold you can of course decorate them with icing if you wish.

Cajsa Warg's 'Små Pepparkakor'

Anna Christina Warg (1703–1769), better known as Cajsa (or Kajsa) Warg, was a Swedish cookbook author and one of the best-known cooks in Swedish history. She published her *Guide to Housekeeping for Young Women* in 1755. It was translated into German and Estonian, and remained in print well into the nineteenth century.

Swedish historian Maud Ekblad,[33] who has written extensively on gingerbread herself, kindly translated Cajsa's recipe for these intensely crisp, aromatic 'small gingerbreads'. If you can source grains of paradise[34] and grind your own spice mix it really is worth the effort.

Ingredients (Makes around 24, 6 cm biscuits)
3–4 cm piece cinnamon stick
4 cloves
18 cardamom pods
½ tsp grains of paradise
½ tsp ground nutmeg
200 g / 7 oz plain flour
Finely grated zest of ½ lemon
Finely grated zest of ½ orange
85 g / 3 oz granulated sugar
85 g / 3 oz golden syrup
50 g / 2 oz unsalted butter
½ tsp bicarbonate of soda
1 tbsp rosewater

Method
1. Place the cinnamon stick, cloves, cardamom pods and grains of paradise (if using) in a spice grinder then grind to a fine powder. Pass

the powder through a sieve to remove any larger fragments then stir in the ground nutmeg (I have found it easier to add pre-ground nutmeg rather than trying to cut a portion from a whole nutmeg and grind it myself). If you don't have a spice grinder see the notes section for quantities of pre-ground spices.

2. Sieve the flour into a bowl, Stir in the ground spices and finely grated zests.

3. Heat the sugar, syrup and butter together over a gentle heat until liquid. Dissolve the bicarbonate of soda in the rosewater then add to the melted syrup.

4. Stir the warm foaming syrup into the flour. Mix well to combine and bring the dough together in a ball. Wrap in clingfilm then leave at room temperature for at least four hours or overnight.

5. Preheat the oven to 200 °C. Lightly flour a board then roll the dough to a thickness of 2–3 mm. Stamp out squares and place on a lined or greased baking sheet. Gather up the trimmings then re-roll to cut out more biscuits. Bake for 6–8 minutes. The biscuits should be a golden colour. Leave on the baking sheet to firm up before transferring to a wire rack. Store in an airtight container.

Taai-taai[36]

Taai is Dutch for 'tough' but don't let the name put you off. These aniseed scented slabs are delicious. They are one of the oldest spice cakes in the Netherlands (a forerunner of the popular *Speculaas*).

Ingredients (Makes 8 large biscuits)
125 g / 4 ½ oz honey
125 g / 4 ½ oz treacle
25 g / 1 oz water
125 g / 4 ½ oz rye flour
125 g / 4 ½ oz plain flour
¾ tsp ground cinnamon
¾ tsp ground aniseed
¼ tsp ground ginger

Speculaas (left) and Taai-taai (right).

⅛ tsp ground nutmeg
1 tsp bicarbonate of soda

Method
1. Warm the honey, treacle and water in a small pan over a gentle heat, stirring occasionally, until fairly liquid. Sieve the flours into a bowl.
2. Add the honey mixture to the flours to make a dough. Knead the dough briefly until the ingredients are fully combined then leave in a cool place overnight (room temperature rather than the fridge is best).
3. Preheat the oven to 200 °C. Line a baking sheet with baking parchment.
4. Mix the spices and bicarbonate of soda together. Knead this into the dough ensuring there are no streaks or lumps.
5. Roll the dough out on a lightly floured board. Ultimately, you want to create a rectangle that is 14 x 20 cm / 6 x 8 in and around 1 cm / ½ in thick (or a smidge less). If you roll the dough out slightly larger than this you can trim it to form a neater rectangle. Divide the larger rectangle into smaller rectangles measuring 5 x 7 cm / 2 x 3 in. Place on the baking sheet, brush with water to remove any excess flour then cook for 7 minutes.
6. Cool on a wire rack but leave them for 24 hours before eating to allow the flavours to develop.

Speculaas[37]

There appears to be no 'definitive' recipe for *speculaas,* or *speculoos* as they are known in Belgium. Whatever recipe you follow the end result should be buttery and crisp, making them an ideal accompaniment to a cup of coffee or tea.

There are a number of theories regarding the name *speculaas.* One is that it is derived from the Latin *speculum* (mirror) because the biscuits are a mirror image of the moulds traditionally used to shape the dough.[38] Another is that the name is a combination of *spek* meaning titbit and *klaas,* the diminutive of Nicholas, as these biscuits are popular during *Sinterklaas* season.[39]

FIRST CATCH YOUR GINGERBREAD

I have to confess to chickening out of pressing the dough into a mould to create interesting shapes. I'm assured if you use flavourless oil on the moulds (which have been dusted off with a clean toothbrush – never use water as it will make the moulds split) the biscuits should come out fine. The recipe below makes a good sized batch which is no bad thing as they soon disappear.

Ingredients
250 g / 9 oz plain flour
½ tsp baking powder
1 ½ tsp ground cinnamon
½ tsp ground cardamom
¼ tsp ground ginger
¼ tsp ground aniseed
¼ tsp ground cloves
⅛ tsp ground nutmeg
⅛ tsp ground mace
175 g / 6 oz unsalted butter, diced
200 g / 7 oz soft dark brown sugar
Pinch of salt
1 large egg, beaten
50 g sliced almonds

Method
1. Preheat the oven to 180 °C. Butter a 33 x 23 x 2 cm / 13 x 9 x ⅞ in Swiss roll tin.
2. Sieve the flour, baking powder and spices into a bowl. Add the butter then rub it in with your fingers (or process in a food processor) until the mixture resembles fine breadcrumbs.
3. Stir the sugar and salt into the mixture followed by the egg. Bring the mixture together into a dough then press into the prepared tin as evenly as possible. Scatter with the almonds.
4. Bake for 20–30 minutes. Allow to cool slightly in the tin then cut into squares (I made 32 in this size tin but you could make the biscuits larger or smaller as you prefer). Lift the biscuits onto a wire rack to cool completely.

COEURS EN PAIN D'ÉPICE (GINGERBREAD HEARTS)[40]

Ingredients
125 g / 4 ½ oz honey
125 g / 4 ½ oz treacle
75 g / 3 oz caster sugar
125 g / 4 ½ oz unsalted butter
400 g / 14 oz plain flour
1 ½ tsp baking powder
1 tsp ground cinnamon
½ tsp ground cardamom
½ tsp ground cloves
100 g / 4 oz ground almonds
1 tsp orange zest, finely grated
1 tsp lemon zest, finely grated
100 g / 4 oz chopped mixed peel
1 large egg
1 x quantity basic icing

Method
1. Heat the honey, treacle and caster sugar until the sugar has dissolved. Add the butter stirring until it has melted. Allow to cool slightly.
2. Sieve the flour, baking powder and spices into a bowl. Stir in the almonds, zests and chopped mixed peel.
3. Add the egg to the honey and treacle mixture then pour the liquid mixture onto the flour. Mix well then refrigerate over night.
4. Preheat the oven to 200 °C. Grease or line a baking sheet with baking parchment.
5. Roll the dough to a thickness of 5 mm to 1 cm. Place on the prepared baking sheet then cook for 7 minutes.
6. As soon as they come out of the oven brush the icing over the top of each biscuit giving them two coatings. Allow to cool completely before transferring to a wire rack (as the biscuits cool the icing will harden). You can embellish the hearts further with royal icing if you like.

Coeurs en Pain d'Épice (Gingerbread Hearts).

Gingerbread House[41]

Ingredients (Makes 1 house)
700 g / 1 ½ lb plain flour
2 ½ tsp baking powder
3 tsp *lebkuchen* spice mix (see page 219)
Pinch of salt
250 g / 9 oz honey
400 g / 14 oz caster sugar
55 g / 2 oz unsalted butter
4 tbsp lemon juice (about 1–1 ½ lemons)
Grated zest of 1 lemon
1 large egg plus 1 large egg yolk

Icing
2 egg whites
340 g / 12 oz icing sugar, sieved
Sweets, nuts and sprinkles for decorating the house

Method
1. First of all you need to create a template for the gingerbread house. A large empty cereal packet is good for this (or any other thin cardboard). You will need two roof panels measuring 18 cm / 7 in x 14 cm / 5 ½ in and two side panels measuring 11 cm / 4 ¼ in x 7.5 cm / 3 in. To make the front and back elevations (which have the same measurements) draw two more boxes on your cardboard measuring 11 cm / 4 ¼ in x 7.5 cm / 3 in. Halfway along the longest side draw a line directly upwards measuring 17 cm / 6 ½ in then draw diagonal lines from the top corner of the box to meet this line at the apex (thereby creating a triangle on top of the box). For the corner posts (which will help support the house) cut out a strip of cardboard measuring 28 cm / 11 in x 1.5 cm / ½ in. Leave the strip whole but mark it into four equal sections (it is less fiddly to cut out one long piece of gingerbread then divide it into four).
2. Sieve the flour, baking powder, spice and salt.
3. Place the honey, sugar and butter in a saucepan large enough to accommodate the dough. Bring these ingredients to the boil, stirring frequently, until the sugar has dissolved. Remove from the heat the add

the lemon juice and zest. Cool to room temperature.

4. Beat in around one third of the flour followed by the whole egg and yolk. Add the remaining flour and mix thoroughly. Divide the mixture into three roughly 500 g portions, cover each ball of dough with clingfilm then refrigerate over night.

5. Grease and flour three 20 x 30 cm / 8 x 12 in Swiss roll tins (if you only have one tin measuring this size you will need to cook the cakes in batches. Preheat the oven to 150 °C.

6. Roll each piece of dough into a rectangle a little smaller than the tin. Lay the dough in the prepared tin then use your fingers to press to the dough up to the sides of the tin. Bake for 15–20 minutes or until the top is golden brown and the cake is firm. Allow to cool in the tin for five minutes before using your template to cut out the pieces of the house.

7. To make the icing, beat the egg whites in a free-standing mixer until frothy. With the motor running gradually add the icing sugar, continuing to beat until you have a stiff icing. Spoon into a lidded plastic container to stop it drying out. Spoon enough icing into a piping bag to decorate the house.

To assemble the house
Use the icing to decorate the different facades of the house remembering to leave enough to 'glue' the house together. If possibly do this several hours before you plan to build the house to allow the decoration to set. You can store the royal icing in a lidded container in the fridge. The following day, ice the bottom end of one side wall and one of the ends of the house. Place it carefully on the board using a little icing to cement them in place. Ice the bottom and two sides of a corner post and place it between them (effectively inside the house) Hold the pieces upright for 3–4 minutes or until the icing begins to set. Ice the opposite end of the site wall and the bottom of the other end wall, and fit that wall onto the house for the front. Ice and add the post in the corner. Hold these pieces until set.

Ice the remaining corner posts and put them in position in front and back, allowing space for the side wall. Now ice the bottom ends of the remaining side wall and put into place. I usually leave the house for another 24 hours before adding the roof. Ice the sloping edges of the front and back of the house. Carefully place the roof panels on each side. They will overlap the front and the back of the house slightly and they will leave a V-shaped indentation along the top of the roof. You can fill this with icing and decorate it with more sweets if desired.

Elisenlebkuchen

When you delve into the world of *lebkuchen* you quickly realise that there is far more to these spicy biscuits than meets the eye. The name is believed to be derived from the Latin *libum* meaning flat cake.

Lebkuchen have been made in Nuremberg since the fourteenth century. Franconia, the area of Germany where Nuremberg is situated, was renowned for its honey. Nuremberg itself had a thriving spice trade courtesy of the *Pfeffersäcke* or pepper sacks as the city's medieval spice merchants were called. But it was enterprising monks who combined the honey, spices and nuts to develop the recipe for these delicious gingerbreads.[42]

Today there are several varieties of *lebkuchen* each of which must meet specific requirements to live up to its PGI status designated by the EU. *Elisenlebkuchen*, said to be the finest of the *lebkuchen*, must contain at least 25 % nuts and no more than 10 % flour or starch (if any is included

at all). According to legend, *Elisenlebkuchen* are named after the beautiful daughter of a Nuremberg gingerbread maker. The biscuits are usually glazed either with chocolate or sugar icing and are often topped with three almonds or hundreds and thousands. Personally, I find the sugared variety too sweet so have provided a chocolate icing below. However, if you would like to use a sugar icing instead use the recipe on page 124. Commercial manufacturers guard their recipes closely and even the recipes you find in books or online vary immensely (most modern recipes omit the honey altogether). This is my interpretation.

Evidently, the monks used small circular wafers called oblaten as a base for the *lebkuchen* to stop the mixture from sticking to the baking sheet. Although you can buy these discs in the United Kingdom it's far more economical to cut out rounds from a sheet of edible rice paper. Providing you use a wheat-free paper these biscuits are gluten free.

Ingredients (Makes around 16 7–8 mm *Elisenlebkuchen*)
2–3 A4 sheets edible rice paper
2 large eggs
100 g / 4 oz sugar
25 g / 1 oz honey
100 g / 4 oz diced mixed peel
2 tbsp rice flour
100 g / 4 oz ground almonds
100 g / 4 oz roasted and ground hazelnuts
2–3 tsp *lebkuchen* spice blend (see page 219)
¼ tsp baking powder
150 g / 5 ½ oz dark or milk chocolate
2 tbsp golden syrup
50–60 blanched almonds and/or multicoloured sprinkles

Method
1. Using a 7 cm / 3 in non-fluted cookie cutter draw 16–20 circles in pencil on your edible rice paper sheets (it's always a good idea to cut a few more than you need just in case). Cut the circles out and keep to one side until required.
2. Place the eggs and caster sugar in the bowl of a free-standing mixer

or use an electric hand whisk. Whisk on a high speed until the mixture is pale and thick. The whisk should leave a trail when removed.

3. Toss the mixed peel in the rice flour. Fold in the ground nuts, mixed peel, *lebkuchen* spices and baking powder. Leave to one side while you preheat the oven to 150 °C.

4. Place the discs on a lined or well greased baking sheet (I would strongly recommend the former as the biscuits will spread beyond the rice paper). Place 1 ½ to 2 tablespoons of the *lebkucken* mixture on each disc flattening slightly with the back of a teaspoon. Make sure there is a margin around the outside of the disc. Place the *lebkuchen* in the oven for 13–15 minutes. The biscuits will spread during this time. They should be lightly golden when they come out of the oven and will still be very soft. Leave them to cool on the tray to firm up before removing them to a wire rack to cool completely.

5. To make the chocolate glaze, put the chocolate and syrup in a heatproof bowl. Place the bowl on top of a saucepan with a few centimetres of barely simmering water in the bottom (the bowl should not touch the water). Stir frequently. Once the *Elisenlebkuchen* are cool, spoon the chocolate over the top, spreading it gently as far as you can towards the edges. Place three almonds on the top of each one then wait (patiently!) for the icing to set before eating.

SWISS BIBERLI BARS[43]

This recipe for Marzipan-Filled Gingerbread Bars comes from Sharon Hudgins a food writer who enjoys eating her way around Switzerland, the country where she was married. I absolutely adore marzipan so couldn't resist including it in this book. Be warned – Biberli are exceedingly rich so a little goes along way.

Ingredients (Makes 32 very rich Biberli bars)
340 g / 12 oz runny honey
150 g / 5 oz dark brown sugar, firmly packed
1 egg, unbeaten
1 tbsp fresh lemon juice
1 tbsp freshly grated lemon zest

2 tsp ground cinnamon
½ tsp freshly grated nutmeg
¼ tsp each of ground cloves, ginger, coriander, cardamom, and anise
280 g / 10 oz plain flour
½ tsp baking soda
¼ tsp salt
400 g / 14 oz marzipan
Icing sugar (for rolling out marzipan)
1 tbsp milk (for brushing on the dough)

Icing:
125 g / 4 ½ oz cup icing sugar
2 tbsp milk
½ teaspoon vanilla extract

Method:
1. Heat the honey and brown sugar together in a small saucepan over low heat, stirring constantly, for about 20 minutes or until the sugar is completely dissolved (no longer gritty) and the mixture is thin. Pour the honey mixture into a large heatproof bowl and let it cool until only slightly warm, stirring occasionally to keep it smooth. Whisk in the egg, scraping down the sides of the bowl, until the mixture becomes thinner. Stir in the lemon juice, grated lemon zest, and all the spices. Mix well.
2. Sift the flour, baking powder, and salt together into another bowl. Stir the flour mixture into the honey mixture, half a cup at a time, mixing well after each addition, until all the ingredients are thoroughly combined. Cover the bowl with plastic wrap and refrigerate the dough for 24 hours. (Don't even think about tasting the dough or you won't have enough for this recipe.)
3. The next day, preheat the oven to 160 °C. Heavily butter two 20 cm / 8 in square metal baking pans. (It is important to use the correct pan size for this recipe). Use a knife to divide the dough in half, and put one of the halves back into the refrigerator. Divide the remaining dough in half again. Dip your fingers in cold water and use your hands to spread the dough in a thin, even layer in each of the pans. (The dough will be very sticky.)

4. Dust a flat surface and rolling pin with icing sugar. Roll out one 7-ounce package of marzipan to a square measuring 20 x 20 cm / 8 x 8 in. Carefully place it on top of the dough in one of the pans. Repeat with the other portion of marzipan. Take the remaining dough out of the refrigerator and divide it in half. Working quickly, dip your fingers in cold water and use your hands to spread the dough in a thin, even layer on top of the marzipan in each pan. Brush the entire surface of the dough lightly with milk.

5. Bake on the middle rack of the oven at 160 °C for 25 minutes, or until a skewer inserted in the center comes out clean. Do not overbake.

6. While the dough is baking, make the icing by combining the icing sugar, milk, and vanilla, stirring until smooth. As soon as the Biberli come out of the oven, use a sharp knife to mark the surface of the dough into 16 equal-size bars (each 50 mm / 2 in square) in both pans. Brush the icing evenly over the hot dough. Let the Biberli cool completely in the pans, then cut into bars.

7. Store the bars in a tightly covered container, with parchment paper or wax paper between each layer of cookies, for at least a day to let the flavours ripen and the cookies soften.

MY PRYANIKI

Over the centuries Russian gingerbreads known as *pryaniki* have taken many forms from the hand-shaped gingerbread (*lepnye pryaniki*), *pechatyne pryyaniki* which are pressed into wooden moulds to create highly decorative shapes and the most modern type, silhouette (*siluetnye*) which are typically cut into shapes like horses or deer.[44] Russian culture is instilled with *pryaniki* and they were once popular wedding gifts or served at funerals as a way to honour the dead. They even feature in everyday maxims, such as 'it is impossible to lure him even with a *pryanik*', which is used to describe someone who is incorruptible, as well as in popular folk stories such as *Baba Yaga*.[45]

Early *pryaniki* were made with honey, rye flour and berry juice to which spices were later added producing something 'dense, unleavened, very sweet and highly spiced'. As a result they have not endeared themselves to the modern palates.[46] Having tried a few of Elena Molokhovets' *pryaniki* recipes from *A Gift to Young Housewives* it is understandable that *pryaniki* needed to evolve in order to survive.[47] Some modern recipes are decidedly biscuit like and can be iced or plain. Others are spongier falling into that no man's land between cookie and cake which provides scope to include on occasion a jam filling or dried berries.

This is my homage to *pryaniki*. It may not be able to trace its ancestry directly back to Molokhovets but hopefully it captures the flavours that have infused *pryaniki* over time including those berries.

Ingredients (Makes 20)
125 g / 4 ½ oz runny honey
40 g / 1 ½ oz unsalted butter
170 g / 6 oz plain flour
55 g / 2 oz rye flour
1 tsp baking powder
½ tsp ground cardamom
½ tsp ground cinnamon
⅛–¼ tsp ground cloves
1 large egg
55 g / 2 oz dried berries e.g. cranberries, blueberries or a mixture of the two
1 x basic icing recipe
Freeze dried raspberry pieces

Method
1. Gently warm the honey and butter until the latter is melted.
2. Sieve the flours, baking powder and spices into a bowl. Add the liquid honey mixture, the egg and the berries. Mix well then bring the dough together as a ball. Cover with clingfilm then refrigerate for at least one hour.
3. Preheat the oven to 180 °C. Divide the dough into 20 equal pieces. Place on a buttered or lined baking sheet leaving a good amount of space between each ball. Flatten the spheres slightly with the palm of your hand then place in the oven for 10–15 minutes until risen and golden.
4. Make the icing while the biscuits are cooking. When the *pryaniki* come out of the oven transfer them to a cooling rack then brush with the icing. Quickly scatter freeze dried raspberry pieces over the *pryaniki* before the icing sets.

Gingerbread Buns.

Bread & Yeasted Cakes

This chapter includes recipes for those gingerbreads that fall into the category of tea breads, as well as those leavened with yeast. Generally speaking, tea breads produce a firmer cake which means they can be sliced and buttered.

Mrs Millington's Sponge Parkin[1]

Ingredients
55 g / 2 oz unsalted butter or margarine, diced
55 g / 2 oz lard or vegetable fat, diced
225 g / 8 oz black treacle
100 ml / 3 ½ fl oz milk
225 g / 8 oz plain flour
225 g / 8 oz fine or medium oatmeal
2 tsp mixed spice
1 tsp ground ginger
¼ tsp ground nutmeg
1 tsp baking powder
110 g / 4 oz Demerara sugar
½ tsp bicarbonate of soda
1 large egg, lightly beaten

Method
1. Preheat the oven to 170 °C. Grease and line a 900 g / 2 lb loaf tin.
2. Heat the fats, treacle and milk together, stirring from time to time, until warm and thoroughly combined.
3. Sieve the flour, fine oatmeal (if using medium oatmeal add to the other ingredients after they have been sifted), spices and baking powder into a large bowl. Then stir in the sugar.
4. Stir the bicarbonate of soda into the warmed treacle mixture, then immediately add it to the dry ingredients. Mix well before

adding the beaten egg.

5. Spoon the mixture into the prepared tin then bake for 45–60 minutes. The parkin will spring back when you press it. Allow to cool in the tin before turning out. This parkin keeps well stored in a tin so cut off portions as and when you want it.

BRÜNI[2]

This was the first recipe Scottish folklorist F. Marian McNeill collected as a child in Orkney. It is more affectionately known as 'Broonie'. Brüni means a thick bannock and is a survivor of the local Norn language, which itself was derived from old Norse. This oatmeal gingerbread reminds me of a malt loaf rather than a squidgy cake, which is why it is in the 'Bread' section. I like it buttered with sliced banana and drizzled with heather honey for breakfast. It's also remarkably good with cheese.

Ingredients
170 g / 6 oz plain flour
2½ tsp ground ginger
1 tsp baking powder
½ tsp bicarbonate of soda
170 g / 6 oz medium oatmeal
55g / 2 oz butter, diced (either salted or unsalted will do here)
110 g / 4 oz soft light brown sugar
60 g / 2 oz treacle
1 large egg
250–300 g buttermilk

Method
1. Preheat the oven to 180 °C. Grease and line a 900 g / 2 lb loaf tin.
2. Sieve the flour, ginger and raising agents into roomy bowl. Add the oatmeal. Rub the butter into the flour then stir in the sugar.
3. Gently heat the treacle in a small bowl (10–15 seconds on high in a microwave should do it – you want it warm and slightly runny rather than hot). Beat the egg into the treacle then add to the dry ingredients along with enough buttermilk to make the mixture sufficiently soft to

drop off a spoon. Mix thoroughly before spooning into the prepared tin. 4. Bake for 60–90 minuets or until well risen and brown. If it seems like it's catching, cover the cake with some greaseproof paper. A skewer should come out more or less clean when inserted. Leave the cake to cool in the tin before turning out.

Mrs Forth's Pepper Cake[4]

Mrs Forth was a vicar's wife from Yorkshire born in 1765. After her marriage to the Reverend John Forth in 1791,[5] she, like many women of the eighteenth and nineteenth centuries, kept a household book. Pepper Cake was traditionally eaten at Christmas in the North Riding. It is sometimes known as Carol Singing Cake because it was given to children doing the rounds singing festive songs, along with the following rhyme:

A little bit of pepper cake
A little bit of cheese,
A cup of cold water
And a penny if you please.[6]

The cutting of the Christmas cheese was done with great ceremony by the master of the house and was offered to visitors, along with some pepper cake.[7] As with many cakes of this period, yeast is used as a leavening agent. You need to start this at least one day ahead.

Ingredients
2 tsp coriander seeds
1 tsp caraway seeds
1¼ tsp ground ginger
1¼ tsp ground allspice
340 g / 12 oz treacle
2 tbsp brandy
340 g / 12 oz white bread flour
55 g / 2 oz unsalted butter, cubed
110 g / 4 oz dark brown sugar
2 tsp dried fast action yeast

200 ml / 7 fl oz lukewarm water
55 g / 2 oz candied peel (optional)

Method
1. Crush the coriander and caraway seeds with a pestle and mortar (or put them in a bowl and use the end of a rolling pin). You want the seeds coarsely ground rather than a fine powder. Add the ground ginger and allspice to the crushed seeds.
2. Spoon treacle into a small pan then add the spices. Heat gently until the treacle is runny then take off the heat, add the brandy and leave over night. Grease and line a 900 g / 2 lb loaf tin ready for the morning.
3. Sieve the flour in the bowl of a free-standing mixer with a dough hook attached. Rub the butter into the flour then stir in the yeast and dark brown sugar. With the motor running on slow gradually add the lukewarm water then mix until combined. Keep the motor running for five minutes to knead the dough. Scrape the mixture off the dough hook, cover the bowl then place in the fridge over night.
4. The next day remove the dough from the fridge. It should have risen overnight despite the cool temperature. Gently warm the treacle mixture to loosen it up slightly (it should be barely warm), Return the bowl containing the dough to the mixer stand then slowly knead the dough using the dough hook, carefully adding the treacle (and candied peel if using) until it is thoroughly amalgamated.
5. Pour the dough into the prepared tin and leave in a warm place for around 30 minutes while you preheat the oven to 170 °C. It will not rise a great deal during this time but you should see a few small bubbles on the surface of the dough.
6. Bake the bread for 75–90 minutes. A skewer when inserted should come out clean. Leave to cool in the tin before turning out. Serve sliced and buttered (and yes, a nice bit of cheddar on the side doesn't go amiss either!).

THE DUKE OF WINDSOR'S GINGERBREAD[8]

This recipe comes from Elizabeth Craig's collection of royal recipes. As a boy, the Duke of Windsor was particularly fond of gingerbread and this recipe was made in the kitchens of Buckingham Palace and St James'

Pepper Cake (top) and The Duke of Windsor's Gingerbread (bottom)

Palace for His Royal Highness. Craig does not say whether the prince liked his gingerbread buttered but the texture of this cake definitely lends itself to that purpose.

Ingredients
225 g / 8 oz plain flour
4 tsp ground ginger
1 tsp ground allspice
½ tsp bicarbonate of soda
110 g / 4 oz unsalted butter, cubed
55 g / 2 oz brown sugar
110 g / 4 oz blanched almonds, roughly chopped
2 tsp caraway seeds
25 g / 1 oz chopped mixed peel
225 g / 8 oz treacle
2 large eggs

Method

1. Preheat the oven to 180 °C. Grease and line a 900 g / 2 lb loaf tin.
2. Sieve the flour, ground spices and bicarbonate of soda into a bowl. Add the butter then rub in with your fingertips until the mixture resembles breadcrumbs.
3. Stir in the brown sugar, chopped almonds, caraway seeds and mixed peel.
4. Slightly warm the treacle to loosen it (10–20 seconds on high in a microwave should do this). Add the eggs to the treacle then beat to mix. Pour this mixture onto the flour then mix thoroughly to combine.
5. Spoon the cake mix into the prepared tin then bake for 45–60 minutes. A skewer should come out clean when inserted. Allow to cool in the tin completely before turning out. Wrap in greaseproof or foil and ideally leave for 24 hours before cutting.

GINGERBREAD BUNS

In *Caviar to Candy*[9] Alice Martineau suggests adding ginger and lemon peel to milk bread dough for an afternoon tea treat. This dough can easily be transformed into a riff on a Scandinavian style cinnamon bun with gingerbread flavours instead. These buns are a lovely treat for afternoon tea or for an extra special breakfast.

Ingredients (Makes 8 large buns)
300 ml / ½ pt whole milk
50 g / 2 oz unsalted butter plus 50 g / 2 oz really soft unsalted butter, cut into small pieces
500 g / 1 lb 2 oz plain flour
7 g / ¼ oz sachet easy blend yeast
1 tsp ground ginger
50 g / 2 oz caster sugar
Grated zest 1 lemon
1 tsp salt
100 g / 4 oz soft dark brown sugar
Gingerbread spice mix: 2 tsp ground ginger, 1 ½ tsp ground cinnamon, ½ tsp ground nutmeg and ⅛ tsp ground cloves.

Method

1. Grease and line a 20 x 30 cm / 8 x 12 in tin with baking parchment.

2. Gently heat the milk and 50 g / 2 oz butter until the latter has melted. Allow to cool until it is lukewarm.

3. Put the flour, yeast, ginger, caster sugar, lemon zest and salt into the bowl of a food mixer with a dough hook attached. Start the motor then gradually pour in the cooled milk and butter. Knead until the dough is smooth and springy (about 5–10 minutes). Alternatively, mix the dry ingredients together in a bowl then add the milk. Once the dough has come together knead by hand on a lightly floured work surface or board until the desired consistency is reached (this will take a little longer than using a food mixer). Cover, then leave to prove for an hour to ninety minutes when it should have doubled in size.

4. While the dough is proving mix the dark brown sugar with the gingerbread spices. Turn the dough out onto a lightly floured work surface or board. Knock back the dough, then roll into a rectangular shape. Ultimately you are looking to create a rectangle roughly 30 x 40 cm / 12 x 16 in. I usually aim to roll the dough into a shape a little larger than these dimensions then trim the excess to produce a rectangle of the size required. Save the trimmings as you will need them later.

5. Dot the dough rectangle with pieces of really soft butter then use a palette knife to spread the butter over the dough, leaving a margin of a centimetre or so around the edge of the rectangle. Sprinkle the spiced sugar over the buttered dough. Roll the dough up from the long side as you would a Swiss roll keeping the cylinder shape as tight as possible without extending length. Square off the ends of the cylinder and add these offcuts to the trimmings you saved earlier.

6. Carefully place the dough roll to one side. Briefly knead all of the trimmings together, then roll them out to a rough rectangle the same size as the base of your baking tin. Press this dough into the bottom of the greased and lined baking tin. This base will prevent the butter and sugar in the buns from oozing out and over caramelising on the base of the tin as the buns bake. Divide the dough cylinder into eight even pieces. Place these cut side up and evenly spaced on the dough base. Cover again and prove for a further 20–30 minutes while you preheat the oven to 180 °C. Don't worry if there are still gaps between the buns after this time. They

will expand further in the oven as they bake.

7. Bake the buns for 35–40 minutes checking them after 20–25 minutes. If they look like they are getting too brown on top, place a piece of baking paper or foil over the tin for the remainder of the cooking time. Allow them to cool in the tin for 10 minutes before turning out onto a wire rack. They will need to cool a bit more before serving although they are best enjoyed warm.

M.F.K. Fisher's Pain d'Épice de Dijon[10]

'But all year and everywhere we smelled the Dijon gingerbread, that *pain d'épice* which came perhaps from Asia with a tired Crusader.

Its flat strange odour, honey, cow dung, clove, something unnameable but unmistakeable, blew all over the town…It was a smell as thick as a flannel curtain.'

Fisher claims the 'magic' in this particular recipe lies in the seasoning. I've read many recipes for *pain d'épice* but have never come across any containing mustard. It actually works remarkably well here, no doubt serving a similar purpose to the *quatre épices* in the recipe below. Fisher also recommends using one third rye flour but I have opted for all wheat flour (which is in keeping with other Dijon *pain d'épice* recipes I have seen).

Ingredients
450 g / 1 lb honey
450 g / 1 lb white bread flour
1 large egg
100 ml / 3½ fl oz milk
1½ tsp baking powder
½ tsp bicarbonate of soda
1 tsp ground anise
½ tsp dry mustard
Zest of a lemon

Method
1. Gently heat the honey then stir in the flour. Put the paste in a

cool place then leave for at least a week (longer won't hurt – Fisher recommends at least eight days).

2. Preheat the oven to 180 °C. Grease and line a 900 g / 2 lb loaf tin.

3. Mix the egg, milk, raising agents, anise, mustard powder and lemon zest together. Break the honey dough into pieces then place in a freestanding mixer with a K beater attached. Add the egg mixture and beat until you have a smooth paste. Pour into a prepared tin.

4. Bake for 60–75 minutes. You may need to cover the loaf half way through as the high level of honey means the top can catch easily. When the loaf is done a skewer should come out clean when inserted. Leave in the tin to cool for a time then turn out onto a wire rack. Once completely cool store in an airtight container wrapped in greaseproof paper.

PAIN RÉMOIS DE SANTÉ[11]

The French had definite ideas about the health benefits and uses for their style of gingerbread. The philosopher Denis Diderot (1713–1784) said a slice of *pain d'épice* soaked in milk could be used as a poultice to treat abscesses in the mouth. In 1814 a Parisian gingerbread vendor called Picholet claimed his *pain d'épice* was an effective de-wormer at a very fair price.[12] While agreeing with earlier writers about the digestive benefits of eating gingerbread Alexandre Dumas would warn his readers to eat it in moderation, as it also possessed laxative qualities.[13] This *pain d'épice* recipe from Reims tastes great – that's as bold a statement as I'm prepared to make.

Ingredients
300 g / 10 ½ oz rye flour
225 g / 8 oz wheat flour
15 g baking powder
190 ml / 6 ½ fl oz water
150 g / 5 oz brown sugar
300 g / 10 ½ oz honey
2 large egg yolk
1 tsp each *quatre épices* (see page 220) and ground anise
Zest of an orange
Zest of a lemon

Method
1. Preheat the oven to 180 °C. Grease and line a 900 g / 2 lb loaf tin.
2. Sieve the flours and baking powders into the bowl of a free-standing mixer with a K beater attached.
3. Heat the water, sugar and honey until the sugar has dissolved. The mixture should be warm when you add it to the flour but not too hot. With the motor running on slow, gradually add the honey solution to the flours. Then add the egg yolks, spices and zests. Mix on a medium speed until the paste is smooth.
4. Transfer the paste to the prepared tin, then smooth the top with the back of a wet spoon. Bake for 70–90 minutes. You may need to cover the loaf halfway through, as the high level of honey means the top can catch easily. When the loaf is done a skewer should come out clean when inserted. Leave in the tin to cool for a time, then turn out onto a wire rack. Once completely cool store in an airtight container wrapped in greaseproof paper.

Berry Pryaniki[14]

There is a style of *pryaniki* that uses toasted breadcrumbs rather than flour combined with a berry syrup. It is somewhat reminiscent of the gingerbread available in Britain during the medieval era. Of all the breadcrumb-based gingerbreads I have tried this is the one I like best. Elena Molokhovets uses white breadcrumbs in her raspberry gingerbreads (*malinovye pryaniki*)[15] but I think Lesley Chamberlain's suggestion of using rye breadcrumbs counteracts some of the sweetness supplied by the berry syrup. A little bit of work is required at the beginning of the recipe to make the breadcrumbs but it is essential to get the texture just right.

Ingredients (Makes 16 squares)
450 g / 1 lb rye bread or good quality white bread, slightly stale is fine
200 g / 7 oz blackcurrant or raspberry jam
2 tbsp hot water
1 tbsp honey
½ tsp ground cinnamon

¼ tsp ground anise
¼ tsp ground ginger
½ tsp baking powder
1 large egg yolk

Method
1. Preheat the oven to 150 °C.
2. Slice the bread about 1 cm / ½ in thick and place on a baking sheet in a single layer. Place in the oven for five minutes then turn the slices over and cook for a further five minutes. Keep repeating this process until the bread is crisp (and golden if using white bread). This can take as little as 10 minutes if your bread is stale or longer if the bread is fresh.
3. Break the toasted bread into pieces then place in a food processor. Blitz to crumbs then tip these back onto the baking sheet and return the sheet to the oven. Cook for a further 5 to 10 minutes or until the crumbs are really crisp (keep a close eye on them as they can quickly burn if you leave them for too long). Return the crumbs to the food processor and process until you have super fine, sand like breadcrumbs. The weight of the bread will have reduced considerably but you will need 225 g / 8oz for this recipe (any leftover crumbs can be stored in an airtight container and used to coat things like fish or chicken goujons. This can be done a few days ahead in which case you will need to preheat the oven again to 150 °C in order to finish the recipe.
4. Place the jam in a bowl. Stir in the hot water and honey until you have a really thick syrupy consistency (add more water if absolutely necessary but you do not want the syrup to be too runny). Add the spices, baking powder and egg yolk. Mix thoroughly before adding 225 g / 8 oz toasted fine breadcrumbs continuing to stir the ingredients together until thoroughly combined.
5. Line an 18 cm / 7 in shallow square tin with foil or foil backed baking parchment. Tip the mixture into the tin and press into an even layer. Place in the oven then immediately turn off the heat and leave the *pryaniki* in the oven as it cools down over several hours or even overnight.
6. Cut the *pryaniki* into squares then store in an airtight container.

Mrs Millington's Sponge Parkin (top)
and Fochabers Gingerbread (bottom).

GINGERBREAD CAKES

If I were categorically made to choose which side of the cake/biscuit fence gingerbread should sit on I would probably err towards biscuits as many early gingerbread recipes are on the denser side. Those fluffy, spongy delights we call cakes are a relatively modern invention made all the more feasible by the advent of commercial baking powder in 1843, courtesy of Alfred Bird. That said there are many spice laden cakes out there which can be classed as types of gingerbread (although admittedly a fair few contain no ginger, as we shall see) so I offer a selection of this style of cake here from Britain and further afield. Gingerbread cakes are generally made by the creaming method, where the butter and sugar are beaten together before the rest of the ingredients are added, or the melting method. This latter technique is sometimes referred to as the boiling method. However, this is misleading as the treacle or syrup and butter mixture should only be warm when you add it to the other ingredients (nobody wants scrambled eggs in their cake). If you think the treacle and butter mixture is too hot, allow it to cool for a little while before proceeding with the recipe.

You'll notice that I haven't included the number of servings on the larger cakes. This is because I'm not one to dictate how big a slice should be. In my opinion (and you are free to disagree with me) a 20 cm / 8 in cake will give you at least eight generous slices, although it could be divided into ten or twelve if needs be.

A few hints on baking gingerbread cakes…
Gingerbreads contain a high proportion of sugar so can burn easily. If you are concerned that the cake is getting too brown in the oven, lightly cover the top with a piece of greaseproof paper to prevent it from browning too much. On the upside, the treacle, syrup and honey content of these recipes means that the cakes keep well. In some cases it is even advisable to leave the cake a day or two before eating to help the flavours really mature.

To test whether the cake is done insert a skewer into the centre of the cake in several places. When the cake is thoroughly baked the skewer will come out clean. If it doesn't, return the cake to the oven for a further 5–10 minutes then repeat the test (give it a little additional cooking time if necessary).

Always leave the cake to cool completely in the tin, unless the recipe states otherwise.

Teisen Fêl[1] (Welsh Honey Cakes)

Evidently there are two versions of this honey cake – one which uses cinnamon and the other that uses ginger.[2] I have used both to make these small cakes which are perfect tea time treats. The honey ensures they keep moist for a good time too.

Ingredients (Makes 12)
225 g / 8 oz plain flour
½ tsp bicarbonate of soda
1 tsp ground cinnamon
1 tsp ground ginger
110 g / 4 oz brown sugar (light or dark according to preference)
110 g / 4 oz unsalted butter, softened
1 egg yolk
110 g / 4 oz runny honey
3 tbsp milk
1 egg white
Caster sugar for dredging

Method
1. Preheat the oven to 180 °C. Generously butter a non-stick 12-hole muffin tin.
2. Sieve the flour, bicarbonate of soda and ground spices into a bowl.
3. Cream the sugar and butter together to a light fawn colour, then beat in the egg yolk followed by the honey.
4. Add one third of the spiced flour followed by a tablespoon of milk. Add another third of the flour followed by another tablespoon of milk

then repeat until all of the flour and milk has been incorporated.

5. In a clean bowl whisk the egg whites to stiff peaks then gently fold into the flour mixture. Divide the cake batter equally between the muffin holes. Lightly dust with caster sugar then bake for 15–20 minutes (a skewer should come out clean when inserted).

6. Remove the cakes from the tin and transfer to a cooling rack. When ready to serve sprinkle with more caster sugar.

NONNETTES

These small round cakes are made from a dough similar to that used for *pain d'épice* and are usually filled with some kind of jam. They are particularly well known in the Champagne, Alsace and Burgundy regions of France. In the north-east of the country they are delivered to children by Saint Nicholas on 6th December.[3] Like so many honey-based gingerbreads on the continent it is believed these little treats were originally created by nuns (hence the name). Certainly in Dijon, orange jam is a popular filling but I have opted for blackcurrant as a nod to one of the city's other 'gourmandises', crème de cassis.

Ingredients
80 g / 3 oz unsalted butter plus extra for greasing
100 g / 4 oz dark brown sugar
200 g / 7 oz honey
150 ml / 5 fl oz water
1 tsp *quatre épices* (see page 220)
1 tsp ground anise
1 tsp ground cinnamon
125 g / 4 ½ oz rye flour
125 g / 4 ½ oz plain flour
10 g / ⅓ oz bicarbonate of soda
12 tsp blackcurrant jam or marmalade
Juice of half a lemon
50–75 g / 2–3 oz icing sugar, sifted

Method

1. Preheat the oven to 200 °C. Thoroughly butter a non-stick 12-hole muffin tin.

2. Mix the butter, sugar, honey and water in a saucepan. Bring to the boil and cook for a minute or two. Add the spices and remove from the heat.

3. Pour the honey mixture into a bowl. Add the flours and bicarbonate of soda. Use an electric whisk to beat the mixture until you have a smooth paste. Half fill each muffin hole, then allow to cool.

4. Use the back of a teaspoon to make an indentation in each cup of dough. Place a teaspoon of jam in the centre of each one. Bake for 15–20 minutes. A skewer inserted into the edge of the nonnettes should come out clean. Allow the nonnettes to cool in the tin for a few minutes before turning out. Most of the jam should have 'sunk' into the cakes but some may have bubbled over. If this happens it is sometimes helpful to run a round bladed knife around the edge of the cake to ease it out of the hole. They should be completely cold before you ice them.

5. To ice the nonnettes, mix lemon juice with the icing sugar. Brush over the top of each cake. According to many a French cook, these cakes taste even better after 48 hours but they rarely last that long in our house!

DICKENS' GINGERBREAD[4] WITH YUZU ICING & CRYSTALLISED GINGER

Some years ago I acquired a copy of *Dining with Dickens,* described as 'a ramble through Dickensian foods', compiled by Charles Dickens' great grandson, Cedric. Within its pages I found a recipe for Pussers Gingerbread (Pussers is a brand of rum) which is described as 'an old Dickens recipe'.[5] It's easy to see why it was popular in the Dickens household as the hefty slug of rum takes this ginger cake to another level. The original recipe calls for the cake to remain as naked as the day it was baked but I believe the icing elevates it further still. I doubt very much that Charles Dickens would have ever encountered a yuzu[6] but citrus and ginger have long been partners in crime, so I thought why not?

Ingredients
110 g / 4 oz unsalted butter

225 g / 8 oz treacle
225 g / 8 oz self raising flour
3 slightly rounded teaspoons ground ginger
175 g / 6 oz dark brown sugar
2 large eggs
75 ml / 2 ½ fl oz dark rum
75 ml / 2 ½ fl oz milk
175 g / 6 oz icing sugar
2 tbsp bottled yuzu juice or fresh lemon juice
55 g / 2 oz crystallised ginger, roughly chopped if in large chunks (i.e. sugar coated rather than the stuff in syrup, although this can be used if this is the only preserved ginger available)

Method
1. Preheat the oven to 180 °C. Grease and line a 900 g / 2 lb loaf tin.
2. Gently warm the butter and treacle in a small pan until the butter has melted.
3. Sieve the flour and ground ginger into a large bowl. Stir in the brown sugar followed by the butter and treacle.
4. Beat the eggs with the rum and milk in a jug then mix this thoroughly into the cake batter. Pour the batter into the prepared tin then bake for around 40–50 minutes (a skewer will come out clean when inserted). Allow the cake to cool in the tin before turning out and removing the lining paper.
5. To ice the cake, sieve the icing sugar into a bowl. Stir in 1 ½ tablespoons of yuzu or lemon juice. Mix to a paste – you need the icing to be thick but spreadable. If it is too thick add the remaining juice (plus a little water if absolutely necessary). In the event that it becomes too thin (i.e. dripping consistency) add a little more sieved icing sugar.
6. Spread the icing over the top of the loaf then scatter with chopped crystallised ginger while the icing is still tacky. Wait until the icing has set before slicing and serving.

FOCHABERS GINGERBREAD[7]

Like so many regional gingerbreads the true origins of this Scottish gingerbread have been lost in time. Its high fruit content and the use of beer makes it stand out from other gingerbreads, although it still manages to be much lighter than the traditional 'plum' fruit cake we associate with Christmas.

Fochabers is a small town located on the east bank of the River Spey not far from Elgin. I've put my own spin on Miss Bella Mitchell's recipe. A free-standing mixer is a great help here.

Ingredients
225 g / 8 oz dried mixed fruit
75 g / 3 oz diced candied peel
2 pieces candied stem ginger in syrup, drained and finely chopped
Grated zest of 1 lemon
3 tbsp whisky
225 g / 8 oz treacle or 110 g / 4 oz treacle and 110 g / 4 oz golden syrup
450 g / 1 lb plain flour
3 tsp ground ginger
2 tsp mixed spice
1 tsp ground cinnamon
¼ tsp ground cloves
1 tsp baking powder
75 g / 3 oz ground almonds
225 g / 8 oz unsalted butter, softened
110 g / 4 oz dark brown sugar
2 large eggs
1 tsp bicarbonate of soda
300ml dark beer (e.g. porter) or ale

Method
1. Soak the dried fruit, candied peel, chopped ginger and grated zest in the whisky overnight.
2. Preheat the oven to 140 °C. Grease and double line a 20 cm / 8 in round or 15 cm / 6 in square, deep cake tin. Also cut out a length of brown paper to wrap around the tin and a 20 cm / 8 in circle or 15 cm / 6 in square of brown paper for the top of the cake. This will stop the edges and top becoming overdone before the centre of the cake is cooked.

3. Gently warm the treacle (and golden syrup if using) in a pan until slightly warm. Sieve the flour, spices and baking powder into another bowl. Stir in the ground almonds.

4. Beat the butter and sugar together in a large bowl or a free-standing food mixer until light and fluffy. Add the warm treacle then beat in the eggs.

5. Add the spiced flour to the butter and treacle mixture followed by the macerated fruit.

6. Stir the bicarbonate of soda into the beer then add this to the cake mixture. Stir thoroughly to combine, then transfer to the prepared cake tin. Depending on the size of your tin this cake will take anywhere between 75–120 minutes to bake. Start checking it after 75 minutes. A skewer will come out clean when the cake is done. Allow to cool in the tin before turning out.

GOLDEN GINGERBREAD[8] WITH STREUSEL TOPPING

I freely admit to dismissing the original recipe for Spongy Gingerbread as uninspiring when I started researching this book. But then I noticed it contained no treacle. While I'm rather partial to the black stuff I do appreciate that some people find it abhorrent. These treacle haters may harbour no grudge against ginger itself, but their aversion to one of the common ingredients used in gingerbread means this style of cake and biscuit can be off limits. This cake, with I hope a more alluring title, provides a solution to the treacle problem. The streusel topping can be omitted if you prefer a plainer cake (although it does lend a satisfying contrast to the spongy cake).

Ingredients for the cake
340 g / 12 oz golden syrup
110 g / 4 oz caster sugar
175 g / 6 oz butter
55 g / 2 oz marmalade
175 g / 6 oz plain flour
175 g / 6 oz wholemeal plain flour
2 tsp ground ginger
2 tsp ground mixed spice

A pinch of salt
1 tsp bicarbonate of soda
A good pinch of cayenne
2 large eggs
225 ml / 7 ½ fl oz milk

Ingredients for the streusel topping
75 g / 3 oz wholemeal plain flour
½ tsp ground ginger
½ tsp mixed spice
¼ tsp baking powder
25 g / 1 oz unsalted butter, at room temperature, cubed
75 g / 3 oz demerara sugar
1 ½ tbsp cold water
25 g / 1 oz blanched almonds, roughly chopped
25 g / 1 oz preserved ginger, roughly chopped

Method
1. Preheat the oven to 180 °C. Grease and line the base of a 23 cm / 9 in square non-stick baking tin (you may want to line the sides too leaving some parchment overhanging to make it easier to remove the cake once it is cooked).
2. Warm the syrup, caster sugar, butter and marmalade until melted.
3. Sieve the flours, ground spices, salt, bicarbonate of soda and cayenne, tipping any left over bran from the wholemeal flour into the bowl. Make a well in the centre.
4. Beat the eggs with the milk then pour onto the well in the flour followed by the warmed syrup mixture. Mix thoroughly then pour into the prepared tin. Place in the oven for 20 minutes.
5. To make the streusel topping, sieve the wholemeal plain flour, spices and baking powder into a small bowl, adding any bran left in the sieve. Rub the butter into the flour mixture then stir in the sugar and water (the latter should cause the mixture to form larger clumps). Finally stir in the chopped almonds and preserved ginger.
6. After 20 minutes remove the cake from the oven and quickly scatter the streusel mixture over the top as evenly as possible. Return the cake

to the oven for a further 25–35 minutes. A skewer will come out clean when it is done. If you are not using the topping, bake the cake for 35–45 minutes in total (there is no need to take it out of the oven after 20 minutes).

7. Allow the cake to cool completely in the tin before removing. Serve cut into slices or squares.

SPICED WHITE PARSNIP & GINGER CAKE

The germ of inspiration for this recipe came from Hugh Plat's Dry Gingerbread in *Delightes for Ladies* (1602):

> Take half a pound of Almonds and as much grated cake, and a pound of fine Sugar, and the yolks of two new laid eggs, and juice of a lemmon, and 2 graines of musk, beat these all together til they come to a paste, then print it with your moldes, and dry it upon papers in an oven after your bread is drawne.[9]

The corresponding recipe for 'cake' that Plat uses in this recipe contains dried parsnips.[10] I imagine drying parsnips so that they can be finely grated would be a bit of a faff so I have used fresh here. Think of this as the fairer cousin of a carrot cake, its complexion enhanced by the use of egg whites rather than whole eggs.[11] Whenever I have leftover egg whites (say from making ice cream) I freeze them for future use in recipes like this or meringues. If you are using fresh eggs the yolks can be scrambled or used to enrich sauces or mashed potato.

Ingredients
125–150 g / 4 ½–5 oz grated parsnips, prepared weight (roughly 2 medium sized parsnips)
200 g / 7 oz self raising flour
2 tsp ground ginger
1 tsp ground cardamom
¼ tsp ground white pepper
25 g / 1 oz ground almonds
225 g / 8 oz soft unsalted butter
225 g / 8 oz caster sugar

6 large egg whites (defrosted if frozen)
1 tsp grated fresh ginger
225 g / 8 oz icing sugar
¾ tsp ground ginger
250 g / 9 oz cream cheese such as Philadelphia

Method
1. Preheat the oven to 170 °C. Grease and line the base of two 20 cm / 8 in sandwich tins.
2. Peel and quarter the parsnips. Remove the tough core from each quarter then coarsely grate.
3. Sieve the flour and the ground spices into a bowl. Stir in the ground almonds and set aside until required.
4. Cream the butter and sugar together until pale.
5. In a separate, clean bowl beat the egg whites to stiff peaks (you could use a free standing mixer for this if you have one). Mix a quarter of the egg whites into the butter mixture then beat in the flour, a spoonful or two at a time. Once all the flour has been incorporated mix in the grated parsnip and fresh ginger then carefully fold in the remaining egg whites.
6. Divide the batter between the two prepared tins. Bake for 20–25 minutes or until the sponges feel springy and a skewer inserted into the middle comes out clean. Allow to cool in the tin for 10 minutes or so before turning out onto a wire rack and cooling completely before icing.
7. To make the icing, sieve the icing sugar and ground ginger into a bowl. Add the cream cheese and beat using an electric hand whisk until thick (initially it may appear runny but keep beating until it thickens up.
8. Use about one third of the icing to sandwich the two cakes together. Spread the remaining icing over the top and sides of the cake. Refrigerate until ready to serve.

CHOCOLATE STUFFED LEBKUCHEN[12]

If you love chocolate and spice you will adore this decadent cake.

Ingredients (Makes 16 pieces)
75 g / 3 oz honey

50 g / 2 oz unsalted butter
75 g / 3 oz dark brown sugar
75 ml / 2 ½ fl oz milk
225 g / 8 oz plain flour
25 g / 1 oz cocoa powder
5 g baking powder
½ tsp ground cardamom
½ tsp *quatre épices* (see page 220)
50 g / 2 oz mixed peel
50 g / 2 oz raisins or sultanas
2 tbsp brandy
100 g / 4 oz dark chocolate plus 25 g / 1 oz
3 tbsp double cream
25 g / 1 oz roasted ground hazelnuts
25 g / 1 oz white chocolate chips

Method

1. Heat the honey, 25 g / 1 oz butter, sugar and milk in a small saucepan until the butter has melted.

2. Sieve the flour, cocoa powder, baking powder and spices into a bowl. Stir in the mixed peel then add the liquid ingredients to the dry. Mix well to combine then leave in a cool place (like the fridge) over night.

3. Soak the raisins or sultanas in the brandy overnight.

4. The following day, prepare the filling. Place 100 g dark chocolate, the double cream and remaining 25 g butter in a heat proof bowl suspended over a small pan of barely simmering water. Stir occasionally until the chocolate has melted.

5. Use a food processor to finely chop the brandy soaked raisins (or do this by hand). Add to the melted chocolate along with the roasted ground hazelnuts. Mix well then allow to cool and firm up a little (do not put it in the fridge).

6. Preheat the oven to 180 °C. Butter and line a shallow 18 cm / 7 in square tin.

7. Divide the dough in two. Roll half the dough out to a square of approximately 17 cm. Lay this in the base of the prepared tin and use your fingers to press the dough to the edges of the tin so that the base

is completely covered.

8. Brush the surface of the base with a little water then spread the filling over the base leaving a margin of at least 5 mm around the edge. Roll out the remaining dough to a square of around 18 cm / 7 in, then lay this over the filling and ease the dough to the edges pressing down to effectively seal the filling inside.

9. Bake for 20–25 minutes or until firm and well risen. Allow to cool in the tin before removing to a rack.

10. Melt the remaining dark chocolate and white chocolates in separate bowls. Channel your inner Jackson Pollock by using a fork to flick white and dark chocolate over the top of the *lebkuchen*. Allow the chocolate to set before cutting into 16 pieces.

Lapis Legit[13] (Layered Spice Cake)

This Indonesian-Dutch spice cake is known as *spekkoek* in the Netherlands, which translates as bacon cake because it looks like streaky bacon when cut. It is a labour of love so you need to allow yourself plenty of time (an hour or more) to make it and ensure you have everything you need to hand when you start cooking. Unlike a conventional cake which is baked, each layer of this cake is grilled. Far from being a modern invention, recipes for *spekkoek* have been appearing in Dutch cookbooks from at least the end of the nineteenth century. A legacy from the former Dutch East Indies, *Lapis Legit* is a wonderful marriage of eastern and western flavours.

Ingredients
125 g / 4 ½ oz plain flour
¼ tsp salt
250 g / 9 oz really soft unsalted butter
200 g / 7 oz caster sugar
5 large eggs, separated
1 tsp vanilla extract
A squeeze of lemon juice
1 tsp ground cinnamon
½ tsp ground cardamom

⅛ tsp ground cloves
⅛ tsp ground nutmeg
55 g / 2 oz melted butter (for brushing)

Method

1. Grease and line a 20 cm / 8 in springform baking tin. Make sure that the paper you use to line the sides of the tin is trimmed level with the top, otherwise it may burn when you start to grill the cake.

2. Sieve the flour and salt into a bowl then put aside until required.

3. Use an electric hand whisk or free standing mixer to beat the butter until smooth then add 100 g / 4 oz caster sugar and continue to beat until light and fluffy. Add the egg yolks and the vanilla extract then beat to combine.

4. Place the egg whites in a separate spankingly clean bowl with a squeeze of lemon juice. Whisk the egg whites until frothy. Reduce the speed of the motor then gradually add the remaining caster sugar. Keep whisking until all the sugar has been added. Increase the speed of the motor, then whisk until the egg whites are stiff and voluminous.

5. Add a generous tablespoon of the egg whites to the butter mixture and mix well. Then fold in one third of the flour followed by one third of the remaining egg whites repeating this process until all of the ingredients are used up and no egg white or flour is visible.

6. Place half the cake batter in another bowl then gently fold in the spices ensuring they are thoroughly combined. You should have two bowls of batter – one pale yellow and one light brown.

7. Preheat your grill. Unless you have a particularly mild mannered grill I would err on the side of caution and go for medium high rather than the maximum temperature. You can always increase the temperature if it doesn't seem hot enough but it will be disaster if the grill is so hot that it burns one of the layers (especially if this happens half way through the process). If you have a grill pan that can be removed (or at the very least the grill pan trivet) take it out as you do not want the cake to be too close to the heat source.

8. Now spread a quarter of the plain batter over the bottom of the cake tin, ensuring a flat, smooth layer (a small angled spatula or dough scraper is good for this). The batter should be evenly distributed,

without thick or thin spots, and it should be pushed to the edge of the tin although the side should be kept clean.

9. Place the cake tin under the grill. In terms of cooking time it really does depend on how ferocious your grill is. It may be as little as two minutes or as much as five as this layer is the furthest away from the heat source. When it is done it should be golden brown and spongy but you need to keep a very close eye on it as it will quickly burn.

10. Brush the cooked layer with melted butter then spread a quarter of the spiced batter over the original layer and return to the grill. This layer will take less time to cook perhaps only ninety seconds to two minutes. When the spiced layer is cooked, brush with more butter and repeat the process alternating between the light and dark batters until both mixtures are exhausted. Bear in mind that each layer may cook more quickly than the previous one. You should have eight layers in total. The very last layer should cook in a very short time indeed as it will be quite close to the heat source.

11. Once the last layer is cooked release the sides of the springform tin and leave to cool on a wire rack. Traditionally this cake is served in very thin slices and will store for up to a week in a cool place (a larder rather than a fridge) if well wrapped in clingfilm.

LEKACH[14] (JEWISH HONEY CAKE)

Sweet foods, particularly those containing honey, are traditionally eaten at the new year celebration of Rosh Hashanah in hope for a sweet year ahead.[15] This deeply aromatic cake is adapted from Marlena Spieler's recipe.

Ingredients
175 g / 6 oz plain flour
½ tsp ground ginger
1 tsp ground cinnamon
1 tsp ground mixed spice
1 tsp bicarbonate of soda
75 g / 3 oz caster sugar
225 g / 8 oz runny honey
4 tbsp vegetable or olive oil

Grated zest and juice of 1 large orange
2 large eggs
2 tsp grated fresh ginger

Method
1. Preheat the oven to 180 °C. Grease and line a 23 cm / 9 in square tin.[16]
2. Sieve the flour, spices and bicarbonate of soda into a large bowl. Stir in the caster sugar.
3. Mix the honey, oil, orange zest and eggs in a jug. Pour onto the flour then use an electric whisk or wooden spoon to beat the mixture to a smooth batter. Add 75 ml / 5 tbsp orange juice (this should be about the juice of 1 large orange – add a little water if necessary to make it up to this level) and the grated ginger.
4. Pour the batter into the prepared tin. Bake for 25–30 minutes or until the cake is firm to the touch (an inserted skewer will come out clean).
5. Leave to cool completely in the tin before turning out. Wrap the cake in foil then store at room temperature for two to three days. This may seem like an agonising wait but it really does help the flavours develop.

MAPLE SYRUP GINGERBREAD[17]

Although the USA didn't have to endure the privations of food rationing during the Great War, Americans were encouraged to reduce their consumption of meat, wheat, fats and sugar in order to support their troops and their European allies. The programme was led by Herbert Hoover who had been appointed as Head of the Food Administration by President Woodrow Wilson.[18] Campaigns across America encouraged people to voluntarily adopt 'Meatless Tuesdays' and 'Wheatless Wednesdays'.[19] Hoover's initiative worked. By the end of the war food shipments were doubled to Europe and continued well after the war had finished.

Publications like the *Win the War Cook Book* by Reah Jeannette Lynch were designed to show the American housewife just how food could help win the war. Various substitutes were suggested such as using maple syrup in place of all or some of the sugar in certain recipes. This is a great recipe for anyone who doesn't like treacle. As this is not wartime I have taken the liberty of increasing the butter and eggs in the original recipe. Maple syrup has a very pronounced flavour so despite what may seem like a lot of spice it is quite a subtly scented cake.

Ingredients
125 g / 4 ½ oz unsalted butter, softened
125 g / 4 ½ oz caster sugar
2 large eggs
250 g / 9 oz plain flour
3 tsp ground ginger
1 ½ tsp ground cinnamon
¼ tsp fine sea salt
1 tsp baking powder
250 ml / 8 ¾ fl oz maple syrup
½ tsp bicarbonate of soda
60 ml / 4 tbsp milk

Method
1. Preheat the oven to 180 °C. Grease and line a 20 cm / 8 in square cake tin.
2. Cream the butter and caster sugar together until light and fluffy using an electric hand whisk. Add the eggs one at a time, beating well after each addition.
3. Sieve the flour with the spices, salt and baking powder. Beat in a couple of spoonfuls of flour, followed by a little of the maple syrup, alternating between the two until all of the flour and syrup have been incorporated.
4. Dissolve the bicarbonate of soda in the milk then add to the cake mixture. Spoon into the prepared tin then bake for 30–35 minutes. Check the cake after twenty and cover if it is getting too brown. The cake should be golden and springy to the touch when done (and a skewer should come out clean when inserted). Allow to cool in the tin before turning out.

PIERNIK WITH PLUM JAM AND CHOCOLATE

Piernik originates from the old Polish term describing spice known as '*pierna*', which was added to flour and honey to make gingerbread. *Piernik* has been made in Toruń since the thirteenth century and the city is particularly renowned for its 'carved' gingerbreads formed in elaborately carved wooden moulds. The Polish composer Frédéric Chopin was especially fond of Toruń gingerbread which made the 'greatest impression' on him when he visited the city in 1825.[20]

Rather like the Russian *pryaniki* there are several forms of *piernik* which have evolved over the centuries. Some resemble biscuits. Others are of a more cake like persuasion. My version takes its lead from the spice cake recipes popular in Poland and further afield today (which I suspect are more modern recipes than that traditionally made in Toruń). I'm not sure whether Mr Chopin would approve, but it's certainly a hit in the Bilton household. If you can bear it, it is a good idea to start this a day or two ahead of when you plan to eat it to allow time for the icing to set.

Ingredients
150 g / 5 oz unsalted butter
110 g / 4 oz runny honey
225 g / 8 oz soft light brown sugar
200 g / 7 oz plain flour
110 g / 4 oz rye flour
2 tbsp cocoa powder
1 ½ tsp ground cinnamon*
1 tsp ground ginger*
½ tsp ground cardamom*
½ tsp ground anise*
¼ tsp ground cloves*
1 tsp baking powder
1 tsp bicarbonate of soda
2 large eggs
200 g / 7 oz buttermilk
250 g / 9 oz plum jam, home made or shop bought
150 g / 5 oz dark chocolate (70% minimum cocoa solids)
2 tbsp runny honey
110 g / 4 oz double cream

*Or use 3½–4 tsp *lebkuchen* spice blend (see page 219)

Method

1. Preheat the oven to 180 °C. Grease and line the base and sides of a 20 cm / 8 in round cake tin (a solid rather than a springform tin is better for this recipe).

2. Gently warm the butter, honey and light brown sugar until the butter has melted and the sugar has dissolved. Allow to cool slightly before proceeding.

3. Sieve the flours, cocoa powder, spices, baking powder and bicarbonate of soda into a large bowl (tip in any bits of bran left in the sieve). Pour the warm honey mixture onto the spiced flour then mix well.

4. Beat the eggs with the buttermilk then add this mixture to the cake batter. Pour the batter into the prepared tin then bake for 30–40 minutes. Allow to cool in the tin before turning out. The cake must be absolutely cold before you fill and ice it, so I like to make it a day or two before I plan to serve it.

5. When you are ready to fill the cake divide it into three pieces as evenly as possible. Spread half the jam on the bottom segment (if the plum jam is particularly firm you can warm it briefly in the microwave to loosen it but make sure it doesn't get hot otherwise it will be too runny). Top with the middle section then spread this with the remaining jam. Cut two 5 cm / 2 in wide 30 cm / 12 in long strips of greaseproof then place on top of a wire rack leaving a gap of 5 cm / 2 in or so between the two strips (it is best to sit the rack over a large chopping board or work surface you don't mind getting messy). Place the jam layered cake on top of the strips so that you have two tabs sticking out either side of the cake. This will help you move the cake to a serving place once it is iced.

6. To make the icing, break the chocolate into small pieces and place in a heat proof bowl along with the honey. Suspend this over a pan of barely simmering water. Stir the contents occasionally until the chocolate and honey has melted. Pour the cream into a jug and microwave for a few seconds on high to warm it (do not boil). Pour the warm cream over the chocolate then mix well until you have a smooth, glossy icing. Remove the pan from the heat and leave to cool and thicken slightly (it needs to be spreadable rather than runny).

7. Spoon the icing over the top of the cake then use a palette knife

to spread it around the sides until the top and sides are completely covered. Inevitably some of this lovely chocolatiness is going to drip which is where the wire rack comes in. Leave the icing to set (it will firm up as it cools but at room temperature this could be several hours depending on the time of year). The process is much quicker in the fridge, so feel free to move the cake there if you have enough space to accommodate the wire rack and chopping board. Otherwise I'm afraid you will just need to be patient!

8. When you are ready to serve the cake, use the paper strips to lift the cake off the wire rack and onto a serving plate or cake stand. Once in place, you will need to use the tip of a knife to gently tease the paper away from the icing at the base of the cake. You should then be able to pull the strips from under the cake, leaving it ready to serve.

Toto

I first heard about this cake in a podcast[21] featuring Catherine Ross and Lynda-Louise Burrell, founders of Museumand: The National Caribbean History Museum.[22] Catherine used a phrase to describe how sweet treats like this spiced coconut cake were cooked 'Hell a top, hell a bottom and hallelujah in the middle!'[23] The hell refers to the hot coals that were used underneath and on top of the metal container in which the Toto cake or a Jamaican sweet potato pudding were cooked (vegetables could be simultaneously roasted over the coals while the cake or pudding was baking).

The sugars and some of the spices included in gingerbreads were grown in the Caribbean and it is an upsetting fact that slaves were used in the production of these ingredients. The slaves of course had to feed themselves and would use whatever fruit, vegetables and grains they had to hand to create dishes with the minimal resources available to them. While cakes such as Toto were not everyday fare it was the sort of thing that every girl was expected to master before getting married, albeit without a written recipe. There were no precise measurements for the components (which can vary considerably from island to island as well as individual households) just the judgement of the cook in terms of quantities and the availability of ingredients. However, two items are essential to make Toto – coconut (ideally fresh) and spices (which could be adjusted according to taste). The other elements in the cake can vary with some people including rum or wine, while others add raisins.

Eliza Acton has a recipe for a rather dense coconut gingerbread in her *Modern Cookery for Private Families* (1845) which follows the more traditional British model using treacle. Personally, I prefer this Caribbean spiced coconut cake and I am grateful to Catherine and Lynda for sharing their family's recipe with me – the end result is the epitome of hallelujah indeed.

Ingredients
1 whole fresh coconut
250 g / 9 oz plain flour
2 tsp baking powder
1 tsp cinnamon
½ tsp nutmeg
½ tsp allspice (optional)[24]
225 g / 8 oz shredded fresh coconut
grated zest of 1 lime
110 g / 4 oz unsalted butter
200 g / 7 oz light brown sugar
1 large egg, beaten
2 tsp vanilla
120 ml / 4 fl oz milk

Method
1. First deal with the coconut. Preheat the oven to 180 °C. Pierce one of the 'eyes' at the end of the coconut (one always gives more easily than the others) and drain as much of the coconut water as you can. Place the coconut on a baking tray and cook for around 20–25 minutes. This should cause the shell to crack. Once the coconut is cool enough to handle wrap it in a clean tea towel and give it a bash with a rolling pin or hammer to split it completely. The flesh should come away easily from the shell. Place the flesh in a food processor then blitz until finely shredded. You will need 225 g / 8 oz shredded coconut for this recipe but the rest can be frozen for use at a later date. This first step can be

done a day or two before you make the cake if you wish.[25]

2. If you haven't already done so preheat the oven to 180 °C. Grease and line a 20 cm / 8 in cake tin or a 900 g / 2 lb loaf tin.

3. Sieve the flour, baking powder and spices together. Mix in 225 g / 8 oz shredded coconut and the lime zest.

4. Beat the egg, vanilla and milk together in a jug.

5. In a large bowl cream the butter and sugar until pale. Beat in a few spoonfuls of the flour and coconut mixture followed by some of the liquid ingredients. Keep alternately adding the dry and wet ingredients until both are used up and you have a fairly stiff dough.

6. Transfer the cake batter to the tin then bake for 40 to 50 minutes or until a skewer comes out clean when inserted. Allow to cool in the tin before turning out. I like to dust this cake with icing sugar and scatter with a little grated coconut before serving.

SAVOURIES

Britain seems to have lagged behind its European neighbours when it comes to using gingerbread in savoury dishes. This is a bit of a surprise given our penchant for combining sweet and savoury (think of the original mince pie with its meat and dried fruit; cheese and chutney or pork and apple sauce). For some reason gingerbread has never made the leap backwards from dessert to main course. Hopefully, this chapter will remedy that. Some of the recipes here are based on classic European dishes which use gingerbread given a British spin. Others are a result of my own experimentation.

In terms of which gingerbread to use in the following recipes any of the plainer biscuits, such as ginger snaps, *pepparkakor,* or 'parlies', or cakes like parkins or brüni, will work (hopefully it goes without saying that you should never use an iced gingerbread or one that contains dried fruit or chocolate!). Depending on which gingerbread you use you will get a slightly different result according to the sugar product or spices contained in the biscuit or cake, so feel free to experiment. In some cases I have been very specific about the type of gingerbread required (such as those using the French *pain d'épice*) simply because this is the best ingredient for that particular dish.

The quantity of gingerbread used in the following recipes may seem very small but its purpose is to enhance the dish rather than envelop it in sweetness. Don't forget that if you are making a gingerbread house you can reduce the offcuts to crumbs and store them in a jar for inclusion in sweet and savoury recipes. It's amazing what a transformation a few gingerbread crumbs can make when added to a breadcrumb coating for a chicken goujon for example.

GAME TERRINE WITH PRUNES

Pain d'épice is a popular accompaniment to *foie gras* in France but this terrine answers well as a more politically correct substitute for the goose liver. Many butchers and some supermarkets sell packs of prepared mixed game meats which are perfect for this recipe.

Ingredients (Serves 8–10)

250 g / 9 oz fatty pork belly, minced (a butcher should be happy to do this for you, otherwise buy strips of pork belly and finely chop it yourself)

250 g / 9 oz veal mince

450 g / 1 lb mixed game (e.g. pheasant, partridge, rabbit, venison), coarsely chopped

3 tsp *quatre épices* (see page 220)

2 cloves garlic, crushed

2 tbsp chopped mixed herbs e.g, thyme, parsley and rosemary

2 large eggs, beaten

6 tbsp brandy

110 g / 4 oz *pain d'épice*, reduced to crumbs (either of the recipes in this book are fine)

Juice ½ lemon

2 fresh bayleaves

2 x 80 g / 3 oz packs pancetta slices

170 g / 6 oz soft, pitted prunes

Method

1. If you haven't been able to get minced pork belly, finely chop the belly using a food processor or a mincing attachment fitted to a freestanding mixer.

2. Place all of the ingredients except the bay leaves, pancetta slices and prunes in a large bowl and mix well. Cover the bowl and marinate over night in the fridge.

3. The following day preheat the oven to 140 °C.

4. Place the two bay leaves in the bottom of a 900 g / 2 lb loaf tin or terrine dish. Use the pancetta slices to line the tin leaving some of the pancetta overhanging the edges to wrap over terrine before you place it in the oven. Give the terrine mix a stir, then place half of it in the loaf tin. Smooth the terrine, then cover with a layer of prunes followed by

the remaining terrine mixture. Use the overhanging strips of pancetta to cover the top of the terrine. Use your hands to press the terrine to ensure it is compact.

5. Place the terrine dish in a deep roasting tin. Pour boiling water into the tin until it comes roughly half way up the terrine. Cover the roasting tin with foil then cook for 90–120 minutes. Any juices running out of the terrine when pressed should be clear (i.e. contain no bloody residue – just like poultry).

6. Once the terrine is cooked remove it from the bain marie and leave to cool. The cooled terrine should be re-covered with foil then refrigerated overnight before serving. Ideally it should also be pressed. This can be done by balancing a couple of weighty tins on top of it while it is in the fridge overnight. However, if you can't fit the terrine in the fridge with the tins on top put it in the fridge without.

7. Serve the terrine in slices with plenty of *pain d'épice*.

Langoustine & Crayfish Stew

I've always been envious of the tales my Finnish friend Mitti used to regale me with of her family's crayfish parties during the summer months. This family celebration takes place in the late summer at their cottage in Heinola. In neighbouring Sweden these gatherings are called *kräftskiva*. Mitti's family eat the boiled crayfish 'au naturel' but eighteenth-century Swedish cookbook author Cajsa Warg turns them into a stew thickened with gingerbread crumbs.[1] English writer Hannah Glasse also includes a recipe for crawfish stew in *The Art of Cookery Made Plain and Easy*.[2] My version takes inspiration from all of these ladies. Fresh crayfish can be tricky to find in Britain but langoustine are a great substitute.[3] Some people object to having a beady eyed audience while they eat their dinner. If you or your guests fall into this category skip the suggested garnish and put all of the shellfish into the stew.

Ingredients (Serves 4 as a starter or light lunch)
2 x 500 g / 1 lb 2 oz packs frozen langoustine, defrosted (or 1 kg / 2 ¼ lb fresh langoustine or crayfish)
2 tbsp sunflower oil

1 small onion, chopped
1 small carrot, peeled and finely chopped
1 clove garlic, crushed
1 tbsp tomato puree
600 ml /1 pt dry white wine
600 ml /1 pt fish stock or water
1 x 20 g / ¾ oz pack fresh dill
1 bay leaf
30 g / 1 oz soft butter
50 g gingerbread crumbs such as *Smä Pepparkakor*
2 x 80 g / 3 oz packs cooked crayfish tails
Juice of 1 lemon
Salt, white pepper and grated nutmeg to season
4 tbsp double cream (optional)

Method

1. Reserve four of the whole crayfish or langoustine for garnish. Remove the tails from the remaining crayfish or langoustine and devein them keeping the shells, heads and claws separate. Lightly crush the shells etc so that they can release as much flavour as possible. Keep the peeled tails to one side while you make the base of the stew.

2. Heat the butter in a large saucepan. Add the onion and carrot then cook until the vegetables are starting to brown. Add the reserved crayfish or langoustine shells, heads and claws followed by the crushed garlic and tomato puree. Continue to cook until everything is taking on a rosy hue before adding the white wine, stock, half the dill (there's no need to chop it) and the bay leaf. Bring to the boil then simmer for thirty minutes. Stir every ten minutes or so crushing the shells as you go. This stage can be done in advance.

3. While the stew base is cooking, finely chop the remaining dill. Mix the butter with the breadcrumbs to form a paste of sorts. Bring a separate pan of well salted water to the boil, large enough to accommodate the remaining whole crayfish or langoustine.

4. Plunge the remaining crayfish or langoustine into the boiling water and cook for three to four minutes. Remove with a slotted spoon then drain well.

5. Strain the liquor into a clean pan (you need at least 600 ml – if you don't have this amount, top it up with water). Bring the strained sauce back to the boil then whisk in small dollops of the butter and gingerbread mixture, stirring constantly until the sauce is slightly thickened. Keep the sauce simmering then add the raw crayfish or langoustine meat. Cook for a couple of minutes before adding the cooked crayfish tails, simmering until all of the shellfish is thoroughly cooked and heated through.

6. Add the lemon juice and dill, then season the stew with salt, white pepper and grated nutmeg. Divide between four bowls garnishing each one with a drizzle of double cream (if using) and a whole cooked langoustine. Serve immediately with lots of crusty bread to mop up the juices.

POTTED MACKEREL WITH FRESH RHUBARB CHUTNEY & PARKIN

I still have nightmares about the fish paste sandwiches which used to appear in my lunchbox during my primary school days. This is why I have opted for a coarser texture for this lightly spiced 'pâté'. I have used a mixture of smoked and poached mackerel but you could use just one type if you prefer. Yorkshire is renowned for both its parkin and tangy rhubarb, and both sit well with this oily fish. I've used the parkin pigs recipe although you can obviously choose an alternative shape if you like.

I had my doubts when I first read the recipe for a No Cook Rhubarb Chutney in *Farmhouse Fare* (1935), but it is a great accompaniment to this potted mackerel (and so much easier to make than a cooked chutney). This recipe will make one 500 ml Kilner jar, rather more than you need for four servings but it will keep for a good few weeks so long as you store it in the fridge. Try it with barbecued lamb.

Ingredients for the potted mackerel (Serves 4)
2 fresh mackerel fillets
3 cloves garlic, sliced
1 slice fresh ginger
1 bay leaf (fresh if possible)
300 ml / ½ pt water
1 tbsp vinegar

½ tsp salt
2 tsp coriander seeds
1 tsp cumin seeds
250 g / 9 oz salted butter
2 plain smoked mackerel fillets
½ tsp ground ginger
Pinch cayenne pepper
1 tbsp snipped chives
Juice of ½–1 lemon
Salt and pepper to season

Ingredients for the chutney
225 g / 8 oz fresh rhubarb
1 tsp grated fresh ginger
1 red chilli, deseeded and chopped
110 g / 4 oz onions, peeled and chopped
55 g / 2 oz currants
55 g / 2 oz raisins

55 g / 2 oz granulated sugar
75 ml / 2 ½ fl oz white wine vinegar
½ tsp dried mustard
½ tsp salt
1 x quantity parkin pigs recipe on page 108

Method
1. Place the fresh mackerel fillets (skin side up), a sliced clove of garlic, slice of ginger, bay leaf, water, vinegar and salt in a large shallow saucepan. Heat gently until the water reaches boiling point then turn off the heat and leave the fish to poach for at least ten minutes. Remove the fish and allow to cool to room temperature.
2. Roast the coriander and cumin seeds until fragrant then coarsely crush with a pestle and mortar.
3. To clarify the butter cut it into thick slices then melt the butter over a gentle heat with the other two sliced cloves of garlic. Pour off into a bowl as much of the clear oil on the surface as possible, leaving the milky residue and garlic in the pan.
4. Take out any stray bones in the poached and smoked mackerel fillets. Remove the skin then break the poached and smoked mackerel fillets into large pieces and place in a bowl. Add the crushed seeds, ground ginger, cayenne, chives and the juice of half a lemon. Mix briefly with a fork before pouring in 100 g / 4 oz of the clarified butter (the remainder will be used to top the pots). Mix again to combine and test the seasoning adding more salt, pepper and lemon juice according to taste. All of the ingredients should be evenly distributed before you pot the pâté and the fish should have broken down further but you are not looking for a smooth paste (hence no food processor action). Spoon the pâté into four 9 cm / 3 ½ in ramekins, then top with a thin layer of the clarified butter. Refrigerate until required.
5. To make the chutney, place all of the ingredients in a food processor and blitz to a fine consistency (it won't be smooth but that's fine). Pour into a sterilised jar then refrigerate until required.
6. To serve the potted mackerel it is best to remove it about an hour or so beforehand to allow the butter to soften slightly. Serve with some chutney and a couple of parkin biscuits on the side (oatcakes are also lovely).

Poached Pear & Roquefort Salad with Pain d'Épice Croutons

Ingredients (Serves 2 as a light lunch)
4 slices *pain d'épice*, each about 1 cm thick (c. 200 g / 7 oz)
2 tbsp olive oil
¼ tsp fine sea salt
¼ tsp white pepper
3 tbsp walnut oil
1 tbsp tarragon or white wine vinegar
1 tsp Dijon mustard
Pinch of caster sugar
Salt & black pepper to season
140 g / 5 oz pack red chicory
1 little gem lettuce
50 g / 2 oz pecan nuts or walnuts, roughly chopped
100 g / 2 oz Roquefort or other strong blue cheese, crumbled
½ quantity of unstuffed poached pears on page 196.

Method

1. Preheat the oven to 180 °C.

2. Remove the crusts from the *pain d'épice* and cut into 1 cm / ½ in cubes. Toss the cubes in the olive oil, fine sea salt and white pepper. Tip onto a baking tray and cook for 10–15 minutes. They should turn a deep mahogany colour but keep an eye on them so that they do not burn. If any do catch discard them as they will taste bitter. Once cooked they will crisp up as they cool.

3. Whisk the walnut oil, tarragon or white wine vinegar, Dijon mustard, caster sugar, salt and black pepper in a bowl until amalgamated (or you could place these ingredients in a jar and give it a good shake).

4. Remove the stalky base from the chicory and little gem lettuce. Separate and wash the leaves then ensure they are as dry as possible (e.g. give them a turn in a salad spinner or dry them on some absorbent kitchen paper).

5. Place the salad leaves in a bowl along with the pecans or walnuts and crumbled cheese. Toss the salad with one tablespoon of the vinaigrette dressing adding more according to your preference.

6. Divide the dressed salad between two plates. Top each pile with two halves of poached pear and as many *pain d'épice* croutons as you fancy then serve immediately. You will probably have some dressing and croutons left over. Both will keep for around a week in airtight containers (separately, of course).

Carbonnade of Beef

Also known as Carbonnade à la flamande this beef and beer stew from Belgium is probably the quintessential savoury gingerbread recipe (granted some nations may beg to differ on this point). In Britain we have been on familiar terms with this dish for many years although we have always shied away from including the gingerbread which, I believe, gives the carbonnade its characteristic flavour. *Pain d'épice* really is the best type of gingerbread to use in this recipe, which is a hybrid between the British and Flemish versions. You need to start this at least one day ahead, but as with many stews this is better reheated a good 24–48 hours after it has been cooked to truly let the flavours develop.

Ingredients (Serves 4 generously)
800 g / 1 ¾ lb cubed stewing beef
2 cloves garlic, squashed
A few sprigs of thyme
500 ml / 16 fl oz dark beer such as porter or stout
½ tsp coarse sea salt
2–3 tbsp vegetable oil
3 medium onions, chopped
70 g / 3 oz pancetta or lardon pieces
300 ml / ½ pt beef stock
1 fresh bouquet garni (parsley, thyme, bay leaf)
1 star anise
55 g / 2 oz *pain d'épice*, crumbled
½ tsp *quatre épices* (see page 220)
2 tbsp Dijon mustard
2 tbsp tarragon or red wine vinegar
Salt and pepper to season

Method
1. Place the beef, squashed cloves of garlic, thyme sprigs and beer in a lidded, non metallic container and leave in the fridge to marinate overnight.
2. The following day, strain the meat, reserving the beery juices. Discard the thyme. Roughly chop the garlic from the marinade then crush with ½ teaspoon of sea salt.
3. Preheat the oven to 140 °C.
4. Pat the beef dry using paper towels or clean disposable kitchen cloths. Heat two tablespoons of the vegetable oil in a large casserole. Brown the meat in batches draining each batch on absorbent paper as you go. After the beef has been browned, add another tablespoon of oil then brown the onions and pancetta pieces before adding the crushed garlic and cooking for a minute or two.
5. Pour the strained beer onto the onions, pancetta and garlic, giving everything a good stir to deglaze the pan. Add the browned beef, bouquet garni, star anise, crumbled *pain d'épice, quatre épices*, Dijon mustard and vinegar. Bring to the boil then place in the oven for 90 minutes.
6. Test the seasoning before you serve the casserole which can be eaten

immediately. However, it really does benefit from being left a day to two to allow the flavours to mature. Reheat the carbonnade slowly on the hob or in a low oven (140 °C) for 30–40 minutes, ensuring it is piping hot before serving.

Cheesy Spätzle Crumble

Spätzle are, broadly speaking, a sort of German pasta, so you could say this is that nation's version of Mac 'n Cheese. I first tried this particular recipe at one of the Cook the Books meetings I go to in Lewes. A bunch of us gather once a month at a local pub for a pot luck supper which is guided by a theme. On this particular occasion the theme was 'preserved', so for this dish, prepared by my friend Helen Dando, she used pre-made sauerkraut. Please don't be put off by the use of pickled cabbage here. I wasn't convinced either until I tried this and now I'm a convert!

Ingredients (Serves 4 as a main course or 6 as a generous side dish)
350 g / 12 oz plain flour, sifted
a pinch of salt and a good grating of nutmeg
4 large eggs
100–150 ml warm water
1 tbsp salt
1 tsp vegetable oil
½ 680 g / 24 oz jar sauerkraut, drained
2 tsp caraway seeds
1 generous tbsp snipped chives
110 g / 4 oz Emmental, finely grated
110 g / 4 oz Gruyère, finely grated plus 55 g / 2 oz for the topping
Salt, pepper, nutmeg and a squeeze of lemon juice
30 g / 1 oz unsalted butter, cut into small diced
250 ml / 8 ½ fl oz single cream
75 g / 3 oz gingerbread crumbs

Method
1. Sieve the flour into a bowl. Add a pinch of salt and a good grating

of nutmeg. Make a well in the centre and break in the eggs. Using the electric hand whisk start to mix in the eggs then gradually add enough warm water until you have a thick, smooth batter. It should run slowly off a spoon. Leave the dough to stand for at least thirty minutes.

2. Preheat the oven to 180 °C. Generously butter a baking dish.

3. Three quarters fill a large saucepan with water and bring to the boil. Add a tablespoon of salt and a teaspoon of vegetable oil. Have the bowl of batter as close as possible to the boiling water. Once the water is boiling, spoon a ladleful of the batter into a potato ricer with spätzle disk or use a colander with 3–5 mm holes. Whichever implement you are using don't fill it over the boiling water otherwise it can become blocked. Once filled, hold the spätzle device over the water and slowly push the batter through the holes using the pusher or with the back of a ladle. As soon as the little dumplings bob to the surface remove them with a slotted spoon and place them in a warm dish.

4. Squeeze as much moisture out of the sauerkraut. Mix the sauerkraut with the caraway seeds, snipped chives and cheeses.

5. Once all of the spätzle have been cooked season well with salt, pepper, nutmeg and lemon juice. Toss them with the sauerkraut mixture until thoroughly combined.

6. Dot the base of the baking dish with half of the butter. Spoon a layer of the cheesy spätzle followed by a drizzle of cream and a little salt and pepper to season. Keep repeating these layers until all of the spätzle is in the dish finishing with cream.

7. Mix the gingerbread crumbs with the remaining Gruyère. Scatter the topping over the spätzle and dot with the remaining butter. Bake for 20–25 minutes until golden and bubbling.

CHESTNUT & APPLE WELLINGTON

Chestnuts, like gingerbread, should not be reserved only for Christmas. This is a lovely meat-free 'roast' which, thanks to the wonders of packaged chestnuts and pre-made pastry, is really easy to prepare.

Ingredients for the Wellington (Serves 4)
50 g / 2 oz blanched whole hazelnuts

2 tbsp vegetable oil
1 medium onion, finely chopped
1 clove garlic, crushed with a little salt
1 tsp grated fresh ginger
½ tsp ground cumin
½ tsp ground coriander
Pinch cayenne pepper
200 g / 7 oz pack chestnut purée
1 Granny Smith apple, unpeeled, cored and grated
1 small carrot (c. 75g/3oz), grated
50 g / 2 oz dark gingerbread, crumbled (e.g. parkin)
50 g / 2 oz white or wholemeal breadcrumbs
1 tsp lemon juice
1 tbsp mushroom ketchup
Salt and pepper to season
375 g / 13 oz ready rolled puff pastry
1 beaten egg, for brushing (optional)

Ingredients for the shallot gravy
200 g / 7 oz shallots, peeled and finely chopped
25 g / 1 oz butter or margarine
25 g / 1 oz gingerbread crumbs
100 ml / 3 ½ fl oz red wine
500 ml / 17 ½ fl oz vegetable stock
1 tsp mushroom ketchup
Salt, pepper and a good squeeze of lemon juice to season

Method
1. Preheat the oven to 200 °C. Line a baking sheet with a silicone liner or baking paper, and roast the hazelnuts until golden (about 5–10 minutes). Remove from the oven and set aside until required.
2. Heat the oil in a frying pan over a medium heat. Add the onion and fry until softened (roughly 5 minutes or so). Add the garlic, fresh ginger, ground spices and cayenne. Cook for a minute or two then tip into a bowl.
3. Add the chestnut purée, grated apple, grated carrot, gingerbread

and regular breadcrumbs, then mix in the lemon juice, mushroom ketchup and roasted hazelnuts until everything is thoroughly combined. Spoon onto a large piece of clingfilm then shape into a thick 'sausage' roughly 20–24 cm / 8–9 in long. Wrap the chestnut roll in the clingfilm and place in the fridge for 30 minutes.

4. To prepare the gravy, cook the shallots in the butter over a low to medium heat until they are golden. Stir in the red wine then bring to the boil and reduce by half. Add the gingerbread crumbs followed by the vegetable stock and mushroom ketchup. Cover and simmer gently for around 20–30 minutes until slightly thickened. Season with salt, pepper and a squeeze of lemon juice. This can be done ahead of time if you wish.

5. To finish the Wellington, unravel the puff pastry on a lightly floured board with a long edge nearest to you. Place the chestnut roll along the length of the pastry leaving a gap of 5 cm / 2 in between the roll and the edge. Brush all around the roll with beaten egg (if using) or water then begin to roll the pastry up and over the chestnut filling (a bit like making a Swiss roll) until the filling is encased. There should be an overlapping seam of pastry underneath the chestnut roll but trim away any excess pastry (if you like you could cut out leaves from the trimmings to decorate the Wellington). Seal the short ends of the Wellington by pressing the top and bottom edges together then transfer to the baking sheet. Bake for 25–30 minutes or until golden brown and thoroughly heated through.

6. To serve the Wellington cut off the pastry ends then divide into four pieces. Serve with some mashed potato and shallot gravy.

Gingered Buttermilk Goujons

Ingredients (Serves 4)
800 g / 1 ¾ lb chicken breast (3–4 large pieces)
150 ml / ¼ pt buttermilk
1 large egg, beaten
1 large clove garlic
½ tsp sea salt flakes

A couple of generous pinches of cayenne pepper
1 ½ tsp *quatre épices* (see page 220)
150 g / 5 oz dried natural breadcrumbs
75 g / 3 oz fine gingerbread crumbs
Salt and pepper
3 tbsp vegetable oil (or a little more if you are using more than one
   baking tray)

Method
1. Cut the chicken breasts into long goujons about 1 cm thick.
2. Mix the buttermilk, egg, garlic, a pinch of cayenne and *quatre épices* in a bowl or dish large enough to accommodate the chicken and marinade. Add the chicken slices and coat with the buttermilk. Leave to marinate for several hours.
3. Preheat the oven to 180 °C. Pour the oil onto a large baking tray (or divide between two if required to accommodate all of the chicken strips in a single layer) and place in the oven to heat up.
4. Mix the dried breadcrumbs with the gingerbread crumbs in a large bowl or ziplock plastic bag. Add a pinch of cayenne and a little salt and pepper. Shake off the excess buttermilk marinade from the chicken strips and toss in the crumb coating. Place on a board or plate while you coat the remaining goujons.
5. Place the breaded chicken on the preheated baking tray in a single layer. Return to the oven for 15 minutes. After this time turn the chicken over and place back in the oven for a further 5–10 minutes or until the chicken is cooked through. Serve immediately.

MEATBALLS WITH TOMATO & GINGER SAUCE

Ingredients for the meatballs
500 g / 1 lb 2 oz pork mincemeat
1 tbsp chopped mixed herbs e.g. parsley, thyme, chives
¼ tsp fine sea salt plus extra if needed
½ tsp ground black pepper
¾ tsp ground cinnamon
1½ tsp ground ginger

15g finely grated parmesan
1½ tsp cumin seeds
1 egg yolk
150 g / 5 oz gingerbread crumbs
Juice from half a lemon
3–4 tbsp vegetable oil for frying

Ingredients for the sauce
2 tbsp olive oil
2 cloves garlic, crushed
1 x 3 cm / 1 in piece root ginger, grated
2 x 400 g / 14 oz tins chopped tomatoes
1 tbsp sun-dried tomato paste
Pinch chilli flakes
1 tbsp balsamic vinegar
A few sprigs thyme
Salt and pepper to season

Method
1. To make the meatballs mix all of the ingredients together except the vegetable oil for frying. Fry a little of the mixture to test the seasoning adding more salt if necessary. Shape into 30 g / 1 oz balls then refrigerate while you make the sauce.
2. Heat the olive oil over a medium heat in a large shallow, lidded casserole or saucepan. Fry garlic and ginger in oil until fragrant but not coloured. Add the chopped tomatoes, sun-dried tomato paste, chilli flakes, balsamic vinegar and thyme. Turn the heat down low and slowly bring to a simmer while you fry the meatballs.
3. Heat two tablespoons of the vegetable oil in a frying pan. Cook the meatballs in batches until browned all over, adding more oil when required. Remove the cooked meatballs from the oil with a slotted spoon and drain them on absorbent kitchen paper.
4. Add the browned meatballs to the tomato and ginger sauce then simmer for around 20–30 minutes or until throughly cooked. Serve with pasta or rice.

Salmon Poached in Cider

Ingredients (Serves 4)
300 ml / ½ pint dry cider
300 ml / ½ pint water
1 onion, peeled and halved
2 cloves
1 bay leaf
A couple of pieces of lemon peel
600 g / 1 lb 5oz salmon fillet, skin on
40 g / 1 ½ oz gingerbread crumbs
75 ml / 2 ½ fl oz double cream
½ tbsp Dijon mustard
Salt, pepper and lemon juice to season
1 tbsp chopped parsley

Method
1. Place the cider, the onion halves stuck with the cloves, the bay leaf, lemon peel and the salmon in a large shallow, lidded casserole

186

or saucepan. Bring to the boil then turn the heat off and leave for 20 minutes or until the salmon is just cooked.

2. Remove the salmon out of the pan with a fish slice and keep warm while you finish the sauce. Discard the onion, cloves, bayleaf and lemon peel. Add the gingerbread crumbs then bring to the boil. Simmer until the sauce has reduced by half and has thickened. Pass the sauce through a sieve or chinois, pressing any residual gingerbread crumbs though with the back of a ladle (this will ensure the sauce is smooth). Add the cream and mustard. Bring back to boiling point to heat through. Season with salt, pepper and lemon juice. Stir in the parsley just before serving.

Proud Henry (Sausages in Beer Sauce)

This dish goes by the name of Stolzer Heinrich[4] (Proud Henry) in its hometown of Berlin. The traditional version uses Bratwurst and dark wheat beer. I've given it a British spin using brown ale and good old bangers.

Ingredients (Serves 4)
2 tbsp vegetable oil

12 good quality butchers' sausages or 8 Bratwurst

4 onions, peeled, cut into half and sliced

75 g crumbled gingerbread e.g. ginger snaps, men or leftovers from
  making a gingerbread house

1 large sprig thyme

1 large bayleaf (fresh if possible)

2 cloves

700 ml brown ale or dark wheat beer

Salt and pepper to season

1–2 tbsp lemon juice

1 tbsp honey (optional)

Method

1. Heat the oil over a medium heat in a large, lidded frying pan. Prick the sausages then brown them in the oil. Keep to one side while you make the sauce.

2. Add the onions to the pan and cook until starting to turn golden. Sprinkle over the crumbled gingerbread, the herbs, cloves and pour in the beer. Bring to the boil then add the sausages. Reduce the heat to bring the casserole to a gentle simmer. Cover and leave to bubble gently for 20–25 minutes or until the sausages are cooked.

3. By the time the sausages are cooked the gingerbread should have done its job of thickening the sauce. If the sauce is too thick for your tastes add a little water (or stock if you have any to hand). Taste the sauce then add salt, pepper and lemon juice, according to your liking. Generally speaking British ale is more bitter than German wheat beer so you may want to add a little honey to counteract this.

4. Serve with mashed potato and green vegetables.

PUMPKIN TORTELLONI

The inclusion of a little crumbled amaretti biscuit in pumpkin-filled tortelloni is a long established tradition in some areas of Italy.[5] Ginger biscuits make an admirable alternative to the amaretti. If you've ever eaten a pumpkin pie you'll know how much this vegetable fruit loves spice. There is no reason why you can't roll the pasta by hand with a rolling pin but a pasta machine or pasta attachment for a food mixer does make life a lot easier. Making filled pasta may seem like a quite a complex process but it is actually fairly straightforward and quite therapeutic in its own way, once you get a rhythm going.

Ingredients for the pasta[6] (Serves 3–4)
500 g / 1 lb 2 oz prepared pumpkin or butternut squash, in 2.5 cm / 1 in cubes
2 tbsp water
200 g / 7 oz '00' Italian flour
1 large egg plus 1 beaten egg for brushing the pasta later
A pinch of salt
1 tbsp olive oil plus a little extra for brushing
A scattering of polenta or semolina

Ingredients for the filling
225 g / 8 oz pumpkin purée
1 clove garlic, crushed
45 g / 1 ½ oz crushed ginger biscuits (e.g. ginger snaps)
25 g / 1 oz fresh white breadcrumbs
45 g / 1 ½ oz finely grated parmesan
⅛–¼ tsp ground ginger plus a little freshly grated nutmeg
1 large egg yolk
Salt, pepper and lemon juice to season

To serve
100 g / 4 oz salted butter
1 small clove garlic, squashed
2 tbsp chopped mixed herbs, e.g. basil, parsley, chives
Good squeeze of lemon juice
3–4 tbsp gingerbread crumbs (optional)
Plenty of freshly grated parmesan

Method
1. Preheat the oven to 180 °C.
2. Place the pumpkin and two tablespoons of water in a roasting pan.

Cover with foil then bake for 60–90 minutes or until the pumpkin is really tender. Leave the pumpkin to cool then purée in a food processor or blender. You need 275 g / 10 oz for this recipe so you will probably have more than you need (a certain amount of moisture will evaporate from the pumpkin as it cooks so it will weigh considerably less than when it was fresh). The remaining purée can be served with the cooked pasta or could be added to a soup later on. This stage can be done a day or so ahead.

3. Sieve the flour onto a clean work surface. Make a well in the middle then add 50 g / 2 oz of the cold pumpkin purée, one egg, a pinch of salt and the olive oil. Using a fork start beating the contents of the well together gradually drawing in the flour from around the edges. Eventually you will need to abandon the fork and use your hands to bring the dough together. If the dough seems particularly dry, wet your hands with cold water and keep kneading until you have a stiff dough (it won't matter if there is a little flour left on the work surface). Brush with a little extra olive oil, wrap in clingfilm and refrigerate for at least 30 minutes.

4. To make the filling combine all of the ingredients in a bowl starting with an ⅛ of a teaspoon of ground ginger, adding more of the spice to taste (you don't want to obliterate the pumpkin or squash flavour). Season well with salt, pepper and lemon juice.

5. To make the tortelloni, divide the dough into four pieces. Take one of these pieces (keep the other three covered) roll it slightly into a rough rectangle on a lightly floured board so it will pass through the widest setting of your pasta machine. Pass it through the pasta machine then fold one third of the pasta towards the middle of the strip, followed by the opposite end over this one so that you have a smaller rectangle. Pass the dough, open end first to squeeze out any air, through the machine and repeat the folding and rolling process three more times, always using the widest setting.

6. When you pass the pasta through the machine for the fifth time on the widest setting continue passing the strip through the machine reducing the settings one at a time (there is no need to fold the pasta now). The pasta parcels are going to be double thickness when formed so the strip needs to be pretty thin (this will mean going down to the lowest or second lowest setting on your machine). The strip is going to get pretty long so make sure you have plenty of space to work on.

7. Lay a couple of clean damp tea towels on your work surface. Place the

pasta strip on the towels. Use a 7 cm / 3 in non fluted cookie cutter to stamp out rounds of pasta. Lightly brush each round of pasta with beaten egg. Place a scant teaspoon of the pumpkin filling on half of each circle. Fold the other half of the circle over the filling to enclose it then press down to seal the edges to create a semicircle. Bring the two corners of the semicircle together to form the tortelloni, squeezing the ends gently together to seal (use a little more beaten egg if necessary). Place the tortelloni on a tray dusted with polenta or semolina (or flour if you don't have either of these to hand) and leave for at least 30 minutes before cooking.

8. Repeat this process with the remaining pieces of dough. The shape of this pasta means there is a lot of wastage. Do not throw these trimmings away – keep them covered to one side. Every Italian in the world will probably be aghast at this next suggestion but I take the trimmings and knead them into another ball of dough, passing it through the machine once as directed from stage 5, then continuing onto stage 6 etc. Personally, I can't detect any difference in the quality of the tortelloni made with the trimmings and those made initially. However, if you would rather not do this stage (and I would only recommend doing it once in any case) you will have a slightly lower yield of tortelloni.

9. To cook the tortelloni bring a large pan of salted water to the boil. Add the tortelloni to the pan and reduce the heat so that the water is bubbling gently rather than rolling. The tortelloni are done when they rise to the surface (about three to five minutes). It is better to cook the pasta in batches rather than crowd the pan but you can remove the cooked tortelloni with a slotted spoon and keep them covered in a warm oven while you cook the rest. It's also a good idea to have some plates warming in the oven for when you are ready to serve the pasta.

10. To serve the tortelloni, melt the butter and squashed clove of garlic in a large frying pan. When the butter is gently bubbling remove from the heat and discard the garlic (this is used to scent the butter rather than be a dominant flavour). Stir in the chopped herbs and lemon juice. Depending on how much pumpkin purée you have left, you could season it with salt, pepper and nutmeg then spread over each serving plate and scatter with the remaining gingerbread crumbs (this a step too far as regards sweetness for some people). Toss the tortelloni in the herby butter, then spoon over the purée and crumbs Sprinkle with finely grated parmesan and serve immediately.

Gingered Scotch Rabbit

'You mightn't happen to have a piece of cheese about you, now? No?
Well, many's the long night I've dreamed of cheese – toasted, mostly.'[7]

Who doesn't share Ben Gunn's obsession with toasted cheese in Robert
Louis Stevenson's classic tale of treasure hunting pirates? Providing you
use a firm gingerbread like the brüni recipe on page 136 or one of the *pain
d'épices* you will discover that toasted cheese makes an excellent topping.
Don't try using a spongier cake as the slices are liable to crumble.

'Rabbits' or rarebits were traditionally served as a savoury at the end
of a meal. As to how this dish of toasted cheese came to be referred to
as a 'rabbit' nobody really knows. Hannah Glasse provides variations for
this type of rabbit in her cookbook, so the name certainly has its origins
in the eighteenth century at the very least.[8]

Ingredients (Serves 1–2)
½ tsp English mustard powder
2 tbsp/30 ml porter
15 g / ½ oz butter
85 g / 3 oz finely grated mature cheddar
1 large egg yolk

Black pepper and a good pinch cayenne to season
Several thick slices of brüni or other firm gingerbread

Method

1. Mix the mustard powder, porter, butter and cheese in a saucepan. Heat gently to melt the cheese and butter but do not boil. Allow to cool slightly before beating in the egg yolk and seasoning. Allow to cool then refrigerate until required. It must be completely cold in order to allow the mixture to firm up before use.

2. Once the 'rabbit' is cold, preheat your grill then lightly toast the gingerbread slices on both sides. Keep a close eye on it. The sugar content of the gingerbread means it will burn easily.

3. Spread the 'rabbit' over one of the toasted sides then place under the grill again until the cheese is golden and bubbling.

BAKED CAMEMBERT WITH GINGERBREAD

Ingredients (Serves 2–4, depending how hungry you are)
250 g whole camembert (ideally in a box)
1 clove garlic, cut into 4 or 5 slithers
A few small sprigs of rosemary

2 tbsp brandy or calvados
Gingersnaps, parkin or other firm gingerbread for dipping

Method
1. Preheat the oven to 180 °C.
2. Remove the camembert from its plastic wrapper. Place it back in the bottom of the box (or put it in a small roasting dish). There is no need to replace the lid of the box. Place the boxed cheese in the centre of a piece of foil large enough to enclose the box.
3. Pierce the top of the cheese in several places then place slithers of garlic or small sprigs of rosemary into each incision. Drizzle the top of the cheese with the brandy or calvados. Bring the edges of the foil up to create a tent-like structure over the cheese. You don't want the foil to touch the top of the cheese otherwise it will stick.
4. Place the tented parcel on a baking tray and cook for 25–30 minutes. After this time the cheese should be molten (and very hot). If for some reason it isn't runny enough return it to the oven uncovered for another five minutes or so.
5. Serve immediately with a selection of gingerbread and perhaps some slices of apple or pear and a few walnuts.

Desserts & Sweetmeats

Here you will find recipes to add a sweet finale to your meal. Some are gingerbread creations in their own right. Others incorporate gingerbread recipes included in this book. All of them I can thoroughly recommend.

Desserts

Carrot & Ginger Roulade with Honeyed Ricotta

I went through a vegetarian phase in my early twenties. The first vegetarian cookbook I owned was a Family Circle publication. It is incredibly battered now, but I still make some of the recipes in the book today, although I'm no longer a vegetarian. It contained a recipe for a honey and carrot roll which quickly became a favourite dessert. I've tweaked it over the years to arrive at the recipe you see here.[1]

Ingredients for the cake (Serves 8)
4 large eggs, separated
60 g / 2 oz plain flour
2 tsp ground ginger
½ tsp ground cinnamon
½ tsp ground allspice
110 g / 4 oz caster sugar
2 tbsp runny honey
1 large carrot (about 170 g), peeled and finely grated
Caster sugar for dusting

Ingredients for the filling
250 g / 9 oz tub ricotta

2 tbsp runny honey
2 pieces candied stem ginger in syrup, finely chopped.

Method
1. Preheat the oven to 180 °C. Grease and line a 23 x 33 cm / 9 x 9 in Swiss roll tin with baking paper (I usually grease the top of the paper too just to make sure the cake doesn't stick). Have another piece of baking paper ready at least as long as the Swiss roll tin. Liberally dust this with caster sugar.
2. Sieve the flour and spices for the cake. In a separate bowl, use an electric whisk to beat the egg yolks with the caster sugar and honey until thick. In another bowl, whisk the egg whites until stiff.
3. Fold the spiced flour into the egg yolk and sugar mixture, followed by the carrot then gently fold in the egg whites until fully incorporated. Spoon the mixture into the prepared tin. Spread the mixture evenly with a palette knife then bake for 10–15 minutes or until well risen and golden. As soon as it comes out of the oven, tip the cake onto the sugar-dusted baking paper. Remove the lining paper, then roll the cake into a spiral from one of the short sides. Allow to cool before filling.
4. To make the honeyed ricotta, beat the ricotta with two tablespoons of honey until amalgamated. Fold in the chopped candied ginger. Unravel the cake and spread the honeyed ricotta over the surface leaving a 2.5 cm / 1 in gap at the edge furthest away from you. Roll the cake away from you then place on a serving plate, seam side down. Dust with more caster sugar (or icing sugar if you prefer), then refrigerate until required.

STUFFED POACHED PEARS

It is better to use slightly under ripe than over ripe pears for this recipe, otherwise there is a danger they will collapse in the poaching liquor. This recipe is good for using up any left over ginger cake you have lying around (although 'cake' and 'stale' are two words that rarely appear in any sentence uttered in our house). Unstuffed, these pears are lovely in a salad with blue cheese and nuts.

Ingredients (Serves 4)
300 ml / ½ pt ginger wine
200 ml / 7 fl oz water
10 cm / 4 in cinnamon stick
3 slices fresh ginger
10 cm / 4 in pared piece of lemon zest
50 g / 2 oz granulated sugar
4 x ripe but firm pears
4 soft, dried figs, roughly chopped (c. 60g/2oz)
50g ginger cake crumbs
1 piece stem ginger in syrup, roughly chopped
2 tbsp ginger syrup
1 tsp arrowroot
2 tsp water

Method
1. Place the ginger wine, water, cinnamon stick, fresh ginger, lemon peel and sugar in a large saucepan and slowly bring to the boil while you prepare the pears.
2. Peel the pears leaving any stalks intact. Halve each one and remove the core containing the pips to create a small hollow. This can be done with a teaspoon or a melon baller if you have one. Place the pears halves in the poaching liquor then simmer very gently for 10 to 20 minutes depending on the ripeness of the pears. You should be able to insert a knife easily into the flesh with very little resistance when they are done.
3. While the pears are cooking prepare the filling. Place the figs, ginger cake crumbs, stem ginger and ginger syrup in the bowl of a small food processor. Process until everything is finely chopped and thoroughly mixed.
4. Once the pears are cooked remove them from the liquor and place in a serving dish. Also remove the cinnamon, ginger and lemon zest. Bring the liquor back up to the boil and reduce by roughly a half. Mix the arrowroot with two teaspoons of water. Stir this into the wine mixture while it is bubbling, stirring constantly until slightly thickened. Pour the sauce around the pears ensuring that none goes into the hollows.
5. Divide the stuffing between the eight halves of pear piling it into

each crevice (each half will be topped with a veritable mound of the gingery filling). Refrigerate the pears until you are ready to serve them. Serve with whipped cream or ice cream.

Dulcia Piperata
(Roman Peppered Honey Cake)

'Pound pepper, pine nuts, honey, rue and passum. Cook with milk and tracta. Cook the thickened mixture with a little egg. Serve drenched in honey and sprinkled in pepper.' *Apicius, 7.11.5*[2]

The recipe above is from a brief section on 'Homemade Sweets and Honeyed Cheeses' in Book Seven of *Apicius,* on Gourmet Recipes. With such sparse instructions, it's hard to know exactly what this recipe should look like. Is it a cake, paste, or even a custard? I've taken a leaf out of Mark Grant's *Roman Cookery* and have whisked the honey and eggs together to create a kind of sponge.[3] As with all early recipes there are no measurements so the spicing is all down to guesswork. I have opted for a subtle approach with the pepper to create a balmy warmth in the mouth rather than a fierce after burn. If using ground black pepper rather than long pepper I would start with half a teaspoon to begin with as this variety seems to be more potent than the long pepper originally used by the Romans.

A note on the ingredients. The recipes in *Apicius* reflect the typical Mediterranean diet of the time. Many of the ingredients used may not have been freely available to people living in Northern Europe.[4] To this end I have substituted certain items listed in the recipes such as using hazelnuts in place of pine nuts. The herb rue has an incredibly bitter taste and can also cause an allergic reaction when picked. For these reasons I have used rosemary as an alternative. *Passum* was a raisin wine made from grapes that have been allowed to dry in the sun. A modern dessert wine such as muscat would be a suitable alternative,[5] although a sweet Sherry such as Pedro Ximenez or Marsala will also work. I have made this recipe using milk and sweet wine (half of each) but in my opinion it doesn't add anything to the end result so have omitted the milk from this version. *Tracta* was a type of dried pastry that could be crumbled into recipes. It is quite labour intensive to make from scratch so I have used spelt flour instead. Very few recipes are not improved by a squeeze or two of lemon but do feel free to omit it if you wish to remain true to the Apician recipe.

Ingredients
175 g / 6 oz blanched hazelnuts or almonds (or 150 g / 5 oz pre ground roasted hazelnuts plus 25 g / 1 oz whole roasted hazelnuts)
3 pieces of long pepper or ½–1 tsp coarse ground black pepper
2 sprigs rosemary 10–12 cm long, leaves removed and finely chopped
4 large eggs
200 g / 7 oz honey
50 g / 2 oz spelt flour, sieved (white for preference but wholemeal will do)
Zest of 1 lemon (optional)
4 tbsp dessert wine (e.g. Muscat), sweet Sherry or Marsala
50 g / 2 oz honey
Juice of ½ lemon (optional) or 1 tbsp water
Generous pinch finely ground black pepper.

Method
1. Preheat the oven to 150 °C. Grease and line the base and sides of a 20 cm / 8 in springform cake tin.
2. Place the hazelnuts or almonds on a baking sheet. Cook for around 8–10 minutes (or longer if necessary) stirring half way through. They should be lightly golden. Reserve 25 g / 1 oz for the topping and finely grind the rest in a food processor (you can skip this stage if using pre-ground hazelnuts).
3. While the nuts are roasting, grind the long pepper using a spice grinder or pestle and mortar. If you are using a spice grinder, you can add the rosemary leaves to the pepper pieces so that they too are finely chopped. If you are using a pestle and mortar, finely chop the rosemary.
4. Break the eggs into the bowl of a free-standing mixer or a large mixing bowl. Add the honey. Whisk the eggs and honey until pale and aerated. The whisk should leave a trail when removed from the mixture.
5. Gently fold in 150 g / 5 oz ground hazelnuts, ground pepper and

rosemary, the spelt flour and the lemon zest (if using). Finally, fold in the sweet Sherry or wine.

6. Pour the mixture into the prepared tin. Place the tin on a baking sheet then bake for 25–30 minutes until well risen and golden. The cake should come away from the edges of the tin and feel springy (a skewer should also come out clean when inserted).

7. Shortly before the cake is done gently heat the remaining honey, lemon juice or water and black pepper until syrupy. When the cake is cooked, pierce it all over with the skewer, then pour over the warm syrup. Allow the cake to cool in the tin before unmoulding. Roughly chop the remaining nuts and scatter over the cake before serving.

GINGERBREAD CREAM[6]

The lyrical Nigel Slater and I have something in common. Both of us were introduced to a version of this gingerbread sundae by an influential lady in our lives. In Nigel's case it was his mother and in mine, my very first boss, Angela. In both cases the 'original' recipe combined ginger nuts and cream (I have a vague recollection that the biscuits were dipped in Sherry first in Angela's version). Nigel uses the domed *lebkuchen* you can buy in supermarkets at Christmas (although the *Elisenlebkuchen* in this book wouldn't work quite as well due to the rice paper base). Any simple spiced ginger biscuit would work here so it's a great recipe to use up excess gingerbread men or the offcuts from a gingerbread house construction. If you are making this for little ones feel free to omit the alcohol.

Ingredients (Serves 4)
175 g / 6 oz dark chocolate, 70% cocoa solids, broken into small pieces
55 g / 2 oz butter
2 tbsp golden syrup or honey
200 ml / 6 ¾ fl oz whole milk
55 g / 2 oz caster sugar
250 g / 9 oz double cream
2 tbsp dark rum or brandy (optional)
200 g / 7 oz crumbled ginger biscuits

Method

1. Place the dark chocolate, butter and golden syrup or honey in a heatproof bowl. Place over a pan of barely simmering water (make the sure the bowl doesn't come into contact with the water) then stir occasionally until all ingredients have melted.

2. Pour the milk into a microwavable jug and heat for 20–30 seconds on high to warm it slightly. Pour the warm milk onto the chocolate mixture along with the caster sugar then stir until glossy. Remove the sauce from the heat and allow to cool slightly before assembling the desserts.

3. Put the cream and rum or brandy (if using) in a bowl. Whip until thickened but still floppy (it should barely keep its shape). Fold in the crumbled ginger biscuits.

4. To assemble the dessert, pour a little chocolate sauce into the base of a sundae dish or large cocktail glass. Spoon some of the ginger biscuit cream over this followed by more sauce. Repeat the layers again finishing with sauce. Place the desserts in the fridge for several hours before you want to serve them to allow all the flavours to mingle. The sauce will thicken considerably (although it won't set hard) but if you prefer a softer consistency remove the desserts from the fridge an hour or so before you want to eat them.

Gingerbread Puddings with Whisky Mac Sauce

You can't beat a proper steamed pudding, especially on a chilly day (by 'proper' I mean one made with suet – you can use a vegetarian variety if you prefer). The notion for this recipe began with a handwritten notebook[7] my grandmother gave me which belonged to her great aunt Eliza. Eliza's gingerbread pudding was very simple so I've added a few bells and whistles, such as a cocktail-themed sauce, to glam it up somewhat.

I have borrowed the ingenious method for steaming the individual puddings in the oven from Regula Ysewijn's *Pride & Pudding*, a wonderfully indispensable book for anyone who loves traditional British desserts.[8]

Ingredients for the pudding (Serves 6)
125 g / 4 ½ oz pitted chopped dates
60 g / 2 oz treacle
180 ml / 6 fl oz hot water
125 g / 4 ½ oz self raising flour
1½ tsp ground ginger
¾ tsp ground mixed spice
110 g / 4 oz dark muscovado sugar
60 g / 2 oz suet
2 large pieces preserved ginger, finely chopped
1 large egg, beaten
1 ½ tbsp milk
Softened butter for greasing the moulds

Ingredients for the sauce
75 g / 3 oz dark muscovado sugar
55 g / 2 oz unsalted butter
1 tbsp preserved ginger syrup
2 tbsp whisky
2 tbsp ginger wine

Method
1. Preheat the oven to 180 °C. Generously butter six individual pudding moulds and select a deep roasting tin which can accommodate all of the moulds. I've never had an issue with these puddings sticking to the bottom of the mould but if you want to be doubly sure of this not occurring you could line the base of each mould with a small disc of baking paper. Boil the kettle so that you have hot water to hand when you are ready to cook the puddings.
2. Place the dates, treacle and water in a small saucepan. Bring to the boil then purée with a stick blender.
3. Sieve the flour and spices into a bowl. Stir in the sugar, suet and finely chopped preserved ginger. In a separate bowl beat the egg with the milk.
4. Add the warm date and treacle purée to the flour, sugar and suet followed by the egg and milk mixture. Mix well together before

dividing between the buttered pudding moulds (they should be about three quarters full at this point).

5. Place the pudding moulds in the roasting tin. Pour enough boiling water around the filled moulds. Cover the tin with a large piece of foil then place in the oven for 30 minutes.

6. When the puddings are cooked, carefully run a round bladed knife around the edge of each pudding. Tip the mould up and give it a shake. The pudding should come out easy enough. If you have used baking paper in the base of the mould don't forget to remove this from the top of your puddings! You can serve the pudding immediately or allow them to cool and reheat them later for a few minutes in a microwave.

7. To make the sauce, gently heat the sugar, butter and ginger syrup in a small saucepan. Once the butter has melted and the sugar has dissolved add the whisky and ginger wine. Continue to heat gently but on no account let the sauce boil or you'll lose the 'heat' from the alcohol. Like the puddings, the sauce can be made in advance and reheated in the microwave.

8. Serve the puddings with some of the whisky mac sauce spooned over the top and whipped cream, crème fraîche or custard.

Honey Tart

Think of this as a take on a traditional treacle tart using medieval crumb-based gingerbread as its muse.

Ingredients (Serves 8)
225 g / 8 oz plain flour
2 tbsp icing sugar
55 g / 2 oz cold unsalted butter and 55 g / 2 oz lard or vegetable fat, cubed (or 110 g / 4 oz unsalted butter)
2 large eggs
280 g / 10 oz runny honey
55 g / 2 oz golden syrup
1 tsp medieval spice powder or ground ginger
Zest of lemon
1 tbsp lemon juice

225 g / 8 oz stale wholemeal breadcrumbs (or you could use white instead but don't use the dried kind used for coating nuggets etc)

Method

1. To make the pastry, sieve the flour and icing sugar into a bowl. Rub the butter and lard (if using) into the flour. Beat one of the eggs and stir this into the pastry base bringing the mixture together to form a firm dough (add a little cold water if the mixture seems too dry). Wrap in film, then leave to rest in the fridge for at least 30 minutes.

2. Preheat the oven to 180 °C.

3. Roll the pastry out and use it to line a 23 cm / 9 in loose bottomed flan tin. I like to leave a little extra pastry overhanging the edge to trim after the base is cooked (this means your tart case will come up to the top of the sides of the tin even after cooking). Prick the base with a fork then line with baking paper and baking beans. Bake for 10 minutes. Remove the paper and beans then return the case to the oven for a further 10 minutes. Use a vegetable peeler or sharp knife to carefully 'shave' off the excess pastry level with the top of the tin.

4. Place the honey and golden syrup in a bowl. Mix well before adding the remaining egg, spice, lemon zest and juice. Beat until thoroughly combined then add the breadcrumbs. Spoon into the precooked pastry case.

5. Bake at 180 °C for around 20 minutes. Allow to cool slightly before serving with vanilla ice cream or custard.

HOT ICE CREAM FOR COLD DAYS

'HOT ICE CREAMS FOR COLD DAYS', it said on the next door.

"Extremely useful in the winter," said Mr. Wonka, rushing on. "Hot ice cream warms you up no end in freezing weather."[10]

This is essentially a take on Baked Alaska inspired by *Charlie and the Chocolate Factory*.[11] In my opinion, this meringue topped dessert works best with a sharp flavoured ice cream rather than the vanilla variety. Admittedly this is a 'cheat's ice cream' but it is devilishly easy to make.

Baked Alaska is one of those desserts which objects to being kept waiting, so make sure you have all of the components ready before you plan to serve it. If you have access to a catering blowtorch I would use this to finish off the dessert. Otherwise give it a brief turn in a hot oven to colour the meringue. A digital or jam thermometer is also useful when making an Italian meringue.[12]

Ingredients for the lemon curd and ginger ice cream (Serves 4)
300 g / 12 oz lemon curd (shop bought is fine)
250 g / 10 oz mascarpone cheese
100 g / 4 oz thick crème fraîche
½–1 tsp ground ginger (according to taste)

Ingredients to finish the dessert
4 x 1–2 cm thick slices of plain ginger cake e.g. Dickens' Gingerbread
  or Golden Gingerbread
4 tsp thin shred orange marmalade
2 large egg whites (about 70 g in weight)
100–150 g / 4–5 oz caster sugar
2 tbsp water
¼ tsp ground ginger
¼ tsp ground cinnamon
2 pieces preserved stem ginger in syrup, very finely chopped in a
  mini food processor

Method
1. To make the ice cream, beat the lemon curd, mascarpone cheese, crème fraîche and ground ginger together. Churn in an ice cream machine according to the manufacturer's instructions then transfer into a container and freeze until required. If you don't have an ice cream machine, pour into a container then freeze for an hour before beating with an electric whisk. Repeat this process two more times. The final ice cream should be as good as a churned variety. This can be done several days ahead.
2. Cut 6 cm / 2 ¼ in rounds from your ginger cake slices. If you plan to use a blowtorch to finish the dessert place each round on its own plate (or all of them on a baking sheet lined with silicone paper, if you plan

to put the dessert in the oven. If you are following this method preheat the oven to 200 °C). Spread each round with a teaspoon of orange marmalade. Scoop four balls of the lemon and ginger ice cream and place on a plate then put them back in the freezer until you are ready to assemble the dessert (if the ice cream is difficult to scoop leave it out of the freezer for ten minutes or so).

3.   Place whichever bowl you intend to make the meringue in on some digital scales (this bowl should be exceptionally clean as any traces of grease will prevent the egg whites from whisking properly). Weigh the egg whites. They should weigh around 70 g / 3 oz give or take a few grams. Whatever the egg whites weigh, you will need double the quantity of caster sugar.

4.   Place the caster sugar in a small sauce pan with 2 tbsp cold water. Gently heat until the sugar has melted. Increase the heat and bring to the boil.

5.   As the sugar comes to the boil, start whisking the egg whites (a free-standing mixer is excellent for this). When the egg whites begin to foam and start increasing in volume, the sugar syrup should have reached a temperature of 121–125 °C. Reduce the speed of the food mixer and very slowly pour the hot syrup down the side of the bowl onto the egg whites. Once all of the syrup has been added increase the mixer speed to high and whisk until the meringue is voluminous and glossy. Once the meringue has reached this stage, whisk in the ground spices then fold in the finely chopped preserved ginger.

6.   Spoon the meringue into a piping bag with a large star nozzle fitted (you don't want one that is too narrow otherwise it could become blocked with the stem ginger pieces). Place a ball of ice cream on each marmalade-topped cake then pipe the meringue around the cake and ice cream so that both are completely covered. Give it a quick once over with the blowtorch or place in the oven for 2–3 minutes to lightly brown the edges. Serve immediately.

Lady Windermere's Gooseberry Tart

This recipe sits somewhere between a crumble and a pie and comes to you via Elizabeth David and Jane Grigson. Both of these great food writers note that the friable texture of the famous Grasmere

Gingerbread lends itself to becoming a topping for a fruit crumble. Mrs David uses apples in her version (which was affectionately known as Lady Windermere's Flan in her family) but I favour gooseberries (although apples are a good substitute when gooseberries are out of season). Like Mrs David, I enjoy this cold with a little thick cream but my boys love it hot with custard.[13]

Ingredients (Serves 6)
500 g / 1lb 1 oz gooseberries (fresh or frozen) or 600–650 g /
   1 lb 5 oz–1 lb 7 oz Bramley apples
75 g / 3 oz granulated sugar (plus extra to taste if required)
1 tsp grated fresh ginger
2 ½–3 ½ tsp ground ginger
2 large egg yolks
125 g / 4 ½ oz plain flour
125 g / 4 ½ oz fine oatmeal
¼ tsp baking powder
150 g / 5 oz unsalted butter, diced
125 g / 4 ½ oz soft light brown sugar

Method
1. Place the gooseberries in a saucepan with the granulated sugar, fresh ginger and half a teaspoon of ground ginger. There is no need to add water to the gooseberries. Heat gently until juice begins to exude from the berries. Cook until the fruit has broken down. Mash the berries to a purée (or uses a stick blender if you want to be really thorough) then pass through a sieve to remove any stray stalks or leaves. Allow the purée to cool , then beat in the egg yolks. This can be done in advance and refrigerated overnight if needs be.
2. Preheat the oven to 180 °C. Butter a 23 cm / 9 in diameter solid flan or pie dish which is at least 2.5 cm / 1 in deep (do not use a loose bottomed flan tin).
3. Sieve the flour, fine oatmeal, baking powder and about two to three teaspoons of ground ginger (depending on how spicy you like your food) into a bowl. Rub the butter into the flour mixture (or use a food processor to make quicker work of the job) then stir in the light brown

sugar. Take half of this mixture and press it firmly and evenly into the base of the flan or pie dish. Spoon the cooled fruit purée over the top of the base then sprinkle over the remaining crumble mixture. There is no need to firm this down.

4. Place the tart on a baking sheet (just in case the fruit purée boils over) then bake for 30 minutes. Serve hot with custard or allow to cool to room temperature and serve with cream.

Variation
If you decide to use apples instead, they will need to be peeled, cored and sliced before they are cooked. Add two tablespoons of water to the apples, then cook until the fruit has broken down. Providing you removed all the pips and tough core before cooking there should be no need to pass the apple purée through a sieve. Proceed with the rest of the recipe as above.

Parkin Ice Cream

This is made along similar lines to the classic brown bread ice cream. Simple to prepare and delicious to eat.

Ingredients
100 g / 4 oz parkin (e.g. sponge parkin or brüni on pages 135 and 136)
300 ml / 12 oz single cream
2 tsp ground ginger
1 tsp vanilla extract
2 large egg yolks
1 tsp cornflour
100 g / 4 oz soft dark brown sugar
300 ml / 12 oz double cream
3 tbsp whisky, brandy or rum

Method
1. Preheat the oven to 180 °C. Place the parkin in a food processor, then process until you have fine-ish crumbs. Place on a baking sheet, then cook for around 5–10 minutes, stirring halfway through but make sure

they don't burn. Depending on how fresh your parkin is, this process may take a little less than 10 minutes or a little longer. The crumbs will feel soft when you first take them out but should crisp up a few minutes after you take them out of the oven. Allow to cool.

2. Place the single cream, ginger and vanilla in a small saucepan and heat to boiling point.

3. Meanwhile, whisk the egg yolks, cornflour and brown sugar until thoroughly combined and slightly paler than when you started. Pour the hot cream over the egg yolks stirring continuously.

4. Return the cream mixture to the saucepan and heat gently until the custard has thickened. Pour into a jug or bowl and cover the surface with clingfilm (to prevent a skin from forming).

5. Whisk the double cream with your alcohol of choice to the soft peak stage (it should be thick but reasonably floppy). Fold the whipped cream into the cold custard prior to pouring into the ice cream machine.

6. Churn the mixture in an ice cream machine according to the manufacturer's instructions. Once frozen (but not solid) fold in the cooled, parkin crumbs then transfer to a container. Place in the freezer until required. Remove it from the freezer around 10–15 minutes before you want to serve it.

RHUBARB AND GINGERBREAD CRUMBLE

This dessert has always been resoundingly popular when I've served it at my supper club. The idea for pre-cooking the crumble topping comes from Raymond Blanc. It avoids the gluey consistency you sometimes get when a crumble has been sitting for a while soaking up the fruit juices. Just make sure you don't spread the crumble mix over the fruit until just before you are ready to bake it.[14]

Ingredients (Serves 6 – 8)
800 g / 1 ¾ lb fresh rhubarb cut into 2 cm lengths
3 tbsp ginger wine or water
110 g / 4 oz granulated sugar plus more if needed
275 g / 10 oz plain flour
3 tsp ground ginger

1 tsp ground cinnamon
¼ tsp ground cloves
110 g / 4 oz soft, dark brown sugar
110 g / 4 oz unsalted butter, cubed
1 tbsp treacle

Method
1. Place the rhubarb in a large saucepan with the granulated sugar and ginger wine (if you have it) or water. Stew gently until the rhubarb is soft and relatively mushy. Test the sweetness adding more sugar if desired. Transfer to an ovenproof dish large enough to accommodate the fruit and the crumble topping. Preheat the oven to 180 °C.
2. Place the remaining ingredients in a food processor and blitz until the mixture looks like fine breadcrumbs. You could do this by hand but I find it easier (particularly where the treacle is concerned) to get a more even mix of the ingredients with a food processor.
3. Spread the crumble topping onto a lightly greased, shallow baking tray. Place in the oven for 10–15 minutes (this will very much depend on how large a tray you use). You want the mixture to have hardened into a large biscuit without being too brown. Allow to cool on the tray (it will continue to harden as it cools).
4. Once the crumble has cooled, transfer it to a plastic bag then bash with a rolling pin (the same as you would if you were making the base for a cheesecake with digestive biscuits). I like my crumble topping to be quite coarse but feel free to pulverise it to a finer consistency if that suits you better. Both the rhubarb and crumble topping can be prepared in advance.
5. Shortly before you are ready to serve the crumble, preheat the oven to 180 °C if you haven't already done so. Spread the crushed crumble over the fruit. Bake for 15 to 30 minutes (dependent on whether you are cooking the crumble from cold or room temperature). Serve hot with ice cream or custard.

SPICED STRAWBERRY SHORTCAKE[15]

We don't tend to think of pairing spices with strawberries but these sweet red fruits take to the warmth of spices surprisingly well.

Seventeenth-century cook Robert May certainly thought so, seasoning them with cinnamon, ginger and sugar before putting them in a tart.[16]

This is an adaptation of a recipe for 'Grasmere Shortcake' I found in one of my grandmother's cookbooks. In truth this shortcake is more like a shortbread in keeping with the friable texture of Grasmere Gingerbread rather than the scone-like consistency found in a classic strawberry shortcake. For this reason I have suggested pre-cutting the cake element before assembling. The original called for a gingery buttercream filling but I prefer cream here spiked with candied ginger.

Ingredients (Serves 8)
225 g plain wholemeal flour (or you could use ordinary plain flour if you prefer)
2 tsp ground ginger
¼ tsp bicarbonate of soda
110 g cold unsalted butter, diced
110 g soft light brown sugar
400 g fresh strawberries, washed and hulled
80 ml Marsala or port
¼–½ tsp ground cinnamon
⅛–¼ tsp ground mixed spice
25 g caster sugar
200 ml double cream
2 tbsp ginger syrup or icing sugar, sieved
1–2 pieces stem ginger in syrup, finely chopped

Method
1. Preheat the oven to 180 °C. Grease and line two 20 cm / 8 in round sandwich tins.
2. Sieve the flour, ginger and bicarbonate of soda into a bowl (tip in any bran left in the sieve). Rub in the butter (or blitz in a food processor) until the mixture resembles coarse breadcrumbs. Mix in the sugar.
3. Divide the mixture between the two tins, spreading it evenly and firming the mixture down with your fingers. Use a round bladed knife to divide each cake into eight even pieces. Bake for around 10–15 minutes or until golden. When the cakes come out of the oven cut them again while

the mixture is still soft. Allow to cool in the tin before turning out.

4. To make the strawberry and red wine sauce: Take 100 g of the strawberries. Place in a food processor with the Marsala or port. Blitz until the fruit is puréed then pass through a sieve into a small saucepan to remove the pips. Add the spices and 25 g caster sugar. Bring the sauce to the boil then simmer until reduced by half. Add more sugar if you think it needs it. Transfer to a bowl and allow to cool to room temperature.

5. Place the cream, ginger syrup or icing sugar in a bowl. Whip together until thick but floppy. Fold in the chopped candied ginger. Quarter the remaining strawberries and toss in the cooled strawberry and wine sauce.

6. To assemble the shortcake, place one of the segmented cakes on a serving plate. Either pipe or carefully spread half of the cream over the segments, ideally leaving a slight gap between each one so that you can still make out each wedge. Top this cake with half of the spiced strawberry compote. Place the remaining shortcake triangles on top, lining them up as closely as possible with the segments on the bottom. Cover the top cake with cream and strawberry compote. You can serve this straightaway or leave it for a few hours (or even overnight if desired, though if you do this the shortbread will inevitably soften).

WHITE CHOCOLATE CHEESECAKE WITH CRANBERRY 'GLÖGG' COMPOTE

Glögg is a mulled wine popular all over Scandinavia during the festive season. If you are not too sure about the taste of cardamom stick with the lower amount of pods suggested below. You can make this cheesecake when cranberries aren't in season by using the raspberry and redcurrant compote on page 112 instead.

Ingredients for the cheesecake (Serves 8–10)
225 g / 8 oz Ginger snaps or other crisp ginger biscuit
110 g / 4 oz unsalted butter
300 g / 10 ½ oz white chocolate
225 g / 8 oz cream cheese e.g. Philadelphia
150 g / 5 oz sour cream

25 g / 1 oz caster sugar
Seeds from 6–10 cardamom pods, crushed with a pestle and mortar
¼ tsp each of ground cinnamon and ground ginger
2 egg whites
A few drops of lemon juice

Ingredients for the compote
300 g / 10 ½ oz cranberries
Juice and zest of 1 large orange
5cm cinnamon stick
4 cardamom pods
2 slices fresh ginger
125 g / 4 ½ oz sugar
125 ml / 4 fl oz red wine

Method
1. Line a 23 cm / 9 in springform cake tin with tin foil. A 20 cm / 8 in tin would also work but you will just have a thicker base and filling for your cheesecake.
2. Crush the biscuits in a food processor or place them in a plastic bag and bash with a rolling pin (the latter is a much better way of relieving stress). Meanwhile, gently melt the butter in a small saucepan. Combine the melted butter and biscuits then put the mixture into the lined tin. Ensure the buttery crumbs are relatively evenly distributed before pressing down firmly with a wooded spoon to form the base of the cheesecake.
3. Place 200 g / 7 oz of the white chocolate in a heatproof bowl and place over a pan of barely simmering water to melt the chocolate. Make sure the bowl doesn't touch the water otherwise your chocolate will go lumpy.
4. Place the cream cheese, sour cream, caster sugar, crushed cardamom, ground cinnamon and ginger in a large bowl and beat until smooth. Beat in the melted white chocolate.
5. In a separate bowl, place the egg whites with a few drops of lemon juice. Beat until the egg whites form stiff peaks. Fold into the cream cheese and chocolate mix then spoon over the base.

6. Grate the remaining 100 g white chocolate and sprinkle this over the cheesecake 'filling'. Refrigerate for several hours or preferably over night.
7. For the compote: Put all of the ingredients into a saucepan and bring to the boil. Simmer gently for around 15 minutes until thickened. Leave to cool to allow the spices a chance to infuse the compote. Remove the spices and ginger before serving. I prefer to serve this at room temperature or warm as it makes a nice contrast to the cold cheesecake (it also becomes rather 'jammy' when cold because of the high pectin content of cranberries but still tastes good).

SWEETMEATS

Sometimes all you want is a little sweet something to round off a meal rather than a full-blown dessert. The following recipes are perfect for that purpose. They also make great edible gifts.

GINGERBREAD TAFFY[17]

Some early recipes for gingerbread were based on a mixture of honey and spices alone making a sort of medieval taffy, a chewy confection laden with spice.

Sugar work is a messy and time-consuming business so make sure you have enough time to complete this recipe when you begin. I'm afraid a digital thermometer is pretty much essential to ensure you get the temperature right (although a jam thermometer will suffice if that is all you have). Please also bear in mind that boiling sugar can be extremely dangerous if handled without care so this recipe is unsuitable for young children to make.

Ingredients for 18 pieces
Flavourless vegetable or sunflower oil
450 g / 1 lb honey
1–3 tsp medieval spice mix or ground ginger

Equipment required
Marble slab or granite worktop (I use the latter)

2 metal spatulas or palette knives
Thermometer (ideally digital)
Teaspoon measure
Small sieve
Dough scraper
Confectionary wrappers (optional) or a tray lined with silicone paper

Method

1.   Lightly oil your marble slab or work surface and the palette knives. It's also useful to have a small dish of oil to hand for your hands.

2.   Pour the honey into a heavy based saucepan and bring to the boil over a medium heat. Once the honey comes to the boil keep a close eye on it. The temperature needs to reach 140 °C but if it goes much over this you will end up with brittle rather than taffy.

3.   Once the honey reaches the required temperature begin pouring it very slowly onto your prepared work surface. Pour a little, then let it settle (it will start to thicken almost the instant it hits the cool surface); then keep adding to the puddle of boiled honey until all of it is on the surface. Make sure there is no danger of the boiling liquid pouring off onto you.

4.   Use the sieve to dredge the spices over the pooled honey. Unless you like your gingerbread super spicy, I would start with two teaspoons (particularly if using the medieval spice mix). Take a palette knife in each hand and begin to push the honey in on itself to work in the spices. Initially it will run back into a pool but pretty soon it will start to form a mass, at which point it should be cool enough to handle (although it will still be fairly warm). Use the dough scraper to scrape up any stray bits of taffy and add them to your mass.

5.   Lightly oil your hands. Form the honey mass into a roll then pick either end up with your hands and stretch it. Fold it back on itself and stretch it again. Keep repeating this process until the taffy turns from a golden brown to a light, speckled tan (the speckles come from the spice mix). This should take around five to ten minutes.

6.   Divide the taffy into three pieces. Create three rolls from these pieces and divide each roll into six pieces. At this point you can roll the taffy into balls and wrap them individually in confectionary wrappers or flatten the balls with the palm of your hand and place them on the tray lined with

silicone paper. If the taffy becomes too hard to handle, place it briefly in a warm oven (we're talking seconds rather than minutes) to soften. Once you have shaped all of the taffy pieces, you can place them in the fridge to firm up (this is less important if they are individually wrapped).

Gingerbread Truffles

Ingredients (Makes around 20)
150 g / 5 oz milk chocolate
100 g / 4 oz dark chocolate
120 ml / 4 fl oz double cream
15 g unsalted butter
1 tbsp treacle
1½ tsp ground ginger
¼ tsp each ground cinnamon and nutmeg
Pinch ground cloves
2 pieces (roughly 40–50 g) preserved stem ginger, finely chopped in a food processor
Crushed ginger biscuits for coating (approx 100 g)

Method
1. Finely grate the chocolates either by hand or using a food processor then place in a heatproof bowl with the butter, cream, treacle and spices. Heat in the microwave on medium power for 30 seconds. Stir, then return the bowl to the microwave for a further 30–60 seconds, stirring every 10–15 seconds. Do not overheat the chocolate as it will 'seize' and become thick and lumpy. Once fully melted, stir in the chopped preserved ginger.
2. Alternatively, gently heat the cream and treacle in a small saucepan then pour over the chocolate. Leave for a few minutes until the chocolate has melted, then stir to combine, adding the spices and the preserved chopped ginger. Transfer to a shallow dish then place in the fridge to firm up.
3. Roll tablespoon portions of the truffle mix into balls, then coat in ginger biscuit crumbs. Keep in the fridge until you are ready to serve them.

PANPEPATO[18]

Panpepato is similar to panforte (described by Gillian Riley as a 'flat, solid, heavily spiced cake, stiff with nuts and candied fruit'[19]) the key difference being the inclusion of chocolate in modern recipes and a good dose of black pepper. After her marriage to the elector of Palatine in 1691, Anna Maria Luisa de' Medici wrote to her uncle that she was looking forward to receiving some panpepato 'for spicy things are much liked in this country'.[20] The only alteration I have made to Christine McFadden's recipe is the use of figs rather than sultanas, purely because I adore dried figs. A little of this confection goes a long way so I serve it as a sweetmeat cut into small pieces rather than a dessert.

Ingredients
110 g / 4 oz soft, dried figs
110 g / 4 oz walnuts
110 g / 4 oz blanched hazelnuts
110 g / 4 oz blanched almonds
85 g / 3 oz candied mixed peel
1 tbsp black peppercorns
200 g / 7 oz runny honey
110 g / 4 oz plain chocolate
30 g / 1 oz unsalted butter
80 g / 3 oz caster sugar
30 g / 1 oz unsweetened cocoa powder
1 tsp ground cinnamon
½ tsp ground nutmeg
¼ tsp ground cloves
100 ml / 3 ½ fl oz hot water
150–175 g / 5–6 oz plain flour

Method
1. Preheat the oven to 170 °C. Line an 18 cm / 7 in square tin with foil-backed baking paper (or just plain foil if you don't have this type in your cupboard).
2. Grind the black peppercorns using a pestle and mortar or spice

grinder. The end result doesn't need to be super fine.

3. Coarsely chop the dried figs and nuts.

4. Warm the honey over a gentle heat in a large saucepan then add in the chocolate, butter and caster sugar, stirring until the chocolate has melted. Add the cocoa, pepper and spices along with the chopped fruit and nuts and mixed peel.

5. The mixture will be quite stiff at this stage so slacken it by adding the hot water. Sprinkle on the flour a little at a time, stirring well after each addition. You should only need 150 g / 5 oz but add a little more if the mixture seems too loose.

6. Spoon the mixture into the prepared tin. Smooth down the surface then bake for 20–25 minutes or until firm. Allow to cool completely in the tin before cutting into small squares. The size is really up to you but I divide this cake into 64 pieces and serve it alongside coffee or tea after dinner.

Miscellaneous Recipes

Basic Icing

Gum Tragacanth is a dried, odourless and tasteless resin which makes this icing set firmly, but also enables it to retain its glossy finish. It is easy enough to source online, but if you prefer not to use it feel free to omit it, although you may need slightly less liquid. Your icing will be softer when set but will still taste as good.

Ingredients
100 g / 4 oz icing sugar
½ tsp gum tragacanth
2–3 tbsp water or lemon juice

Method
1. Sieve the icing sugar and gum tragacanth into a bowl. Stir in two tablespoons of water to make a fairly runny icing (add more water if required to make the right consistency). In most cases this icing can be brushed over the top of each biscuit as soon as they come out of the oven. Give the biscuits a second coating if you want a thicker finish to the icing.

Lebkuchen Spice Mix

Ingredients
4 tsp ground cinnamon
1 ½ tsp ground cloves
1 ½ tsp ground cardamom
1 tsp ground ginger
1 tsp ground nutmeg
½ tsp ground anise
½ tsp ground white pepper

Combine all of the ingredients and use according to the recipe. Store in a jar or lidded container. This will keep for several months at least.

MEDIEVAL SPICE MIX (FINE SPICE POWDER)[1]

Ingredients
1 ½ tsp grains of paradise (*Aframomum melegueta*, a spice closely related to cardamom)
1 tsp whole cloves or ½ tsp ground cloves
10 tsp ground ginger
2 ½ tsp ground cinnamon

Use a spice grinder or a pestle and mortar to grind the grains of paradise and cloves. Mix the ground spices with the ginger and cinnamon. Use as per directed in the recipe.

QUATRE ÉPICES[2]

An indispensable spice blend to have in the kitchen. Try adding a pinch or two to a stew or even sprinkled over your roast chicken.

Ingredients
4 tsp ground white pepper
1½ tsp ground or grated nutmeg
1 tsp ground ginger
½ tsp ground cloves

Combine all of the ingredients and store in an airtight container.

SPICED ALE

Along with gingerbread, spiced ale was a popular beverage at fairs across the country. Fairs were held in all seasons so I have provided a cold and a warm version of this traditional drink. Do they go with gingerbread? Well, in a bizarre way they do, so don't dismiss the combination until you have tried it. Both recipes can be scaled up to serve more people.

TEWAHIDDLE[3]

The name was the original attraction for this recipe, though it's actually rather refreshing. To echo Dr Kitchiner's sentiments: 'Before our readers make any remarks on this Composition, we beg of them to taste it; if the materials are good, and their palate vibrates in unison with our own, they will find it one of the pleasantest beverages they ever put to their lips.'

Ingredients (Serves 1)
½ tbsp brandy
A pinch of nutmeg
A pinch of ginger
½ tsp brown sugar (or more according to taste)
A strip of pared lemon zest
300 ml / ½ pt ale, chilled

Place the brandy, spices, sugar and lemon zest in a large glass. Give them a quick stir, then top up with the cold ale. It will froth, so go easy.

MULLED ALE WITH APPLES

Barnstaple and Widecombe-in-the-Moor, both in Devon, traditionally held fairs in September. The recipe for the spiced ale served in Barnstaple was a closely guarded secret according to Mrs Maude Seldon (the ale there had a piece of toast soaked in it and was served with cheese as well as gingerbread).[4] The recipe below is attributed to Widecombe Fair.[5]

Ingredients (Serves 1)
300 ml / ½ pt ale
1 whole clove
Pinch of mixed spice
⅛ tsp ground nutmeg
¼–½ tsp granulated sugar (or more according to taste)
½ small eating apple, cored and sliced

Place all of the ingredients in a saucepan. Heat slowly until hot but do not allow to boil. Strain into a mug or tankard then serve with a couple of slices of apple floating on top.

Acknowledgements

First Catch Your Gingerbread was written during the Covid-19 crisis of 2020 at a time when travel both within the UK and beyond our borders was impossible. I have been fortunate in being able to vicariously experience the gingerbreads of other nations through the generosity of fellow food historians, writers and museum curators both at home and abroad who have shared their expertise in this field as well as their recipes.

Food writer and culinary historian Sharon Hudgins has been a guiding light throughout my gingerbread journey. She has been magnanimous in helping me gain a better understanding of European gingerbreads as well as Mongolian food culture. Her Biberli Bars have a particular soft spot in my affections as I have such fond memories of Switzerland myself.

Thanks to an introduction by Ami Hovstadius to Dr Richard Tellström and Karsten Thurfjell I was able to benefit from their knowledge of the history of gingerbread in Sweden. I am especially grateful to fellow gingerbread enthusiast Maud Ekblad (see www. historiehuset.se) for her translations of Cajsa Warg's recipes.

The island nations of the Caribbean have played a critical role in the creation of modern gingerbread. Without the sugar industry, and I am sad to say the slave trade, the treacle laden gingerbreads we are so familiar with in Britain would not exist. I am indebted to Catherine Ross and Lynda-Louise Burrell of Museumand, the National Caribbean History Museum, for introducing me to the history of the Toto cake (and sharing their delicious recipe too), and also Judy Bastyra for her insights into Caribbean culture.

The research and extensive recipe development required for this project was made possible by a grant from the Guild of Food Writers Fellowship Fund. In particular I would like to thank Clarissa Hyman for her encouragement over the years and the support of my colleagues on the Guild's committee (especially Jonathan Woods for his kind words). Having joined the Guild a number of years ago I am always struck by how willing its members are to share their expertise with fellow food writers. I am grateful for the encouragement I have received from Guild members Bee Farrell, Emma Kay and Regula Ysewijn, as well as Christine McFadden and Marlena Spieler who kindly consented to me using their recipes for Panpepato and *Lekach* respectively. A special mention also needs to be made to Dr Kim Salmons of St Mary's University for reminding me of Jude Fawley's gingerbread house building skills and reinvigorating my passion for Thomas Hardy.

While I have long been a gingerbread addict I spent many of my younger years living in Horsham, West Sussex in ignorance of the town's gingerbread history. Both Lesley Ward of Horsham Gingerbread and Jeremy Knight, Museum & Heritage Officer for Horsham Museum, assisted me in discovering more about my home town's sweet history and the heritage of gingerbread bakers and vendors in general. My quest to explore the history of gingerbread was largely inspired by the collection of moulds on display at Horsham Museum (on loan from Brighton Museum and Art Gallery).

As a writer it is one thing to have an idea begging to be written in the inner recesses of your mind, it is another thing entirely to find a publisher who agrees with you. I will be eternally grateful to my publisher Catheryn Kilgarriff for recognising the potential of both myself and the subject. I am also indebted to Brendan King for his first class editing.

Without the support and willingness to eat copious amounts of gingerbread of my husband Neil (also known as Billy) and my sons Charlie and Alex this book would never have come to fruition. I'm also grateful to my brother Dr Anthony Farrant and his partner Dr Claudia Capancioni for helping me source academic papers once the British Library had closed its doors, and to my friends and neighbours who have also courageously munched their way through batches of the brown stuff (even when some of the more historic reproductions have been a little odd). Hats off to Helen Dando from Cook the Books in Lewes for introducing me to the wonders of spätzle, sauerkraut and cheese!

Notes

Introduction

1 *Love's Labour's Lost* (1598), Act V. Scene I.
2 Cradock (1965), p. 133. In the follow up to this cookbook, *The Sociable Cook's Book* (1967), Fanny reveals the gingerbread's nickname was 'Night Starvation…because people will come downstairs and raid the tin' (p. 292).
3 Davidson (2005), p. 339.
4 *Pepparkakor* is a type of Swedish gingerbread biscuit.
5 Freeman (1996), p. 217.
6 Hudgins (2019), p. 49.

Chapter One

1 Mayor (2009), pp. 1-2. Mithridates ruled Pontus, a kingdom situated on the Black Sea in what is now North Eastern Turkey, from 120 BCE until 63 BCE.
2 Ibid, pp. 240-1. Mayor says that modern science has shown some substances, such as garlic, can neutralise poisons like arsenic in the bloodstream, and that charcoal can filter and absorb certain toxins.
3 Dalby (1996), p. 138 and p. 250. Pliny lists around fifty ingredients for mithridatium, while Roman medical writer Celsus (c. 25 BCE – c. 50 AD) lists only thirty-eight.
4 Mayor (2009), p. 240.
5 Ibid, pp. 349-50. Mayor concludes that if Mithridates had taken the full dose of poison rather than sharing it with his daughters his suicide attempt would have been successful.
6 Turner (2005), pp. 165-6.
7 Dalby (1996), p. 137.
8 Ibid, p. 191.
9 Grainger (2006), p. 10-11. Dalby and Grainger (2003) note that pepper was a popular seasoning in sweet dishes, p. 69.
10 Dalby (2000), pp. 194-5.
11 Turner (2005), see Chapter 2, pp. 61-109.
12 Dalby (2000), pp. 194-5; Turner (2005), see Chapter 2, pp. 61-109.
13 Dalby (2000), pp. 194-5.
14 Turner (2005), see Chapter 2, pp. 61-109.; Dalby (2000), pp. 194-5.
15 Simoons (1991), Chapter 12, pp. 370-375.
16 Dalby (2000), p. 181. According to Ptolemy, ginger was grown in Sri Lanka, although the Romans also believed it grew in modern day Eritrea and Ethiopia (where it grows today). Simoons (1991) believes ginger was carried west from India to Africa by Arab traders, eventually leading to Zanzibar becoming a major centre of the spice trade by the tenth century AD.
17 Simoons (1991), Chapter 12, pp. 370-5. Ginger is sometimes suggested as a substitute for laser or silphium in modern adaptations of Roman recipes, such as those in *The Roman Cookery of Apicius* (1993), p. xxiv by John Edwards.
18 Dalby (1996), p. 138.
19 Simoons (1991), Chapter 12, pp. 370-5.
20 Goldstein (2015), p. 12. The Greeks and Romans knew of cane sugar from India but it was exceedingly rare and extortionately expensive. Its only use would have been medicinal.

21 Alcock (2006), p. 84. Beekeeping began in Egypt in the third millennium BCE, when honey could be used to pay taxes and wages.

22 Dalby (2000), pp. 141-2; Goldstein (2015), p. 12.

23 Grainger and Grocock (2006), see 'A Glossary To *Apicius*', *Apicius*, 7.11.4. *Alica* is similar to semolina and comes from a type of emmer groat.

24 Edwards (1993), p. 172. In their Introduction to *Apicius*, Grainger and Grocock (2006) suggest the omission of cakes could be because patisserie goods were a completely different genre with bakers and cooks performing completely different functions.

25 Goldstein (2015), p. 12

26 Dalby (1996), p. 23.

27 Goldstein (2015), p. 12.

28 Grant (2008), p. 38.

29 Dalby (1996), p. 126. Chauney (1978) has suggested that ancient honey cakes were not dissimilar to modern-day Greek *loukoumades*, doughnuts soaked in a honey syrup (p. 15).

30 Dalby and Grainger (2003), p. 95. In Roman times *placenta* had nothing to do with afterbirth. The word was adopted for this meaning by a seventeenth-century scientist.

31 Dalby (1996) p. 91; Dalby and Grainger (2003), p. 95.

32 Wilkins and Hill (2006) suggest this question is answered by looking at the context in which the cakes are described (pp. 127-130).

33 Athenaeus (1854), p. 1030.

34 Ibid, p. 1031.

35 Alcock (2009), pp. 107-8.

36 Ibid, p. 105. Alcock adds: 'Modern experiments have shown that when dough, placed in a pan filled with honey, was baked in an oven, the dough absorbed the honey, thus making a delicious sweet bread, somewhat akin to rum baba.'

37 Humble (2010), Chapter 1.

38 Chauney (1978), p. 15.

39 Ibid, p. 16. In her book on the history of Spanish food, *Delicioso* (2019), Maria José Sevilla describes how Roman soldiers carried their own supply of grain which could be ground and made into *panis militaris*, 'a coarse, indigestible bread', but no mention is made honey or spices being added to make this bread more palatable (p. 23).

40 Ibid, p.16.

41 Simoons (1991), Chapter 12, pp. 376-9.

42 Ibid.

43 Ibid. One emperor granted a monthly supply of white honey, a medicine believed to confer immortality, to noted physician T'ao Hung-ching (AD 452-536) on his retirement.

44 Schafer (1977), p. 117.

45 Ibid, p. 109.

46 Ibid, p. 118.

47 Leppman (2005), p. 33.

48 Mayor (2009), p. 244. Foreigners dressed in Persian clothing are depicted offering mithridatium pills to the emperor in Chinese illustrated manuscripts.

49 Mayor (2009), p.244. Elaborate jars were used to store the elixir which often depicted the life of Mithridates, and apothecaries across Europe had to openly display the precious ingredients used to concoct mithridatium. See also Turner (2005), p. 112. The medieval aristocracy had good reason to seek an antidote to poison. There are many examples of nobles and even kings being killed by poison. Louis IV (ruled 936-954) was, somewhat ironically, poisoned by a pepper sauce.

Chapter Two

1 Toussaint-Samat (2008), p. 496. The *Regimen sanitatis Salernitanum* was a set of rules relating to diet and healthy written in the thirteenth century by the medical school in Salerno.

2 Turner (2005), pp. 212-3.

3 Hess (1995), pp. 342-3. The formula is taken from *Livres des Simples Medicines* which itself is purported to be a thirteenth-century translation of an earlier work on pharmocopoeia.

4 Ibid, p. 343.

5 Turner (2005), p.112. Alexandre Dumas was one of the authors who supported the theory of spices being brought back to Europe by the Crusaders.

6 Chauney (1978), p. 16; Toussaint-Samat (2008), p. 32.

7 I am indebted to Sharon Hudgins for this insight into Mongolian food and diet.

8 Banham (2004), pp. 29-42; Hagen (2006).

9 Hieatt (1998), pp. 101-116.

10 Banham (2004), p. 29-42; Hagen (2006).

11 Banham (2004), p. 29-42

12 Hagen (2006), p.180. Cubebs, sometimes referred to as tailed pepper, are related to the pepper family although their flavour is more akin to allspice (unheard of during the medieval period). Although they have a hot, spicy flavour Grains of Paradise are actually related to cardamom. Both cubebs and grains of paradise were popular spices during the middle ages but gradually fell out of favour.

13 Turner (2005), p. 115.

14 Brears (2012), p. 343. Initially the quantities of sugar imported into Britain were small but by the late thirteenth century this had increased to several tons. Sugar would gradually shift from being viewed as a spice to a relatively commonplace ingredient.

15 Loud (2019). Arnold, Abbot of the Monastery of St John at Lübeck was one of the most important chroniclers of the thirteenth century. His accounts cover the years 1172–1209 and includes the German Crusade of 1197-8 (the third crusade). It was published soon after the Benedictine's death around 1214. In his original transcript the 'honeyed bread' is described as '*panis mellitos*'. There is no mention of spices in this bread. However, in another section of the Chronicles describing the pilgrimage of Duke Henry, the Lion of Saxony, the duke is forced to abandon his wagons of supplies when they become bogged down in a swamp leaving behind 'all sorts of carefully prepared delicacies flavoured with spices.'

16 Hagen (2006), p. 416.

17 Ibid. Banham (2004) believes there is a lack of evidence to suggest honey was used as a sweetener for cakes or fine breads. Honey was primarily used to make mead, which was associated with feasting (p. 41).

18 Goldstein (2015), p. 584. Perhaps this is the source of the mysterious honey bread consumed by Genghis Khan's troops?

19 Visit Toruń website, http://www.visittorun.pl/237,l2.html

20 Also known as The Union King

21 Eskilsson (2016). Unfortunately no record has been left of whether this cure worked or not.

22 Chauney (1978), p. 15.

23 Dumas (1988), p. 133. Dumas believed this was merely 'conjecture based solely on the cruel and vindictive character of the prince'.

24 Ibid.

25 Austin (1888) Harlian MS. 279, p. 35.

26 Wilson (1991), p. 247 and p. 305. Although Wilson believes the omission of ginger to be an oversight on the part of the original author. Sanders also known as Red Sandalwood was

used as a food colouring in medieval and renaissance food. Dissolved in alcohol it makes a scarlet colour. Dorothy Hartley says this use of sanders helped make the gingerbread resemble cuir bouilli armour (literally boiled leather). It was leather that had been treated so that it became tough and rigid, as well as able to hold moulded decoration.

27 Brears (2012), p. 405.

28 Hieatt (1998), p. 101-116.

29 Ibid.

30 Brears (2012), p. 344.

31 Brears (2012), p. 344; Colquhoun (2007), p. 68.

32 Brears (2012), p. 344. Comfits are 'strongly-flavoured seeds repeatedly coated in layers of dried [sugar] syrup until they resembled small white peas.

33 Brears (2012), p. 344. Spiced wine sweetened with honey and no doubt a throw back to the scented wines served in Ancient Rome. It is interesting to note that this beverage is now being served after dinner rather than before as the Greeks and Romans had done.

34 Brears (2012), p. 344.

35 Ibid. Gingerbread 'fairings' have long been associated with fairs like the Nottingham Goose Fair which has been held since the late thirteenth century. Presumably somebody outside of the grand house kitchens was making these treats to sell to the general public.

36 Toussaint-Samat (2007), p. 496.

37 Entry on 'Ginger', Buttes (1599).

38 Definition in John Baret's *An Alvearie, or Triple Dictionarie* (1574).

39 Turner (2005), p. 215. Turner adds 'The spicer was one of several libidinous professions born under the sign of Venus, along with singers, jewellers, music lovers and tailors of women's clothing…The spice trade was driven not so much by the palate as by the gullet and the loins.'

40 Ibid.

41 Brears (2015), p. 519.

42 Ibid; Mennell (1996), pp. 86-87. Henry VIII had banqueting rooms at Hampton Court, Greenwich and Nonsuch Palace. Perhaps most famous of all royal banqueting rooms is Banqueting House built in 1622 for James I (it replaced an earlier sixteenth-century structure which burned down in 1619).

43 Philip Stubbes, *The Anatomie of Abuses* (1583), quoted in *The Plays of Philip Massinger* (ed.) W. Gifford, Vol II, London: G. & W. Nicol, 1813, p. 13.

44 Brears (2015), p. 529.

45 Ibid, p. 530.

46 Dawson (1596/7), p. 117.

47 Murrell (1621), Number 31.

48 Gum Tragacanth. This is an odourless paste which is added to icing and marzipan to help them harden but the finish remain glossy.

49 Plat (1617). See recipe 60. That Plat uses a parsnip-based cake for his white gingerbread adds weight to the claim that Montpellier's *gingibrati* is a forerunner of Tudor-style gingerbread.

50 Ibid. See recipe 22.

51 A manchet was a loaf of fine white bread. Elizabeth David (1977, p. 331) explains that a manchet loaf could weigh anywhere between 175 g and 450 g. 'The manchet was hardly more than a large roll and not considered a sufficient allowance of bread for one person at one meal.'

52 'A small pot with a handle and three feet,' *Collins English Dictionary*.

53 I have successfully made a version of this in my own kitchen, using a scaled down recipe. In my opinion liquorice gives it a rather unpleasant flavour, but then I'm not a fan of liquorice so others may beg to differ.

54 Mennell (1996), p. 84.

55 *Elinor Fettiplace's Receipt Book* (1986) edited by Hilary Spurling is a prime example. Sadly it does not include any gingerbread recipes but is well worth reading nevertheless.

56 Marmalades in the sixteenth and seventeenth century tended to be thick fruit pastes (a bit like a fruit pastel) rather than spreads like jam. Typically, they would be made from Seville oranges or quinces. The word is actually derived from marmelo, the Portuguese for quince.

57 Brears (2015), p. 531. Gingerbread must have been made outside the home as it was possible to buy it at fairs.

58 Chauney (1978), pp. 14-32; Scharfenberg (1991), p. 357. The Nuremberg guild for commercial gingerbread makers was called the *Lebküchler* after the cities famous *Lebküchen* gingerbread. In London there was a Guild of Pepperers formed in 1180 to maintain standards for the purity of spices and for the setting of certain weights and measures. This Guild would eventually become the Worshipful Company of Grocers although its crest still contains nine cloves as a reminder of the organisation's roots. The closest thing to a gingerbread guild would be the Worshipful Company of Bakers which was established around the same time as the Guild of Pepperers.

59 Chauney (1978), p. 18. The quantities here seem unbelievably big but commercial bakers have always made dough in bulk. In this instance the apprentice is making three twenty pound loaves of *pain d'épice* from a master batch weighing two hundred pounds. My assumption is that customers would buy a portion of these massive slabs of *pain d'épice* rather than the whole thing. In order to complete his test the apprentice had to turn the remaining dough into several different styles of gingerbread according to their masters desire. Henri IV does not provide any further details of what forms these various sorts of gingerbread should take but presumably the apprentice would have been expected to produce some kind of moulded gingerbread in addition to the pavés.

60 Pagrach-Chandra (2002).

61 Mennell (1996), p. 102.

62 Jane Grigson (1992), p. 342. Grigson describes this type of confection as 'slightly rubbery' and believes it is 'inadequate and misleading' to call it gingerbread, although she concedes there may be a relationship between all gingerbreads no matter where they originate.

63 Drummond and Wilbraham (1991), p. 87; Brears (2015), p. 130.

64 Johnson (1785), see definition of 'Oats'.

65 Glasse (1747), for example Oatmeal Hasty-Pudding on page 80. C. Anne Wilson (1991, p. 200) has noted that even in southern England, oatmeal was a popular thickener for pottages and frequently appeared in household and monastic accounts.

66 *The Closet of the Eminently Learned Sir Kenelm Digbie, Knight* (1669) includes over 100 recipes for mead and metheglin (both made from copious amounts of honey), an attempt perhaps to reignite the popularity these beverages enjoyed among our Anglo Saxon ancestors?

67 Simmons and Goodwin (1983), p. 52.

Chapter Three

1 Sohn (2019) According to visitnorthwest.com, the town of Macclesfield is nicknamed 'treacle town'. Legend has it that a cart of treacle overturned in the town centuries ago resulting in a scramble by the townsfolk to scoop up the sticky cargo from the cobbles. Macclesfield still hosts a monthly Treacle Market where local food producers sell their wares (although presumably the treacle sold in the town today comes in tins from the supermarket).

2 Ibid.

3 Hess (1995), p. 413. She argues that original Venetian treacle was likely made with heavy honey.

NOTES

4   Wilson (1991).pp. 304-5.

5   Mintz (1986), pp. 28-29.

6   Wilson (1991), p. 305; Hess (1995), p. 413.

7   Collingham (2017), p. 46.

8   Ibid, p. 52. By 1700 more than a third of England's imports were tropical groceries like sugar, coffee and tobacco.

9   Ibid, p. 51.

10 Mintz (1986), p. 43.

11 Ibid, p. 45.

12 Collingham (2017), p. 52.

13 Ibid, p. 54.

14 Mintz (1986), p. 35.

15 Wilson (1991), p. 305.

16 May (2012), p. 275.

17 Wilson (1991), p. 305; Hess (1995), p. 200.

18 Nott (1723), p. 219.

19 Carter (1730).

20 Ibid. Nutmeg, mace and cinnamon were still frequently used. Ginger appears too, but perhaps with not so much frequency. Pepper is almost entirely absent.

21 Drummond and Wilbraham (1991), p. 112.

22 Ibid. In his praise for English puddings, the French writer and traveller François Misson (1650–1722) would declare: 'Blessed be he that invented the pudding, for it is a Manna that hits the Palates of all Sortes of People'. See M. Misson's *Memoirs and Observations in His Travels Over England*, translated by Mr Ozell, London: Browne, Bell & Darby, 1710, p. 315.

23 *The Diary of Samuel Pepys*, entry for 28 February 1668. Cocoa beans were ground (sometimes with spices) and pressed into cakes which would be pounded then boiled in water to make a chocolate drink.

24 Mintz (1986), p. 122.

25 Collingham (2017), p. 54.

26 Ibid, p. 89.

27 Ibid. Treacle was often served as an accompaniment to boiled pudding as well as being included as an ingredient when making them.

28 Rundell (1812), p. 241.

29 Having looked at several recipes from the same period by 'drops' I assume Rundell means walnut size balls, which authors like Glasse (1747) and Kitchiner (1817) refer to as 'gingerbread nuts'.

30 Drummond and Wilbraham (1991), p. 269; Brears (1997), p.59

31 Glasse, a Southerner born and bred, includes several oatmeal recipes in *The Art of Cookery Made Plain and Easy* (1747), including one for Oatmeal Hasty Pudding (p. 80). She suggests serving her version with wine and sugar, ale and sugar or cream.

32 Brears (1997), p. 61.

33 Drummond and Wilbraham (1991), p. 332

34 W.E.A. (1997), p. 79.

35 Grigson (1993), p. 340.

36 Grigson (1993), p. 341. The original recipe is kept in a bank vault and has been trademarked.

37 Shepherd (2020). The festival still takes place every year in the village but in more recent times has been moved to mid-July.

38 Byerly and Timbs (1828) p. 295; The Morris Ring (2020). Although young women appear

to have been the original rush bearers The Morris Ring website informs us that their role was largely replaced by male rush-cart bearers in the 1800s. In fact by the middle of the nineteenth century any involvement by women in the rush bearing ceremony was considered controversial. When forty-two women helped pull the Smallbridge rushcart in 1859 the Rochdale Observer received a letter following the festival from John Ashworth, who complained: 'Those persons labouring for the redemption of mankind must be sick at heart. Never could they have conceived that young girls would be seen drawing rushcarts.'

39 The Morris Ring (2020)
40 Hartley (1999), p. 58
41 Bates (1907) p. 59. This account is of a rush-bearing in nearby Ambleside. Bates attended a similar festival in Grasmere a week later. She describes her landlady busy preparing the gingerbread for rush-bearing: 'There were five hundred squares this time, since, in addition to what would be given to the children, provision must be made for the Sunday afternoon teas throughout Grasmere. The rolling out of the dough had not grown easier with the passing of nearly half a century, and she showed us the swollen muscles of her wrist' (p. 61).
42 Kraig (2017), p. 78
43 Hess (1995), p. 7. Martha Washington was widowed in 1757 aged 25. She married George Washington, who became the first president of the United States, a couple of years later.
44 Hess (1995), p. 342.
45 Kraig (2017), p. 78.
46 Ibid, p. 94.
47 Collingham (2017), p. 139.
48 Kraig (2017), p. 75.
49 Simmons (1815), p. 52.
50 Alcott (1873), p. 94.
51 In the context of *The Picayune's Creole Cook Book* the creole cookery in question refers to that of Louisiana born of French, Spanish and African influences (although creole cookery can have a broader meaning, see *Larousse Gastronomique*, p. 325.). It is therefore no surprise that many recipes in this cookery book have French titles.
52 Picayune (2002), p. 307. By today's standards this nickname is downright offensive. However, the book was published in an age where segregation was strictly enforced in the southern States despite slavery being abolished in 1865. I wish I could say Estomac Mulâtre had fallen out of favour soon after the publication of this book, but it appears over half a century later in a reprint of Countess Morphy's *Recipes For All Nations* (1953, p. 550) originally published in the thirties.
53 Norman (1997), p. 50.
54 David (1975), p. 21. As the name suggests 'allspice' was used to fulfil the role of multiple spices leading some people to believe the ground form was in fact a mixture of several spices. I'm inclined to agree with Elizabeth David and say the only spice it reminds me of is clove.
55 Rundell (1812), p. 122.
56 Acton (1864), p. 552.
57 *Queen Victoria's Journals,* entry for 24 December 1833.
58 Ibid, entry for 24 December 1856.
59 Marshall (1888), p. 426
60 Francatelli (1883), p. 417. *The Modern Cook* was originally published in 1846.
61 Favre (1903), p. 857
62 Francatelli (1883), p. 417.
63 *Queen Victoria's Journals,* entry for 6 August 1850. The queen does not say whether her

own children had the opportunity to join in with the games.

64 Dickens (1850), p. 165.

65 Vine (1898), pp. 141-151.

66 Ibid, p. 142. Traditionally continental gingerbread doughs are left to mature for several months. From Vine's words it seems this may have been the case in Britain too, though very few British gingerbread recipes instruct the maker to leave the dough for a period of time.

67 Ibid, p. 143.

Chapter Four

1 Day (2013).

2 Chauney (1978), pp. 45-53; Pinto (1969).

3 Chauney (1978), p. 47; Pinto (1969).

4 Vine (1898); p. 143; Tuer (1897), p. 441; Pinto (1969).

5 Vine (1898), p. 143.

6 Pinto (1969).

7 Toomre (1998), p. 428; Goldstein (2020), pp. 280-1. Elizabeth I is believed to have given her guests gingerbreads moulded in their likeness (Hildebrand (2017), p. 189).

8 Vine (1898), p. 143.

9 Tuer (1897) p. 441.

10 Riley (2001), p. 193.

11 Pinto (1969).

12 These could also be brightly coloured. Vine (1898) compares them to hundreds and thousands.

13 Vine (1898), p. 144.

14 Dodge (1875), p. 448.

15 There are variations of this tale across Europe. In Russia the main character is a ball of dough called 'Kolobok'. In Germany he is a pancake and in Hungary a dumpling.

16 Hoffmann (1993), p. 87.

17 Candlin (1987); Day (2013).

18 Tuer (1897), p. 445.

19 Mayhew (1851), p. 200.

20 Lancaster (1898), p. 81

21 Frazer (1922), p. 490.

22 Frazer (1922). In the Roman town of Aricia, sixteen miles south east of Rome, a special loaf called *maniae* was made, shaped like a man. Frazer questions the suggestion that these dough effigies were a type of sacramental bread eaten by worshippers to replace an earlier practice of human sacrifice, made to appease the ghosts of the dead at the festival of the Compitalia. Over time, human sacrifices seem to have been replaced by woollen effigies of each household member, the hope being that the ghosts would carry off the effigies rather than the living. The connection between the votive offerings and the man-shaped loaves appears to have come about because the name of the latter was also that of the goddess of the dead, Mania (or Manea) being the mother of ghosts and spirits in Roman mythology.

23 Crane (1999), p. 505.

24 The ancient Britons of Wales had pushed back against invaders from the Anglo-Saxon era onwards with varying degrees of success but the country was eventually annexed by England in the thirteenth century. Even after the Statute of Rhuddlan (which introduced English common law to Wales and provided a framework for the governance of the principality), was passed in 1284 Wales retained its own culture and language. In

the following years there were a several rebellions resulting in the Penal Laws against Wales (1402) which prohibited the Welsh from carrying arms, holding office and from living in fortified towns. The Laws in Wales Acts 1535-1542 during the reign of Henry VIII would see the Welsh language and law being banned from the political, legal and educational systems. It is probably no wonder then that the Welsh were, and continue to be, so protective of their heritage and language.

25 *The Diary of Samuel Pepys*, entry for 1 March 1666.

26 Brand (1853), p. 105

27 Smith (1831), p. 140.

28 Sharpe (1846) p. 302. The article goes onto say the skewer was inserted so that children had something to hold onto. The description of 'white "parlement"' implies the figures may have been made from almond paste (rather like marchpane) or possibly a paler, sugar-based gingerbread like those produced in Grantham, Lincolnshire. I would still suggest the innocence of the figure's symbolism is open to debate depending on your nationality. Certainly, when I have mentioned this practice to Welsh friends they have found the very idea of hanging effigies of straw or the skewering of gingerbread Welshmen quite offensive.

29 Adolphe Thiers, the second elected president of France (1871-73) reputedly said 'No man can truly call himself great until seen in gingerbread', quoted by Webb (2011).

30 Chauney (1978), pp. 54-5; Kroen (2000), pp. 222-3. Billy-Baider was not the only person to poke fun at the king in this manner. There are numerous examples of Charles X being depicted as a priest in caricatures and in song from this period. There was a widespread belief during the Restoration in France that the Catholic Church, with the support of the King, was trying to regain some of the power it had enjoyed prior to the revolution.

31 Petch (2009).

32 Hilton (2013).

33 Bondeson (1992), pp. 217-21. The women depicted on the biscuits were the Chulkhurst twins, Mary and Eliza. The popular legend states they were born to wealthy parents in 1100 joined at the hip (some accounts say they were joined at the shoulder too). When they died thirty-four years later they bequeathed some land to the church wardens stipulating the rent should be used to provide an annual dole for the poor of the parish. Although the basic biscuits handed out are not made from gingerbread, Tuer has noted that it was not uncommon for old designs to be appropriated for new uses. It is feasible that the gingerbread mould held in the MERL collection could have been used as the basis of the Biddenden Maids.

34 Marchant (1888), p. 108.

35 White (1968), p. 328. White refers to gingerbread husbands as being a Hampshire speciality while Mason and Brown (1999), mention gingerbread wives in reference to the Barnstaple fair in Devon (p. 253).

36 Hughes (2018).

37 White (1968), p. 328.

38 Keats (2003), p. 179. The reference to gingerbread appears in 'Over the Hill and Over the Dale': 'Over the hill and over the dale, / And over the bourn to Dawlish / Where gingerbread wives have a scanty sale, / And gingerbread nuts are smallish.'

39 Newbery (2013), p. 167.

40 Quoted in the *Taunton Courier and Western Advertiser*, 12 June 1929.

41 Gately (2010). In previous eras the heart shape had different meanings. The Greeks used the symbol to depict ivy or vine leaves the symbols of constancy and regeneration. The Celts used a similar symbol to represent eternity although the corresponding Viking valknut design signified the power of Odin to induce battle-madness in warriors.

42 Ibid. To the common man the heart symbol could still have an erotic meaning evoking breasts, buttocks and genitalia. 'In Shakespearean England, for instance, the plackett – a heart-shaped apron for women with a pocket for the hands below the waist was also the slang name for a vagina.'

43 Hörandner (1982), p. 233. Today we think of cupid as being an adorable chubby cherub who sends love from the gods by means of shooting arrows through our hearts. However, in ancient times these cute archers could also use their arrows to deliver plague.

44 Gately (2010). Florence White (1968) mentions Gingerbread Valentines as being a particular delicacy of Bath (p. 347).

45 Cox (2016).

46 In Ben Jonson's play *Bartholomew Fair*, the esquire Bartholomew Cokes wants to give his wedding guests gingerbread gloves as part of the banquet, a sweet course that used to be served at the close of a feast, claiming 'O me! what a device will there be, to make 'em eat their fingers' ends!' (p. 217).

47 Hörandner (1982), p. 234.

48 lectar.com (2020). Both *lect* and *licitars* are consistently referred to as gingerbreads in Slovenia and Croatia despite the absence of spice in the recipes I have seen which is why I have included them in this section. Evidently, in 2010, UNESCO added the Gingerbread craft from Northern Croatia to the "Representative List of the Intangible Cultural Heritage" for Croatian culture.

49 Nederlands Bakkerij Museum (2020); Pagrach-Chandra (2002). Seventeenth and eighteenth century recipes suggest *hylikmaker* were similar in taste and texture to speculaas although the custom of giving crust and end pieces to suit suggests types of spice loaf may have been used instead.

50 lectar.com (2020). At the gingerbread museum in Radovljica, located in a medieval building, you can watch the *lects* being made from the mixing of the honey dough right through to the decoration, just as they have been made since at least 1766.

51 Hörandner (1982). According to safefood.eu the concern over food colourants is far from a modern preoccupation. A law was passed in France in 1574 that made it illegal to add colourings to pastries and in Germany you could be burned for using saffron as a colourant from 1531 (one suspects that was more due to the spice's value rather than any danger it could pose to health). It was Frederick Accum in 1820 who drew the world's attention to the perils of colouring food with substances like red lead, verdigris and blue vitriol. See https://www.safefood.eu/Food-Colour-Resource/History.aspx

52 Nicholls (2014).

53 Ibid.

54 Chauney (1978), p. 54.

55 Nicholls (2014).

56 Chauney (1978), p. 54.

57 Lebleu (2016)

58 Ibid. Sadly the Austrian giraffe died eight months after she arrived, which makes the survival of gingerbread moulds and cakes so surprising. King George IV of England also received a giraffe in 1827 but she died in October 1829. Fortunately, Zarafa fared much better living until 1845.

59 Petty (1993), p. 101

60 Goldstein (2020), pp. 280-1

61 Toomre (1998), p. 428

62 Mayhew (1851), p. 153-212

NOTES

63 Horsham Museum's impressive collection of gingerbread moulds is on loan from the Brighton Museum and Art Gallery.

64 Tuer (1897), pp. 446-7. A makeweight is something added to the scales to make up a required weight. In the instance here it was given as a freebie to reliable customers. Tuer does not provide any further explanation on what this means. Was the customer who received it a servant perhaps with ideas above their station or perhaps a nagging wife?

65 Mayhew (1851), p. 200

66 Baxter (2018). A trouser-wearing chicken was depicted in a doodle by an eighteenth century schoolboy Richard Beale alongside his maths equations (his book also contains lovely doodles of the family's dog). Archivists at the Museum of English Rural Life, which holds the Beale family diaries, have pondered why the thirteen year old would include such an odd image. Perhaps it was a depiction of his favourite gingerbread fairing?

67 Mayhew (1851), p. 200. In this case the white gingerbread was made with sugar rather than treacle. At the Nottingham Goose Fair you could buy candy cockerels on a stick as recently as 2019 (although minus the trousers). They had been made by the same family since 1872 but look like they may disappear after Ray Brooks, the grandson of the original manufacturer, announced his retirement at the age of 89.

68 Chauney (1978), p. 67.

69 Reader (2011), p. 20.

70 Christiani (1900).

71 Grimm (1920), p. 104.

72 Avey (2013)

73 Hildebrand (2017), p. 189.

74 Turner (2005), p. 149. Unfortunately, the publishers have not specified Turner's exact source and I was unable to find any further information about this fabulous structure.

75 Anon (1968). *The Land of Cockaygne* was probably compiled in Ireland in the first half of the fourteenth century, possibly by a Franciscan friar, for amusement. The poem is followed by a long drinking song indicating perhaps that a monk's life was not quite as austere as we might suppose.

76 Grimm (1920), p. 104.

77 Alcock (2001), p. 12. Given the turbulent times they were living in the Grimm brothers, Jacob and Wilhelm, were keen to preserve their heritage and their homeland's identity. They believed one of the best ways to do this was to record German folk tales in order to capture the spirit and values of German culture. Alcock points out this was 'linked directly to the cult of emerging German nationalism.'

78 Alcock (2001), p. 15. Hansel and Gretel may in fact be a variation of the story of Nennillo and Nennella written by Giambattista Basile in the seventeenth century. The protagonists in this story are also a brother and sister abandoned in the woods by their father and step mother. Basile's tale is even more fantastical involving a prince, pirates and a giant fish but crucially no edible houses.

79 Hörandner (1982), p. 239.

80 Alcock (2001), p.18.

81 Hörandner (1982), p. 239.

82 Todorov (2019)

83 Hardy (1985), pp. 382-3

84 Scharfenberg (1991), p. 349.

85 Prior (1795), p. 464.

86 Brontë (1922), p. 27. Given that Mr Brocklehurst is usually portrayed as being a harsh and unjust school master, one can safely assume that the boy he is referring to is too scared to declare a preference for a biscuit over reciting a psalm. The boy's outward devotion is rewarded as he is given 'two nuts in recompense for his infant piety', so perhaps the child has the right idea after all.

87 Tuer (1897), pp. 4-5; Riley (2001), p. 193

88 Tuer (1897), p. 439. In truth the hornbook would probably be better classified as one of the gingerbread toys discussed by Mayhew in his Labour of London (1861) as their true educational merits are debatable.

89 Tuer (1897) p 439. Hone wrote quite a bit on the subject of hornbooks but his notes were not published until Tuer included them in his own account of the hornbook's history.

90 Pinto (1969).

91 Tuer (1897), p. 442.

92 Hartley (1999), p. 635. The explanation for *cuir bouilli* is covered in Chapter 3.

93 Hone (1826), p.585.

94 Riley (2001), 195.

95 Tuer (1897), p. 442.

96 Riley (2001), pp. 194-195; Luard (1997), p. 17

Chapter Five

1 Jonson (2000). Act II, Scene II. In Jacobean England a punk was slang for a female prostitute and a chapman was a pedlar.

2 University of Sheffield (2020). In addition to these Charter Fairs there were Prescriptive Fairs based solely on trade rather than entertainment, many of which had been operating long before the charters were in place (although a lot of these Prescriptive Fairs, such as the Nottingham Goose Fair, were eventually granted a royal charter). There were also fairs established for the hiring of agricultural staff known as Mop Fairs.

3 Farrer and Brownbill (1907), pp. 238-246

4 Hardy (1994), Chapter 1, pp. 1-14. Furmity or frumenty consists of wheat grains which have been stewed (or cree'd) in water until they swell so much they burst. It can then be eaten plain or have milk added and sweetened with honey or treacle (raisins are sometimes added too). Hardy describes this dish of 'grains of wheat as swollen as lemon pips' (p. 6) as nourishing although Florence White concedes the addition of rum makes it a 'very degenerate type' (1968, p. 365). Wife sales occurred fairly frequently in Britain particularly at fairs and markets. Source: Blakemore 22/8/2018 https://www.history.com/news/england-divorce-18th-century-wife-auction

5 Candlin (1987), p.45.

6 Comfits are sugar coated seeds.

7 White (1968), p. 320, quoting Miss M.W. Rogers of Marazion.

8 Chambers, R. (1881), p. 263.

9 Thornbury (1878), pp. 344-351. On his way to Smithfield it was the custom for the Mayor to call on the keeper of Newgate, and on horseback partake of 'a cool tankard of wine, nutmeg, and sugar'. However, this custom ceased in the early nineteenth century.

10 Thornbury (1878), pp.344-351.

11 Dickens (1905), Chapter YII, 'Greenwich Fair',

12 Ibid. At this time gingerbread nuts were small, fairly hard biscuits about the size of a walnut.

13 *Punch* (1845). Mr Caudle adopts the approach taken by many a henpecked husband claiming not to have heard his wife's tirade: "'Here,' says Caudle, "I dozed off, hearing confusedly the

words – hill – gypsies – rattles – roundabouts – swings – pink bonnet – nuts.'" p. 139.

14 Walford (1873), p. 202.

15 Chauney (1978), pp. 66-8.

16 'Parisian Gingerbread Fair', *North British Daily Mail,* 10 April 1874.

17 Huysmans (2014), p. 87.

18 Ibid, pp. 91-2.

19 Chauney (1978), p. 66-8.

20 Day (2016), Chapter 3.

21 Evelyn (2015). Diary entry for 24 January 1684, p. 121.

22 Selli (2018).

23 Day (2016), Chapter 3.

24 Ibid.

25 Thornbury (1878), pp.344-351.

26 Baggs et al (1994), pp. 269-74.

27 University of Sheffield (2020).

28 Frost (1875), p. 377.

29 University of Sheffield (2020).

30 Hone (1826).

31 Ibid.

32 Ibid. The fair lent its name to the upmarket district of Mayfair in London (Wolford, 1878).

33 Frost (1875), p. 101.

34 Richardson (1875). Catchpennies or 'cocks' contained 'fabricated stories designed for gullible people too ignorant to discern the nature of the transaction, or to buyers who were willing to be gulled of their pennies through sheer enjoyment'. This type of story has existed in one form or another since the middle ages. At the very end of the nineteenth century Mark Twain would fall victim to fake news about his own death although he is often misquoted as saying 'the rumours of my death have been greatly exaggerated'.

35 *The True Briton* (1752), p. 576. *The True Briton* certainly does not read like a catchpenny, which usually featured sensational stories with headlines like 'Young Lady Born with a Pig's Head' (Richardson 2014). *The True Briton* was more likely to discuss court cases than human deformities.

36 Indeed it would be a significant sum today equating to over £2000 in 2017. Source: National Archives.

37 Cox and Dannehl (2007). Thomas Turner kept a detailed diary of his daily routine from 1754 to 1765. There were 20 shillings to one pound.

38 Mayhew (1861), pp. 158-60.

39 Smith (1839), p. 70.

40 The South Sea Bubble refers to the speculation mania that ruined many British investors in 1720. Keen to capitalise on the rising fortunes of the South Seas Company (whose chief business was the slave trade) which had agreed to underwrite Britains debt, many people were inveigled into investing in unprofitable and bogus organisations. When the stock market collapsed some months later many investors, who ranged from the gentry to servants, were ruined. Source: https://www.britannica.com/event/South-Sea-Bubble

41 Smith (1839), p. 70.

42 Ibid.

43 Dibdin (1807), p.94. The original score was by Reeve and was published by Clementi and Co. In the pantomime *Harlequin and Oberon* it is sung by Mr Knight.

44 Hardy (1985), p. 376.

45 *Punch* (1845), p. 209.
46 Jonson (2000). Act II, Scene II.
47 Jonson (2000). Act II, Scene VI.
48 Redding (1844), p. 146.
49 Smith (1839), p. 72.

Chapter Six

1 Goldstein (2015), pp. 190-1.
2 Raffald (1784), p, 187.
3 Goldstein (2015), p. 190-1. Although candyfloss may not be great for our teeth it is actually surprisingly low in calories. A one ounce (roughly 25 g) serving typically contains 105 calories as most of the product is made of air.
4 Hartley (2012). Hartley suggests the original toffee apples may have been windfalls dipped in boiled honey toffee and concludes 'it's one of the most thoroughly old-fashioned English sweetmeats you will find, and thoroughly wholesome and pleasant and to be commended in every way' (p. 167).
5 Kaye-Smith (1916), p. 429.
6 Vesey-Fitzgerald (1955), p. 426. The Hampshire village of Broughton had been granted a charter to hold a four-day fair in 1136 providing an indication of its importance to the local economy. By 2016 the population of village was listed at 1009, presumably a shadow of its former self.
7 At the start of the Great War Britain was importing at least 60 % of its food, especially grain, and other commodities from overseas. Just 12 % of the male population were employed in agriculture at the turn of the century. At the outbreak of war in 1914 1.5 million agricultural workers were unemployed. Source: nfuonline.com
8 For information in this section I am indebted to an interview with Jeremy Knight of the Horsham Museum (June 2020).
9 Knight (2006). By 1700 there would be only one weekly market held on a Saturday.
10 Ibid. The fair began on the 18 July and if that was a Saturday, or any day up to and including the Thursday it ran till the following Saturday. If however the 18th was a Friday it ran until the following week's Saturday.
11 Burstow (1911), p. 71. The stallholders would pitch their tents and caravans in Horsham town centre for the duration of the fair.
12 'A Wealden Causerie', *West Sussex County Times*, 20 March 1942. The account comes from an obituary of Charlie Parsons who had worked for Chatfield, the confectioner as a boy. The recollections are from an anonymous friend who had known Mr Parsons for over seventy years since they were schoolboys, so probably date from around 1870 if not earlier.
13 Medwin (1847), p. 372. Shelley was born at Field Place just outside Horsham in 1792. Thomas Medwin, also from Horsham, was Shelley's cousin. He began writing the poet's biography in 1845 corresponding with family members like Shelley's son (Shelley's wife Mary refused to give Medwin any information on her husband) but it received a tepid reception from critics when it was published two years later. The 'gingerbread' letter is included as an appendix at the back of the book although the original correspondence has sadly been lost. When the Shelley fountain was unveiled in Horsham town centre in 1996 local children were given gingerbread as homage to the dead poet.
14 'A Wealden Causerie', *West Sussex County Times*, 12 May 1939. Charlie Parsons eventually became the caretaker at Horsham Town Hall. On his retirement in 1939 he recalled his

early career at Chatfields: 'It was hard work earning a living in those days. We used to sell our wares at 18 for sixpence and many people insisted on getting 40 for a shilling. When we took £1, after a hard day's work, we thought we had done exceptionally well.' He died three years after giving this interview.

15 Source: Horsham Museum. The museum has a rather splendid collection of gingerbread moulds on loan from Brighton and Hove City Council. Within the Brighton Museum's register there is a photocopy of a typed note from Mr Attree who donated the moulds to the museum providing information on Horsham's gingerbread history.

16 'A Wealden Causerie', *West Sussex County Times*, 20 March 1942. Although many of the goods produced by Chatfield were baked he classes himself as a confectioner rather than a baker. Perhaps the former conveyed more skill than the latter? Abraham's eldest son William Chatfield (1834–1916) is listed as a confectioner in the 1861 and 1881 censuses but appears to have emigrated to Australia in 1887, presumably taking his family knowledge with him. Source: https://en.geneanet.org

17 Source: Horsham Museum

18 Penshurst Place in Kent has been owned by the Sidney family since the sixteenth century. Shelley's grandfather, Sir Byshhe Shelley, married Elizabeth Sidney of Penshurst (his second wife) in 1769 and their son Sir John Shelley-Sidney was the poet's uncle, hence the family connection.

19 Kind thanks is given to Lesley Ward and Jeremy Knight for answering my questions about Horsham and its gingerbread legacy.

20 Horandner (1982), p. 239.

21 Riley (2001), p. 193.

22 Horandner (1982), p. 239.

23 Colquhoun (2008), p. 325; Lethbridge (2013), p. 150. Lethbridge points out that the number in domestic service did not drop as drastically as one might think. In 1914, 1.6 million people were in service and this had fallen to 1.2 million by 1918 (p. 145).

24 Lethbridge (2013), p. 150.

25 Humble (2005), Chapter 2, pp. 47-80

26 Ibid.

27 Ibid.

28 Byron (1915), Chapter 5, pp. 90-129.

29 Jekyll (1922), p. 120.

30 Leyel and Hartley (1927), Chapter 9, pp. 207-216. Dishes include moussaka, stuffed aubergines and a rather unusual suggestion for slowing simmering eggs in their shells in coffee and olive oil (apparently they taste like chestnuts after twelve hours). They also include a recipe for ginger cake in a later chapter.

31 White (1968), p. 9.

32 Ibid., p. 301.

33 McNeill (1974), p. 259.

34 Ministry of Food (2007), pp. 87-92.

35 Horandner (1982), p. 239.

36 Droste (2019), pp. 28-33.

37 Source: https://www.omnihotels.com/hotels/asheville-grove-park/things-to-do/upcoming-events/national-gingerbread-competition

38 Lunsford (2019). At the time of printing the largest gingerbread house was recorded in November 2013, made by the Traditions Club in Bryan, Texas. The house was 18.28 m (60 ft) long, 12.8 m (42 ft) wide and 3.07 m (10.1 ft) tall at its highest point. Source:

Guinness Book of Records.
39 Source: https://www.visitnorway.com/typically-norwegian/christmas/the-worlds-largest-gingerbread-town/
40 Source: https://www.thegingerbreadcity.com
41 Vesey-Fitzgerald (1955), p. 426.
42 Spence, Sanchez and Youssef (2019), pp. 13-33. Brandy snaps are a thin wafer-like biscuit, flavoured with ginger and often rolled into a tubular shape.
43 The Foire du Trône has also survived albeit as an immense funfair come carnival outside of the city. Having never had the opportunity to visit this fair myself I cannot say whether gingerbread is still sold there, or if it is in what quantities. Given the fate of gingerbread at British fairs my assumption would be that moulded *pain d'epice* has given way to more modern confections. Pigs are still very much associated with the fair in the form of a mascot called Troni. Source: https://www.foiredutrone.com
44 Berrington (1999).
45 Slater (2017), pp. 153-5.
46 Oyeyemi (2019), Chapter 1.
47 Lawson (2000), p. 236.
48 Oyeyemi (2019), Chapter 1.

Biscuits, Wakers & Griddle Cakes

1 Pagrach-Chandra (2002).
2 Brears (2015).
3 Ibid. If sailors or soldiers were away on campaigns for long periods they could consume as much as a pound of these bland but durable biscuits per day.
4 Pladis (2018).
5 'Ginger Nut' (2001). Presumably the analogy to a fiery vindaloo curry is due to the spicy nature of the biscuit.
6 See 'Biscuits', Huntley & Palmers Collection (www.huntleyandpalmers.org.uk). In *The Hungry Empire* Lizzie Collingham notes that Ginger Nuts could still cost as much as a labourer could earn in one day. Many of the biscuits manufactured by Huntley & Palmers during the nineteenth century were being exported. In 1874 the company boasted that 'seldom a ship sails from England that does not bear within his ribs a Reading Biscuit'. As well as Europe, Huntley & Palmers exported biscuits as far a field as China and Japan. However, its largest export market was India which accounted for 10% of the company's export trade by 1906.
7 See 'Factory Visitors Book 1892', Huntley & Palmers Collection (www.huntleyandpalmers.org.uk).
8 Glasse (1747).
9 W.E.A. (1997).
10 Kitchiner (1817). One of the most striking things about this recipe is that it provides a guide both on the temperature and the time the recipe should be cooked for, quite a rarity for similar recipes from the same era.
11 See 'Johnny Ginger Mug', Huntley & Palmers Collection (www.huntleyandpalmers.org.uk).
12 Hallam (1979).
13 White (1908).
14 Vine (1898).
15 W.E.A. (1997).
16 Kitchiner (1823).

Notes

17 Pagrach-Chandra (2002).

18 Anon (1880).

19 Unlike most Victorian curries the recipes in this book do not rely on commercial curry powder mixed with flour to produce a generic representation of this dish. While they may not be truly authentic by today's standards they are still delicious and reflect the author's openness to trying the local cuisine.

20 Kleber (1915).

21 McNeill (1974).

22 Ibid.

23 Ibid, Vine (1898)

24 Byron (1915).

25 Mason & Brown (1999).

26 Byron (1915).

27 Brears (1987).

28 Byron (1915).

29 Brears (2012).

30 W.E.A. (1997).

31 Duff (2015), Mason and Brown (1999).

32 Mason and Brown (1999).

33 For further details on Maud's work see her website (in Swedish): www.historiehuset.se

34 Grains of Paradise are sometimes referred to as Guinea Pepper or Melegueta pepper. They are actually related to cardamom rather than pepper although they do have an aromatic, peppery flavour. During the medieval period they were widely used in English cookery but today they are rarely used at all. If you know where to look they can be sourced quite easily. However, for this recipe you could substitute the grains for a quarter teaspoon of finely ground white pepper.

35 If you prefer to use pre-ground spices you will need the following quantities: 2 g ground cinnamon (this is just shy of 1 tsp); ¼ tsp ground cloves; 2 g ground cardamom; 2 g ground nutmeg; ¼ tsp white pepper

36 Pagrach-Chandra (2002).

37 Ibid.

38 Dotsch (2017).

39 Luard (1990).

40 Chauney (1978).

41 Adapted from Hazelton (1970).

42 Scharfenberg (1991).

43 Hudgins (2010).

44 Goldstein (2020).

45 Melikova (1997). In the folk tale *Baba Yaga* two children are given *pryanik* to sustain them on their journey to the witches house (which sits upon hens feet). After being set a number of impossible tasks the children use the cookies and other items of food to encourage the animals to help them escape from the witch.

46 Chamberlain (1982), p. 266.

47 Toomre (1998). Molokhovets, the Russian answer to Mrs Beeton, published her book by curious coincidence in 1861, the same year as Mrs Beeton's *Book of Household Management*. *A Gift to Young Housewives* provides a number of *pryaniki* recipes ranging from the more 'traditional' honey and rye mixture through to those made with sugar syrups or treacle.

Bread & Yeasted Cakes

1 White (1968).
2 McNeill (1974).
3 Ibid.
4 WEA (1997). The original instructions for this cake do not indicate whether the cake should be proved before baking. Like the ladies who compiled this collection of recipes I have tried mixing all the ingredients together then baking, which resulted in a very dense cake, and then proving the dough prior to adding the treacle. I felt the latter, which produced a lighter cake, was preferable so have gone with this method.
5 Ibid.
6 Hughes (2016).
7 Ibid.
8 Craig (1953). Elizabeth Craig had an acquaintance who had access to a scrap book of recipes evidently kept by Queen Victoria as a young girl. It was believed that the young Victoria had transcribed many of these recipes from much older sources (the book includes recipes dating back to the sixteenth century) and the Queen's own daughters continued to add to the book as the years went by. Craig collated these recipes (and a few 'modern' ones like this gingerbread) in a short volume called *Court Favourites* which was released shortly after Elizabeth II came to the throne.
9 Martineau (1927). Eliza Acton had previously suggested adding ginger to bread dough in her *The English Bread-Book For Domestic Use* (1857), stating on p. 163: 'When diarrhoea or other complaints of a similar nature are prevalent, this bread will be found of excellent effect, especially in travelling; far better, indeed, than many of the compounds to which people have recourse to avert disturbance of the system.'
10 Fisher (1963), pp. 80-81. Originally from *Serve It Forth*, published in 1937.
11 Bésème-Pia (2015).
12 Chauney (1978).
13 Dumas (1988).
14 Chamberlain (1982).
15 Toomre (1998).

Gingerbread Cakes

1 Freeman (1996), p.211.
2 Ibid.
3 Bésème-Pia (2015), p. 116.
4 Dickens (1984), pp. 50-51.
5 Ibid.
6 Yuzu is a very sour type of citrus cultivated in Japan, Korea and China. Its flavour has been described as being somewhere between a lemon and a lime although I think grapefruit is closer myself. The fresh fruit is hard to source in the UK but you can buy small bottles of this fragrant juice online and from some supermarkets.
7 McNeill (1974), p. 258.
8 Spry and Hume (1958), p. 816.
9 Plat (1617), No. 23 'To make dry Gingerbread'.
10 Plat (1617), No. 60 'Sweet Cakes without Spice or Sugar'.
11 Silver and gold cake recipes were popular during the Victorian period. Egg whites were used in the silver cake to maintain a pale colour and the yolks (along with a bit of turmeric) in the gold version.

Notes

12 Adapted from Pia-Bésème (2015), p. 125.
13 Pagrach-Chandra (2012).
14 Spieler (2015), p. 55.
15 Rosh Hashanah translates as the head of the year. It is considered a High Holy Day which is observed by most Jews. The sweetness of the festival is preserved by eschewing all sour or bitter foods. Apples dipped in honey are eaten to bring the promise of sweetness for the year ahead. See Spieler (2015), p. 13.
16 Marlena uses a 25 x 20 x 5cm / 10 x 8 x 2 in tin, which unfortunately I do not possess. If using this size tin the cooking time may be different.
17 Lynch (1918), p. 128.
18 Schumm (2018).
19 Schumm (2018).
20 Visit Toruń website.
21 Dearlove (2020).
22 Museumand: The National Caribbean Heritage Museum is a social history and community museum celebrating and commemorating the Caribbean contribution to the UK. As a museum 'without walls' they connect with communities across the UK, through art, music, performance and more. Museumand is dedicated to preserving Caribbean history, tangible and intangible heritage and culture in unusual ways including innovative exhibition-events, television programmes and books.
23 Dearlove (2020).
24 I have to confess to adding allspice by accident while testing this recipe but was more than happy with the end result. Feel free to omit it if you wish to stick to the original recipe.
25 I discovered this method for removing the flesh from a coconut in Mary-Anne Boermans' adaptation of Acton's coconut gingerbread recipe in *Great British Bakes* (2013), p. 112.

Savouries

1 My thanks again to Maud Ekblad for providing a translation of Cajsa's recipe.
2 Glasse (1747), p. 95. Glass suggests serving her stew on top of toasted bread. Her sauce is thickened with butter and flour.
3 The white-clawed crawfish in Britain have become an endangered species due to a plague which has ravaged crayfish population across Europe. The Signal Crayfish from North America was introduced in the 1970s to replenish our dwindling stocks (Britain used to export large numbers of crayfish to Scandinavia) but unfortunately this new variety of crayfish is a carrier of the fatal disease causing further damage to the native crayfish population. Despite the environmental concerns surrounding this alien species you still need to apply for a licence from the Environment Agency in order to capture them. Having said all this, some fishmongers can source fresh crayfish for you. Source: https://www.waterways.org.uk/news_campaigns/campaigns/invasive_species/crayfish/signal_crayfish
4 Scharfenberg (1991).
5 Amaretti biscuits are made from sweet and bitter almonds mixed with egg whites (rather like English macaroons). They can be crisp or soft. They are sometimes included in the pumpkin filling for tortelloni in Emilia-Romagna in Northern Italy. (Riley (2007), pp. 13-14).
6 There are legions of recipes for pasta. After attending one of her cookery classes many years ago I always use this one from food writer and chef Ursula Ferrigno.
7 Ben Gunn on his first encounter with Jim Hawkins, in Robert Louis Stevenson's *Treasure Island* (1883).
8 Glasse (1747).

Desserts & Sweetmeats

1 Family Circle (1990), p. 71.
2 Grainger and Grocock (2006).
3 Grant (2008), p. 144. Grant uses this method for his honey cake called *Enkhytoi* which comes from Lydia in Western Turkey. His recipe is inspired by a quote from *The Deipnosophists* by Athenaeus.
4 Grainger (2006), p. 17.
5 Grainger and Grocock (2006), p. 356.
6 Slater (2017), p. 223, Slater (2000), p. 288.
7 The slender notebook dates from 1871 and was tucked inside an 1894 copy of Mrs Beeton's Cookery Book when my grandmother gave it to me.
8 Ysewijn (2016), p. 69.
9 My grandmother, who died in 2019 at the age of 102, made the best shortcrust pastry I have ever tasted. She swore by using a combination of lard and butter so I do the same. If you are making this for vegetarians use vegetable fat or all butter instead.
10 Dahl (1983), p.p 109-10.
11 Fison and Dahl (1994), p. 58. I have omitted the peach slices in the original recipe as I found them a bit cumbersome when assembling the dessert. The colour and texture of sliced peaches always reminded me of goldfish as a child. Not that it stopped me eating and thoroughly enjoying them.
12 Italian meringue is made with a molten sugar syrup which partially 'cooks' the egg whites as they are being whisked. That said, it is always worth consulting any guests who are pregnant or have compromised immune systems to ascertain whether they are happy to eat semi-cooked egg whites. Italian meringue holds it shape well and can therefore be made a few hours ahead if you are planning to serve this at a dinner party.
13 David (1975), pp. 221-2.
14 Blanc (2011), p. 249.
15 *Farmhouse Fare* (1935), p. 101.
16 May (2012), p. 246.
17 Brears (2012), p. 348.
18 McFadden (2008), p. 224.
19 Riley (2007), p. 358.
20 Ibid, p. 360. The Palatinate is a region in south western Germany. Given the area's proximity to both Alsace in France and Bavaria, home to Nuremberg, both of which have a long history and appreciation of gingerbread, it is perhaps no great surprise that Anna Maria's panpepato was eagerly awaited.

Miscellaneous Recipes

1 Pichon (1846). In the translation of Pichon's text by Janet Hinson the recipe states: 'Take an ounce and a drachma of white ginger, a quarter-ounce of hand-picked cinnamon, half a quarter-ounce each of grains and cloves, and a quarter-ounce of rock sugar, and grind to powder.' As this mixture is being added to sweet dishes the sugar has been omitted. This recipe appears in the section labelled 'Other Odds and Ends'.
2 Hildebrand (2017), p. 206.
3 Kitchiner (1840), p. 386.
4 White (1968), p. 324.
5 Darwin (1950), p19.

Bibliography

Alcock, J.P. 'Folk Tale Memories as Illustrated and Interpreted in the Story of Hansel and Gretel', in *Food and the Memory: Proceedings of the Oxford Symposium on Food and Cookery 2000*, edited by Harlan Walker, Totnes: Prospect Books, 2001.

Alcock, J.P. *Food in the Ancient World*, Westport: Greenwood Press, 2006.

Alcock, J.P. *Daily Life of the Pagan Celts*, Oxford: Greenwood World Publishing, 2009.

Alcott, Louisa May. *Little Women*, London: George Routledge & Sons, 1873.

Anon. *The Land of Cockaygne*, London, British Library, MS Harley 913, ff. 3r-6v, translated by J. A. Bennett and G. V. Smithers, in *Early Middle English Verse and Prose*, Oxford: Clarendon Press, 1968.

Athenaeus. *The Deipnosophists; or, Banquet of the Learned*, Vol IV, translated by C.D. Yonge, London: Henry G. Bohn, 1854.

Austin, Thomas. *Two Fifteenth-century Cookery-books*. Harleian ms. 279 (ab. 1430) & Harl. ms. 4016 (ab. 1450), With Extracts From Ashmole ms. 1429, Laud ma.553, & Douce ms. 55, London: Early English Text Society, 1888.

Baggs, A.P.; Board, B.; Crummy, P.; Dove, C.; Durgan, S.; Goose, N.R.; Pugh, R.B.; Studd, P.; and Thornton, C.C. 'Markets and Fairs', in *A History of the County of Essex*: Vol 9, Borough of Colchester, edited by Janet Cooper and C.R. Elrington, Oxford: Oxford University Press, 1994.

Baggs, A.P.; Currie, C.R.J.; Elrington, C.R.; Keeling, S.M. and Rowland, A.M. 'Horsham: Market and Fairs' in *The Victoria History of the County of Sussex,* Vol VI, Part 2, edited by T.P. Hudson, Oxford: Oxford University Press, 1987.

Banham, Debby. *Food and Drink in Anglo-Saxon England*, Stroud: Tempus, 2004.

Baret, John. *An Alvearie, or Triple Dictionarie in English, Latin, and French*. 1574.

Bates, Katharine Lee. *From Gretna Green to Land's End: A Literary Journey in England*, New York: Thomas Y. Crowell & Co, 1907.

Bondeson Jan. 'The Biddenden Maids: a curious chapter in the history of conjoined twins', *Journal of the Royal Society of Medicine*, 85(4), 1992: 217–221.

Brand, John. *Observations on Popular Antiquities: including the whole of Mr. Bourne's Antiquitates vulgares*, revised by Sir H. Ellis, Vol 1, London: Henry G. Bohn, 1853.

Brears, Peter. *Traditional Food in Yorkshire*, Edinburgh: Donald, 1987.

Brears, Peter. *Cooking and Dining in Medieval England*, Totnes: Prospect Books, 2012.

Brears, Peter. *Cooking and Dining in Tudor & Early Stuart England,* London: Prospect Books, 2015.

Brontë, Charlotte. *Jane Eyre*, London: Dent, 1922.

Buttes, Henry. *Dyets Dry Dinner,* London: William Wood, 1599.

Byerly, Thomas. and Timbs, John. *The Mirror of Literature, Amusement and Instruction*. Vol XI, London: J. Limbird, 1828.

Candlin, Lillian. *Memories of Old Sussex*, Newbury: Countryside Books, 1987.

Chambers, Robert. *The Book of Days: A Miscellany,* Vol II, London: W. & R. Chambers, 1881.

Chauney, Martine. *Le Pain d'Epice de Dijon*, Paris : Christine Bonneton, 1978.

Christiani, Baron. 'Paris Notes: Mid-Lent Festivities', *The Globe*, 24 March 1900.

Collingham, Lizzie. *The Hungry Empire: How Britain's Quest for Food Shaped the Modern World*, London: Bodley Head, 2017.

Colquhoun, Kate. *Taste: The Story of Britain Through Its Cooking*, London: Bloomsbury, 2008.

Cox, Nancy. *Retailing and the Language of Goods, 1550–1820*, London: Routledge, 2016.

Cox, Nancy, and Dannehl, Karin. *Dictionary of Traded Goods and Commodities 1550–1820*, Wolverhampton: University of Wolverhampton, 2007.

Crane, Eva. *The World History of Beekeeping and Honey Hunting*, New York: Routledge, 1999.

Dahl, Roald. *Charlie and the Chocolate Factory*, New York: Bantam Books, 1983.

Dalby, Andrew. *Siren Feasts: A History of Food & Gastronomy in Greece*, London: Routledge, 1996.

Dalby, Andrew. *Empire of Pleasures: Luxury and Indulgence in the Roman World*, London: Routledge, 2000.

Day, Ivan. 'Street cries on the frozen Thames, food hawkers at London frost fairs, 1608–1814', in *Food Hawkers: Selling in the Streets Antiquity to the Present*, edited by Melissa Calaresu and Danielle van den Heuvel, London: Routledge, 2016.

Dibdin, Charles. *Mirth and Metre*, London: Vernor, Hood & Sharpe, 1807.

Dickens, Charles. *David Copperfield*, London: Bradbury & Evans, 1850.

Dickens, Charles. *Sketches by Boz: Illustrations of Everyday Life and Everyday People*, London: Chapman and Hall, 1903.

Dodge, Mary Mapes (ed.). 'The Ginger Bread Boy' in *St Nicholas: A Monthly Magazine for Girls and Boys*, Vol II, Part 2, 1875.

Droste, Magdalena. 'Lydia Driesch-Foucar', in *Bauhaus Women: A Global Perspective*, edited by E. Otto and P. Rössier, London: Bloomsbury Publishing, 2019.

Drummond J. C. and Wilbraham, Anne. *The Englishman's Food: Five Centuries of English Diet*, London: Pimlico, 1991.

Dumas, Alexandre. *Dumas on Food: Recipes and Anecdotes from the Classic Grand Dictionnaire de Cuisine*, translated by Alan and Jane Davidson, Oxford: Oxford University Press, 1988.

Evelyn, John. *The Diary of John Evelyn*, Cambridge: Cambridge University Press, 2015.

Farrer, William, and Brownbill, J. A. *History of the County of Lancaster*, Vol III, London: Constable, 1907.

Favre, Joseph. *Dictionnaire universel de cuisine pratique*, Paris: Chez l'auteur, 1903.

Frazer, J. G. *The Golden Bough*, New York: Macmillan, 1922.

Frost, Thomas. *The Old Showmen and the Old London Fairs*, London: Tinsley Brothers, 1875.

Goldstein, Darra. *The Oxford Companion to Sugar and Sweets*, Oxford: Oxford University Press, 2015.

Grimm, J. and W. 'Hansel and Grethel' in *Grimm's Fairy Tales*, London: William Heinemann, 1920.

Hagen, Ann. *Anglo-Saxon Food and Drink: Production, Processing, Distribution and Consumption*, Little Downham: Anglo-Saxon Books, 2006.

Hallam, Jack. *The Gingerbread Ladies: The Rags-to-Riches Story of Sarah Nelson, the Creator of Lakeland's Celebrated Gingerbread*, Reigate: Jack Hallam, 1979.

Hardy, Thomas. *The Mayor of Casterbridge*, London: Penguin Classics, 1994.

Hardy, Thomas. *Jude the Obscure*, London: Penguin Classics, 1985.

Hartley, Dorothy. *Food in England*, London: Little Brown, 1999.

Hartley, Dorothy. *Lost World: England 1933-1936*, Totnes: Prospect Books, 2012.

Hazelton, Nika Standen. *Cooking of Germany*, New York: Time Life Books, 1970.

Hieatt, Constance B. 'Making Sense of Medieval Culinary Records: Much Done, But Much More to Do', in *Food and Eating in Medieval Europe*, edited by M. Carlin and J.T. Rosenthal, London: Hambleton Press, 1998.

Hildebrand, Caz. *The Grammar of Spice*, London: Thames & Hudson, 2017.

Hoffmann, E.T.A. *The Nutcracker and the Golden Pot*, New York: Dover, 1993.

Hone, William. *The Every-Day Book or Everlasting Calendar*, Vol. 1, London: Hunt and Clarke, 1826.

Hörandner, E. 'Gingerbread Hearts: Symbols of Affection, Popularity and Honour', in *Gold Under The Furze: Studies in Folk Tradition Presented to Caoimhin O Danachair*, edited by Alan Gonley, Dublin: Glendale Press, 1982.

Hudgins, Sharon. 'Gingerbreads Galore!', *German Life* (USA), December 2010/January 2011: 54-56.

Hughes, Glyn. *The Lost Feast of Christmas*, lulu.com, 2016.

Hughes, Glyn. *The Lost Foods of England*. Winster: Foods of England, 2017.

Humble, Nicola. *Culinary Pleasures: Cookbooks and the Transformation of British Food*, London: Faber & Faber, 2005.

Humble, Nicola. *Cake: A Global History*, London: Reaktion Books, 2010.

Huysmans, J.-K. *The Vatard Sisters*, tr. by Brendan King, Sawtry: Dedalus Books, 2012.

Johnson, Samuel. *A Dictionary of the English Language*, in two volumes, London: Rivington et al, 1785.

Jonson, Ben. *Bartholomew Fair*, edited by Suzanne Gossett, Manchester: Manchester University Press, 2000.

Kaye-Smith, Sheila. *Sussex Gorse: The Story of a Fight*, New York: Alfred A. Knopf, 1916.

Keats, John. 'Over The Hill And Over The Dale' in *Complete Poems*, edited by Jack Stillinger, Cambridge: Belknap Press, 2003.

Knight, Jeremy. *Horsham's History*, Horsham: Horsham District Council, 2006.

Kroen, Sheryl. *Politics and Theater: The Crisis of Legitimacy in Restoration France, 1815-1830*, Berkeley: University of California Press, 2000.

Lancaster, J. M. (tr.). 'Mythological forms of bakers' cakes', in *Current Literature*, London: Hutchinson & Co, 1898.

Larousse Gastronomique, New York: Clarkson Potter, 2009.

Lebleu, O. 'Long-necked diplomacy: the tale of the third giraffe', *The Guardian*, 11 January 2016.

Leppman, Elizabeth. *Changing Rice Bowl: Economic Development and Diet in China*, Hong Kong: Hong Kong University Press, 2005.

Lethbridge, Lucy. *Servants: A Downstairs View of Twentieth-Century Britain*, London: Bloomsbury, 2013.

Loud, Graham A. (tr.) *The Chronicle of Arnold of Lübeck*, Oxford; Routledge, 2019.

Lunsford, Mackensy. 'The house that tech built: Bakers use lasers, power tools at Gingerbread House Competition', *USA Today*, 14 December 2019.

Marchant, W.T. *In Praise of Ale*, London: George Redway, 1888.

Mason, Laura, and Brown, Catherine. *Traditional Foods of Britain: An Inventory*, Totnes: Prospect Books, 1999.

Mayhew, Henry. *London Labour and the London Poor*, Vol I, London: Griffin, Bohn & Co, 1861.

Mayor, Adrienne. *The Poison King: The Life and Legend of Mithradates, Rome's Deadliest*

Enemy, Woodstock: Princeton University Press. 2009.

Medwin, Tom. *The Life of Percy Bysshe Shelley,* London: Thomas Cautley Newby, 1847.

Melikova, Natalya. 'Sweet and Spicy Cake Brings Taste of Old Russian Folklore', *Moscow Times,* 27 August 1997.

Mennell, Stephen. *All Manners of Food: Eating and Taste in England and France from the Middle Ages to the Present,* Chicago: University of Illinois Press, 1996.

Miller, J. Innes. *The Spice Trade of the Roman Empire,* Oxford: Clarendon Press, 1969.

Mintz, Sidney. *Sweetness and Power: The Place of Sugar in Modern History,* New York: Penguin, 1996.

[Newbery, John.] *Little Goody Two-Shoes and Other Stories: Originally Published by John Newbery,* edited by Matthew O Grenby, London: Palgrave Macmillan, 2013.

Nicholls, Henry. 'Meet Zarafa, the giraffe that inspired a crazy hairdo', *The Guardian,* 20 January 2014.

Norman, Jill. *The Complete Book of Spices: A Practical Guide to Spices and Aromatics,* London: Dorling Kindersley, 1997.

Oyeyemi, Helen. *Gingerbread,* London: Picador, 2019.

Pagrach-Chandra, Gaitri. *Windmills in My Oven: A Book of Dutch Baking,* Totnes: Prospect Books, 2002.

'Parisian Gingerbread Fair', *North British Daily Mail,* 10 April 1874.

Prior, Matthew. 'Alma: Or, The Progress of the Mind', in *The Works of the British Poets,* edited by Robert Anderson, London: John & Arthur Arch, 1795.

Punch. 'Revival of Brook Green Fair', *Punch,* Vol VIII, London: Bradbury & Evans, 1845.

Reader, Keith. *The Place de la Bastille: The Story of a Quartier,* Oxford: Oxford University Press, 2011.

[Redding, Cyrus.] *Pictorial History of the County of Lancaster,* London: Routledge, 1844.

Riley, Gillian. 'Learning by Mouth: Edible Aids to Literacy', in *Food and the Memory: Proceedings of the Oxford Symposium on Food and Cookery, 2000,* edited by Harlan Walker, Totnes: Prospect Books, 2001.

Riley, Gillian. *The Oxford Companion to Italian Food,* Oxford: Oxford University Press, 2007.

Sevilla, Maria José. *Delicioso: A History of Food in Spain,* London: Reaktion Books, 2019.

Sharpe's London Magazine, Vols 1-2, London: T. B. Sharpe, 1846.

Schafer, Edward. 'T'ang', in *Food in Chinese Culture: Anthropological and Historical Perspectives,* edited by K. C. Chang, New Haven: Yale University Press, 1977.

Shakespeare, William. 'Love's Labour's Lost', *The Complete Works of William Shakespeare,* edited by W.J. Craig, London: Oxford University Press, 1914.

Simmons, Rosemary. and Goodwin, Gillian. *Manchet & Trencher Bread,* London: Gelofer Press, 1983.

Simoons, Frederick J. *Food in China: A Cultural and Historical Inquiry,* Boca Raton: CRC Press, 1991.

Smith, Horace. *Festivals, Games, and Amusements, Ancient and Modern,* London: Henry Colburn and Richard Bentley, 1831.

Smith, John Thomas. *The Cries of London. Exhibiting Several of the Itinerant Traders of Ancient and Modern Times,* London: John Bowyer Nichols and Son, 1839.

Spence, C., Sanchez, C. C., Youssef, J. 'Brandy Snap: Reviving Historica Fairground Foods', in *Petits Propos Culinaires 115,* London: Prospect Books, 2019.

Spurling, Hilary (ed.). *Elinor Fettiplace's Receipt Book,* London: Penguin Books, 1986.

Thornbury, Walter. 'Smithfield and Bartholomew Fair', in *Old and New London*, Vol II, London: Cassell, Petter & Galpin, 1878.

Toussaint-Samat, Maguelonne. *History of Food*, translated by Anthea Bell, Oxford: Blackwell Publishing, 2008.

The True Briton, Vol III, No. XXIV, London: W. Bizet, J. Barnes and N. Gibson, 1752.

Tuer, Andrew W. *The History of the Horn-book*. London: Leadenhall Press, 1897.

Turner, Jack. *Spice: The History of a Temptation*, London: Harper Perennial, 2005.

Various. 'The Lover's Student' in *The Mirror Of Literature, Amusement, and Instruction*, Vol. 13, Issue 372, 30 May 1829.

Vesey-Fitzgerald, Brian. 'A Partial Eclipse of the Fair', in *The Sphere*, 11 June 1955.

Vine, Frederick. *Saleable Shop Goods for Counter-Tray and Window: A Practical Book for All in the Trade*, London: Office of the Baker and Confectioner, 1898.

Walford, Edward. *Old and New London: a Narrative of its History, its People, and its Places*, Vol VI, London: Cassell, Petter & Galpin, 1873.

Webb, Andrew. *Food Britannia,* London: Random House, 2011.

Wilkins, John M. and Hill, Shaun. *Food in the Ancient World,* Malden: Blackwell Publishing, 2006.

Wilson, C. Anne. *Food & Drink in Britain*, London: Constable, 1991.

Online sources

Avey, Tori. 'The History of Gingerbread', The History Kitchen, 20 December 2013 <https://www.pbs.org/food/the-history-kitchen/history-gingerbread/>

Baxter, Guy. 'Why Is A Chicken Wearing Trousers?', Museum of Rural English Life <https://merl.reading.ac.uk/news-and-views/2018/10/chicken-wearing-trousers/>

Berrington, Katie. 'The 16 Best Christmas Markets in the UK For 2019', Vogue, 20 November 2019 <https://www.vogue.co.uk/gallery/christmas-markets-in-the-uk>

British History Online <www.british-history.ac.uk>

Britsh Newspaper Archive <www.britishnewspaperarchive.co.uk>

Day, Ivan. 'Block Gingerbread', foodhistorjottings.blogspot.com, 16 July 2013 <http://foodhistorjottings.blogspot.com/2013/07/block-gingerbread.html>

Dearlove, Lucy. 'Catherine and Lynda', www.leckerpodcast.com, 13 March 2020 <https://www.leckerpodcast.com/episodes/2020/3/13/s3-e2-catherine-and-lynda>

Dotsch, Steven. 'Speculaas Biscuit', The Speculaas Spice Company, 2017 <https://www.speculaasspice.co.uk/speculaas-biscuit Accessed: 27 April 2020

Eskilsson, Lena. 'Snäll kaka med mörk historia', Västerbottens-Kuriren, 6 December 2016 <https://www.vk.se/2016-12-05/snall-kaka-med-mork-historia>

Gately, Iain. 'A Heart-Shaped History', Lapham's Quarterly, 14 February 2010 <https://www.laphamsquarterly.org/roundtable/heart-shaped-history>

'Ginger Nut', Nice Cup of Tea and a Sit Down.com, 4 November 2001 <http://www.nicecupofteaandasitdown.com/biscuits/previous.php3?item=2>

Hilton, Alison. (2013) 'Focus On Collections #2: Collecting Your #Muscake (And Eating It!)', Museum of Rural English Life, 19 June 2013 <https://merl.reading.ac.uk/news-and-views/2013/06/focus-on-collections-2-collecting-your-muscake-and-eating-it/>

Hughes, Glyn. 'Gingerbread Husbands', The Foods of England Project, 2 September 2018 <http://www.foodsofengland.co.uk/gingerbreadhusbands.htm>

Huntley & Palmers Collection <www.huntleyandpalmers.org.uk>

'Live Gingerbread Museum', www.lectar.com <http://www.lectar.com/_en/lectar_muzej.html>

Morris Ring. 'Rush-Bearing & Rushcarts', The Morris Ring, 2020 <https://themorrisring. org/about-morris/north-west>

National Farmer's Union. 'World War One: The Few That Fed The Many', nfuonline.com, 2014 <https://www.nfuonline.com/assets/33538>

Nederlands Bakkerij Museum. 'Kermis en Jaarmarkten', 2020 <http://www.bakkerijwiki. nl/index.php?t=4&h=75&s=269>

Pepys, Samuel. The Diary of Samuel Pepys <https://www.pepysdiary.com/diary>

Petch, Alison. 'Memorial Items', England: The Other Within. Analysing the English Collections at the Pitt Rivers Museum <http://england.prm.ox.ac.uk/englishness-memorial-items.html>

Pichon, Jérôme. Le Ménagier de Paris, 1846 <http://www.gutenberg.org/files/44070/44070-h/44070-h.htm#page_vol-2-122> see English translation by Janet Hinson at http://www.daviddfriedman.com/Medieval/Cookbooks/Menagier/Menagier.html)

Pladis. 'Better Biscuits: Annual Biscuit Review 2018', www.pladisglobal.com <https://www.pladisglobal.com/wp-content/uploads/2019/05/Better_Biscuits_Digital_Version.pdf>

Queen Victoria's Journals <http://www.queenvictoriasjournals.org/home.do>

Richardson, Ruth. 'Street Literature', British Library, 15 May 2014 <https://www.bl.uk/romantics-and-victorians/articles/street-literature>

Safefood. 'The History of Food Colour Additives' <https://www.safefood.eu/Food-Colour-Resource/History.aspx>

Schumm, Laura. 'Food Rationing in Wartime America', History Stories, 23 May 2014 <https://www.history.com/news/food-rationing-in-wartime-america>

Selli, Fabrizio. 'All the fun of the Frost Fair: why, when and how did Londoners party on the ice?', Museum of London, 29 November 2018 <https://www.museumoflondon.org.uk/discover/frost-fairs>

Shepherd, A. 'Grasmere Rushbearing', Calendar Customs, 2020 <https://calendarcustoms.com/articles/grasmere-rushbearing/>

Sohn, Emily. 'Why the Great Molasses Flood Was So Deadly', History Stories, 15 January 2019 <https://www.history.com/news/great-molasses-flood-science>

Todorov, Jordan. 'How a Literary Prank Convinced Germany That 'Hansel and Gretel' Was Real', Atlas Obscura, 3 July 2019 <https://www.atlasobscura.com/articles/is-hansel-and-gretel-real>

University of Sheffield. 'History of the Fairground', National Fariground and Circus Archive, 2020 <https://www.sheffield.ac.uk/nfca/researchandarticles/historyfairs>

Visit Toruń. 'Toruń Gingerbread', 2009 <http://www.visittorun.pl/237,l2.html>

Cookbooks

Acton, Eliza. Modern Cookery for Private Families, London: Longman, Green, Longman, Roberts & Green, 1864.

Acton, Eliza. The English Bread-Book for Domestic Use, London: Longman, Brown, Green, Longmans & Roberts, 1857.

Anon. The Indian Cookery Book, by a Thirty-Five Years' Resident, Calcutta: Thacker, Spink & Co, 1880.

Bésème-Pia, Lise. *Petit Traité Gourmand du Pain d'Épice*, Saint-Remy-de-Provence: Editions Equinox, 2015.

Blanc, Raymond. *Kitchen Secrets*, London: Bloomsbury, 2011.

Boermans, M. A. *Great British Bakes*, London: Square Peg, 2013.

[Cradock, Fanny & Johnnie Cradock]. *Cooking with Bon Viveur*, London: Daily Telegraph, 1965.

[Cradock, Fanny & Johnnie Cradock]. *Sociable Cook's Book*, London: Daily Telegraph, 1967.

Byron, May. *May Byron's Cake Book*, London: Hodder and Stoughton, 1915.

Carter, Charles. *The Complete Practical Cook: Or A New System of the Whole Art and Mystery of Cookery*, London: W. Meadows, 1730.

Chamberlain, L. *The Food and Cooking of Russia,* London: Allen Lane, 1982.

Craig, E. *Court Favourites: Recipes from Royal Kitchens,* London: Andre Deutsch, 1953.

Dalby, Andrew, and Grainger, Sally. *The Classical Cookbook*, London: British Museum Press, 2003.

Darwin, Bernard. *Receipts and Relishes: Being A Vade Mecum for the Epicure in the British Isles,* London: Naldrett Press, 1950.

David, Elizabeth. *Spices, Salt and Aromatics in the English Kitchen*, London: Penguin, 1975.

David, Elixabeth. *English Bread and Yeast Cookery,* London: Allen Lane, 1977.

Dawson, Thomas. *The Good Housewife's Jewel*, with an Introduction by Maggie Black, Lewes: Southover Press, 2002.

Dickens, Charles. *Dining with Dickens*, Goring-on-Thames: Elevendon Press, 1984.

Dods, Margaret. *The Cook and Housewife's Manual*, Cambridge: Cambridge University Press, 2013.

Duff, Julie. *Cakes Regional and Traditional,* London: Grub Street, 2015.

Edwards, John. *The Roman Cooker of Apicius: Translated and Adapted for the Modern Kitchen*, London: Random House, 1993.

Family Circle. *Flavour Fresh Vegetarian Recipes,* Wellingborough: J.B. Fairfax Press, 1990.

Farmers Weekly. *Farmhouse Fare: A Cookery Book of Country Dishes*, London: Farmers Weekly, 1935.

Fisher, M.F.K. *The Art of Eating*, London: Faber and Faber, 1963.

Fison, Josie, and Dahl, Felicity. *Roald Dahl's Revolting Recipes,* London: Red Fox, 1994.

Francatelli, Charles Elmé. *The Modern Cook; A Practical Guide to the Culinary Art in All its Branches*, London: Richard Bentley & Son, 1883.

Freeman, Bobby. *First Catch Your Peacock*, Ceredigion: Ylolfa, 1996.

Glasse, Hannah. *The Art of Cookery Made Plain and Easy*, Totnes: Prospect Books, 2012.

Goldstein, Darra. *Beyond the North Wind: Russia in Recipes and Lore*. New York: Ten Speed Press, 2020.

Grainger, Sally. *Cooking Apicius: Roman Recipes for Today,* Totnes: Prospect Books, 2006.

Grainger, Sally, and Grocock, C. W. *Apicius,* Totnes, Prospect Books, 2006.

Grant, Mark. *Roman Cookery. Ancient Recipes for Modern Kitchens*, London: Serif, 2008.

Grigson, Jane. *English Food*, London: Penguin, 1993.

Hess, Karen. *Martha Washington's Booke of Cookery and Booke of Sweatmeats,* New York: Columbia University Press, 1995.

Hudgins, Sharon. *T-Bone Whacks and Caviar Snacks,* Denton: University of North Texas Press, 2019.

Jekyll, Agnes. *Kitchen Essays* (originally published 1922), London: Persephone Books, 2001.

Kitchiner, William. *The Cook's Oracle*, Edinburgh: Robert Cadell, 1840.

Bibliography

Kleber, L.O. *The Original Suffrage Cook Book* (1915), Twickenham: Aurora Metro Books, 2018.

Lawson, Nigella. *How To Be A Domestic Goddess*, London: Chatto & Windus, 2003.

Leyel, C. F., and Hartley, O. *The Gentle Art of Cookery* (originally published 1925), London: Quadrille, 2011.

Luard, Elisabeth. *European Festival Food*, London: Bantam Press, 1990.

Lynch, R. J. *Win The War Cook Book*, London: Forgotten Books, 2015.

Marshall, A. B. *Mrs A. B. Marshall's Cookery Book*, London: Robert Hayes, 1888.

Martineau, Alice. *Caviare to Candy: Recipes for Small Households From All Parts of the World*, London: Richard Cobden-Sanderson, 1927.

May, Robert. *The Accomplisht Cook*, Totnes: Prospect Books, 2012.

McFadden, Christine. *Pepper: The Spice that Changed the World*, Bath. Absolute Press, 2008.

McNeill, F. Marion. *The Scots Kitchen: Its Lore and Recipes*, St Albans: Mayflower Books, 1974.

Ministry of Food. *Eating For Victory: Healthy Home Front Cooking on War Rations*, London: Michael O'Mara Books, 2007.

Morphy, Countess. *Recipes For All Nations*, London: Neville Spearman, 1953.

Murrell, John. *The Delightfull Daily Exercise for Ladies and Gentlewomen*, London, 1621.

Nott, John. *The Cook's and Confectioner's Dictionary: Or, the Accomplish'd Housewife's Companion*, London: Rivington, 1723.

Pagrach-Chandra, Gaitri. *Het Nederlands Bakboek*, Kosmos Uitgevers: Utrecht, 2012. Translated by Karin Engelbrecht for The Spruce Eats 13/04/2019 <https://www.thespruceeats.com/indo-dutch-spekkoek-recipe-1128478>

Perry, Charles (tr.). *A Baghdad Cookery Book: The Book of Dishes by al-Hasan, M, and al-Karim, M*, Totnes: Prospect Books, 2005.

The Picayune's Creole Cook Book, New York: Dover Publications, 2002.

Plat, Hugh. *Delightes for Ladies to Adorne their Persons, Tables, Closets, and Distillories: with Beauties, Banquets, Perfumes and Waters*, London: Arthur Johnson, 1617.

Rundell, Maria. *A New System of Domestic Cookery Formed Upon Principles of Economy and Adapted to the Use of Private Families*, London: John Murray, 1812.

Scharfenberg, Horst. *The German Kitchen*, Papermac, 1991.

Simmons, Amelia. *American Cookery, or, The Art of Dressing Viands, Fish, Poultry and Vegetables*, Poughkeepsie: Paraclete Potter, 1815.

Spieler, Marlena. *Jewish Festival Food*, London: Lorenz Books, 2015.

Spry, Constance, and Hume, Rosemary. *The Constance Spry Cookery Book*, Letchworth: Reprint Society, 1958.

Slater, Nigel. *Real Food*, London: 4th Estate, 2000.

Slater, Nigel. *The Christmas Chronicles*, London: 4th Estate, 2017.

Toomre, Joyce. *Classic Russian Cooking: Elena Molokhovets' A Gift to Young Housewives*, translated by Joyce Toomre, Bloomington: Indiana University Press, 1998.

White, Florence. *Good Things in England*, London: The Cookery Book Club, 1968.

Workers' Education Association (W.E.A.). *A Ragoo of Ducks: Household Recipes from York Manuscripts*, York: Workers' Education Association, 1997

Ysewijn, Regula. *Pride and Pudding: This History of British Puddings Savoury and Sweet*, London: Murdoch Books, 2016.

RECIPE INDEX

GENERAL INDEX